Poetry & Responsibility

Poetry & ...

Poetry & Responsibility

Neil Corcoran

LIVERPOOL UNIVERSITY PRESS

First published 2014 by
Liverpool University Press
4 Cambridge Street
Liverpool
L69 7ZU

This paperback edition first published 2021

British Library Cataloguing-in-Publication data
A British Library CIP record is available

ISBN 978-1-78138-035-2 cased
ISBN 978-1-80034-877-6 paperback

Typeset in Stone by Carnegie Book Production, Lancaster
Printed and bound by CPI Group (UK) Ltd, Croydon CR0 4YY

for Paul Driver

Contents

Acknowledgements

Some of these chapters, or parts of them, first appeared, usually in substantially different form, in the *Cambridge Quarterly*, the *Edinburgh Review*, a special issue of the *Irish University Review* edited by Peter Denman, *PN Review*, the *Times Literary Supplement* and the *Yeats Annual*, and in collections edited by Fran Brearton, Santanu Das, Terry Gifford, Alan Gillis, Edna Longley and Bernard O'Donoghue. Several originated as lectures and seminars given at the universities of Bristol, Cardiff, Lausanne, Liverpool, Northumbria, Princeton, Queen's, Belfast and York, and at the London Modernism Seminar of the Institute of English Studies of the University of London, the Shakespeare Institute in Stratford-upon-Avon and the Yeats International Summer School in Sligo. I am very grateful for these invitations and for the illuminating comments made in discussion by their participants. I am also grateful to the many undergraduate and postgraduate students who, in Sheffield, Swansea, St Andrews, Liverpool and Sligo, discussed with me over many years some of the issues aired in this book and kept me on my toes.

Neil Corcoran
Liverpool, 2013

Introduction:
The Responsibilities of Poetry

In 1914 – an appropriate year – W. B. Yeats, who figures significantly in what follows, as much in his effect on his successors as in his own work, published a volume called *Responsibilities*. It bears what has since become an extremely well-known epigraph: '*In dreams begins responsibility.*' The quotation is attributed only to an 'Old Play', but this has never been traced and it is widely assumed that Yeats wrote the epigraph himself. If this is so, then he is curiously avoiding responsibility for an epigraph itself evoking responsibility and proposing, strangely, that its origin lies in imagination or unconscious drive or desire. Yeats's evasiveness possibly suggests anxiety that any declaration of the kind may appear sententious or self-serving in a poet. *Responsibilities* has, even so, been frequently read, following its title and epigraph, as the pivotal volume in Yeats's progress from a late nineteenth-century poetry of romantic mytholo-gizing to the more urgent, chastising and self-chastising attitudes of public accountability to be read in his mid- and later period work. The poem 'Among School Children', to which I give considerable attention in this book, is one crucial exhibit of that later phase, originating, as it does, in the public responsibilities which Yeats assumed and dutifully performed as a senator of the recently created Irish Free State; originating, therefore, in the contingencies of contemporary social and political life but eventually including in its breathtakingly widening radius at least the possibility of aesthetic transcendence.

It was his admiration for Yeats's progress that, in the socially disinte-grating American 1930s, impelled Delmore Schwartz to entitle a book in 1938, after Yeats's epigraph, *In Dreams Begin Responsibilities*, signalling a certain strenuousness of social obligation. Frank O'Hara, on the other hand (whose in some ways surprising admiration for Yeats hums intermittently in his work, as does what he identifies in himself in 'Homage to André Gide' as 'the windy course / of an almost Irish remorse', which 'insistently beckon[s] me elsewhere'), modifies Yeats's phrase in 'Memorial Day, 1950' with what seems a note of caustic challenge: 'Our responsibilities', he writes, 'did not begin / in dreams, though they began in bed.' This is wry and witty in the breezily camp mode of which O'Hara made himself such a charmingly attractive master, and it may seem to mirror elements and attitudes of *irresponsibility* in the self-representations on which much of his work depends. Notoriously, 'Ave Maria', written in 1960, when Eisenhower was still president, appears to advise the 'Mothers of America' that it could only be to their advantage to give children still young enough to need it permission to go to the movies so that they might be picked up there and sexually used by adult strangers. Whether 'Ave Maria', although blasphemously entitled, actually advocates any such (of course deplorable) thing is in fact put in doubt by the rhetorical contract which the poem enters into with the reader and the wayward, not easily interpretable, ironies to which that rhetoric gives rise; but, even so, O'Hara's readiness to court outrage is clear.

The strategy ought to be understood, I think, as an alternative form of responsibility, a kind of slant responsibility that challenges the constricting conventions and assumptions of mid-century American conservatism. An imp of the perverse sometimes grins as provocatively from O'Hara's shoulder as it does from Emily Dickinson's when poems of hers such as 'Did the Harebell lose her girdle' anatomize nineteenth-century American sexual hypocrisy with a sharp but still calm, almost amused, disdain; and O'Hara revered Dickinson. Camp in O'Hara, that is, becomes a way of saying what could not otherwise, in this culture and society, get said: that responsibilities of course begin in bed if you are gay in 1950s America and are willing to admit it, even celebrate it, in your poems, and so behave without hypocrisy in relation to your own sexuality: 'our' in the phrase 'our responsibilities' is the possessive pronoun of an elected coterie solidarity. This outsider responsibility sensitizes O'Hara both to the plight of poets in Soviet Russia and to the pre-Civil Rights condition of American blacks, whose culture his work consistently acknowledges and admires; and these loyalties and affections lie behind 'The Day Lady Died', his great elegy for the singer Billie Holiday, which is at the centre of my chapter on his work.

These examples of Schwartz and O'Hara suggest, then, that when poets contemplate matters of social or political accountability or answerability they simultaneously contemplate matters of poetic responsibility and responsiveness too. Both Schwartz's and O'Hara's perceptions are shadowed by Yeats's, whether in acknowledgement or deviation. When they meditate on accountability they meditate also on the ways in which Yeats has already meditated and turned his meditations into admirable, ungainsayable and potentially usable poetic art. The simultaneity is watermarked into the *Responsibilities* epigraph itself, since it makes it plain that when Yeats stiffens his work with social responsiveness he is not merely abrogating the attractiveness of the world of dream. The

2

almost paradoxical strangeness of Yeats's saying that responsibilities begin in dreams indicates that for him they begin in the romantic-symbolist aesthetic itself. The excellence or absoluteness of poetic form, image and symbol, that is to say, and the effortful attempt at transcendence, supply criteria of social judgement; which is one of the reasons why, for Yeats, the social and cultural world he was actually offered was, like the biological necessity itself, so endlessly disappointing, with the consequence that his later work frequently fetches up in extremes of grief and outrage, emotions by which 'Among School Children' is touched. It is appropriate, therefore, that the simultaneity of the demands of aesthetic perfection and ethical obligation should cohere even formally in Yeats's epigraph, since '*In dreams begin responsibilities*' is a regular line of iambic pentameter, the staple diet of traditional English prosody.

That modern poets have occasionally been anguished by the conflicting demands of responsibility is apparent. 'In the midst of what is going on now,' T. S. Eliot said in a private letter in London in October 1942, for instance, while he was writing 'Little Gidding', 'it is hard, when you sit down at a desk, to feel confident that morning after morning spent fiddling with words and rhythms is justified activity ... And on the other hand, external or public activity is more of a drug than is this solitary toil which often seems so pointless.'[1] 'Fiddling' may have the proverbially irresponsible example of Nero within earshot, and may also recall Marianne Moore's poem 'Poetry', with its famously dismissive, even reproving, opening line: 'I, too, dislike it: there are things that are important beyond all this fiddle.' That line gave A. Alvarez his title for a collection of essays published in 1968, *Beyond All This Fiddle*. In my chapter on the politics of translation I discuss his hugely influential Penguin *Modern European Poets* series, which brought new post-war political necessities and urgencies into English poetry from, predominantly, the countries of the Soviet bloc, in ways that seemed to him satisfactorily to go beyond the 'fiddle' of post-war English poetic gentility. As Moore's poem advances, however, what seems dismissive turns out to be merely concessive, as a case for poetry is resistantly made; and in fact in a wartime lecture, which eventually became the essay 'The Social Function of Poetry', Eliot appears less vulnerably ambivalent, more confidently deciding that 'the duty of the poet, as poet, is only indirectly to his people: his direct duty is to his *language*, first to preserve, and second to extend and improve'.[2] The italics are insistent, and this is also very much the attitude to be read out of Eliot's wartime sequence of poems *Four Quartets*, which frequently returns to the subject of poetic language itself, and at a pitch of extremity ('Every poem an epitaph'). The sequence is one to which succeeding poets seeking examples of responsible poetic behaviour have made frequent recourse.

Seamus Heaney, who receives considerable attention in this book, asks in the ninth of his 'Glanmore Sonnets' in his volume *Field Work* (1979), 'What is my apology for poetry?', where the word 'apology' summons the prose essays or manifestos of the poets Philip Sidney and Percy Bysshe Shelley, reminding us that questions of poetic responsibility have a long history, and in poets' prose as well as in their verse. In philosophy the debate reaches as far back as Plato and as far forward as the contemporary Jürgen Habermas. For poets of modernity and postmodernity, two statements on the matter have assumed particular prominence, however. One was articulated once more in relation to Yeats when, in W. H. Auden's great elegy 'In Memoriam W. B. Yeats', written on the poet's death in 1939, he wrote that 'poetry makes nothing happen'. The other is Theodor Adorno's apparent insistence that poetry itself ought no longer to happen since 'To write poetry after Auschwitz is barbaric'.[3] Neither of these observations is, in context, at all straightforward, and both have been extensively debated. I shall return to Auden at the end of this introduction, and although this is not the place to take up Adorno's statement yet again it remains true that its implications, together with his apparently situating modernity as 'the final stage of the dialectic of culture and barbarism', haunt a great deal of thinking about the responsibilities of the post-war lyric; even if his subsequent recantation of his dictum is much less frequently brought into the reckoning: 'Perennial suffering', he then said, 'has as much right to expression as a tortured man has to scream; hence it may have been wrong to say that after Auschwitz you could no longer write poems'.[4] 'A Disused Shed in Co. Wexford', for example, one of the most justly celebrated poems of Derek Mahon, whose work I discuss in Chapter 7, may even be read as an oblique response to Adorno, in its exclamatory but recoiling lyric address to the 'Lost people of Treblinka and Pompeii!'.

Seamus Heaney's essays, notably those collected in *The Government of the Tongue* (1988) and *The Redress of Poetry* (1995), frequently return to the debate, both in critiques of individual poets and in more general thematic pieces. The titles of these books are judiciously similar in grammatical structure: they are to be read as both subjective and objective genitives, with implications and resonances that Heaney delicately and persuasively unpicks. These readings have been highly influential, as have certain of the books' formulations, notably the opposition of, and then the attempted reconciliation between, 'song' and 'suffering' in the context of Irish political violence, and the appropriation of George Seferis's requirement, during the Second World War in Greece, that poetry must be 'strong enough to help'.[5]

When Heaney cites this precept, as he does twice in *The Redress of Poetry*, he in some ways oddly omits the context in which Seferis makes his observation. It is not in fact phrased as positive requirement but as the negative discovery of a lack. A lifelong admirer of C. P. Cavafy, whose work he engages in ongoing dialogue in both his prose and his poetry, Seferis nevertheless finds that at times of greatest stress Cavafy's work is 'not strong enough to help'. This is a judgement that most admirers of Cavafy would strongly dispute: and I touch in this book on the adequately responsive strength, as I see it, of one of Cavafy's poems, and on the way his influence affects one of the most adequately strong of all modern poems, Zbigniew Herbert's 'Elegy of Fortinbras'. Almost despite itself, then, Heaney's citation reminds us that, even in times of stress and even as they search out exemplary instances, poets are liable to misread or wrongly estimate one another, or are even obliged to misread or wrongly estimate one another, in their efforts to make their own necessarily exploratory and inventive original contributions. When poets read painters and paintings in poetic acts of ekphrasis, this may also hold true, as I suggest in Chapter 7. Such rapprochements may be agonistic as well as genuinely accommodating and appreciative, in ways that contribute further to understandings of creative responsibility. As in acts of literary critique, ekphrasis gives rise to both responsible and necessarily irresponsible readings, abjurations of strict justice by means of which alone the new aesthetic object can be created. The relationship is given another provocative twist when poets make new poems by contemplating and analysing their own portraits: such poems live off an almost vertiginous play of representation and self-representation – and of aesthetic critique.

In his essays Heaney is primarily concerned with matters of form; and thinking about poetic responsibility in relation to form provokes in this poet–critic some suggestive formulations, notably when he speaks of 'the jurisdiction of achieved form' and when he adumbrates a view of what might constitute 'lyric action'.[6] Nevertheless, Heaney's prose has also, from the beginning, been taken up with the social behaviour of poets, with the gestures, alignments and public attitudes maintained as modes of both social response and aesthetic self-protection. Heaney seeks to locate in these biographical moments models of what he frequently calls the 'exemplary'. My account of the genesis of his poem 'Casualty', a poem first published only several years after the event it commemorates, the 'Bloody Sunday' shootings in Derry in 1972, examines the way Heaney seeks out appropriate forms of public behaviour in Yeats, finding them in some initially surprising places, and simultaneously derives an appropriate and liberating poetic form from Yeats. Louis MacNeice, on the other hand, wants to maintain certain forms also employed by Yeats, notably the sophisticated use of popular refrain; but, driven by democratic impulse, he abjures the autocratic, hierophantic stances of Yeats's 'last Romantic' forms of modernity. This admirable ethical stance involves him in certain aesthetic difficulties and uncertainties, which he overcomes in his finest and most characteristic work.

Heaney's relationship to Yeats is one of the most remarkable coincidences of social and poetic responsibility treated in this book; and it has its mirror image in Paul Muldoon's coming, in his poem 'Our Lady of Ardboe', to an uneasy but equally enabling accommodation with Heaney himself, in a subtly revisionary formal spirit. This is a poem in which Muldoon is, in turn, simultaneously coming to terms with, even as he offers a critique of, one of the most pressing matters of responsibility for his generation of Irish Catholics, the heritage of Irish Catholicism itself, and in which he also touches on painful personal subject matter which has profoundly exercised him subsequently.

The Civil Rights movement in Northern Ireland in the late 1960s and early 1970s, in which Heaney, then lecturing in Belfast, was involved, took inspiration and learnt tactics from the movement that had originated, in relation to black people, in the USA several years earlier. Some of Bob Dylan's early songs seem umbilically connected to crucially defining moments of that movement, and a very young Dylan ('we still had our puppy fat', said Joan Baez, truly) sang at the march on Washington addressed by Martin Luther King in 1963. Many contemporary poets identify Dylan's lyrics throughout his lengthy subsequent career as strong and influential contemporary poetry. Paul Muldoon, for instance, published a celebratory poem called 'Bob Dylan at Princeton, November 2000' in a collection of essays on Dylan which I edited in 2002, and in the sequence 'Sleeve Notes' in *Hay* in 1998 he admires Dylan as one of those 'great artists' who 'are their own greatest threat, / as when they aim an industrial laser / at themselves and cut themselves back to the root'. [7] In the restless, sometimes radical self-revisions of his career Dylan may seem, then, poetically exemplary. I also attempt in my chapter on him, though, to identify some moments in the public statements and commitments of his life in which he manoeuvres himself into a position of vital artistic independence by refusing what he sees as the constricting views of him maintained by an admiring, even adulatory, but potentially co-opting audience: one of these occasions involves, almost scandalously, his relationship with the Civil Rights movement itself. We might read in this behaviour something not dissimilar to what Heaney defines as exemplary, and creatively self-protective, in the 'intransigence' of Yeats. Considering strategies of self-protection, I examine in Dylan a further form of responsibility: the one he bears, in advancing age, to his own earlier work and genius, to what clearly seems to him, as well as to others, the mystery of his own songs.

When Heaney defines 'lyric action' in *The Government of the Tongue* he is thinking of the 'radical witness' offered in totalitarian Stalinist Russia by the poet Osip Mandelstam. In my chapter on the uses made of *Hamlet* and its hero in that same Russia by Boris Pasternak, and in Warsaw Pact Poland by Zbigniew Herbert, I inquire into some of the effects of a poetry in which, you might say, poetic intertextuality – and not only in relation to Shakespeare – becomes itself a form of 'radical' political responsibility. Since for most readers of poetry in English the reception of Pasternak's 'Hamlet' and Herbert's 'Elegy of Fortinbras' is dependent on translation, reading their work also involves a consideration of the ethics and responsibilities of the act of translation itself, and of its contentious recent history. The versions of these poems made, respectively, by the American poet Robert Lowell and the Polish poet

Czesław Miłosz – like the similarly contentious 'account' of the *Iliad* by Christopher Logue, which I discuss elsewhere – demand, also, to be read in the context of the Cold War period in which they were made. Indeed, the establishing of contemporary context has rarely been more necessary than in relation to poems such as these, and in fact their contexts can be seen as formally and thematically coded into the translations themselves. Thinking about the responsibilities taken by the lyric 'I' when it is dramatized in this context through a literary persona – to consider, that is, the forms taken by irony when it becomes a mode of political engagement and opposition – is to reflect in a new light on the ways in which lyric responsibility may be exercised, and to arrive at a chastened understanding of how lyric sufficiency may be painfully earned and achieved.

These, then, are some of the salient forms in which poetic responsibility has been articulated in modern poetry, but I begin this study where the poetry of responsibility and witness is most obvious in the English language itself: in the poetry of the First World War. Wilfred Owen, Seamus Heaney says, 'has haunted the back of the literary mind as a kind of challenge'.[8] As officer poets, Owen's and Sassoon's ethical and aesthetic responsibilities were at complete odds. As officers they were responsible for the conduct of a war in which orders to their men frequently resulted in their deaths; as poets they regarded themselves as speaking 'for' these same men who were not in a position to speak for themselves. The plight of these poets, then, which is attested in the sometimes fraught forms of their poems, gives evidence of the lyric 'I' undergoing the most extreme form of pressure; and in Owen's hands, in particular, the English lyric becomes newly and differently exemplary as a consequence. Isaac Rosenberg and David Jones, on the other hand, both private soldiers, had no such obligations or compunctions, but in both poets the war is given permanent poetic form: in Rosenberg's outsider, truculent and, under the circumstances, heroic revision of certain available mythologies and social attitudes and types, and in his almost prescient seizing on new modernist opportunities of irony and intensity; and in Jones's patient post-war labour of testimonial recovery and retrieval, his lifelong search for appropriate commemorative means. Persistence against the odds was the immediate necessity for the private soldier; it becomes the permanent obligation for the poet.

Poets reading other poets, both their works and their lives, are, of course, critics too, and all good poems are also acts of good literary criticism. Literary criticism itself has its responsibilities, and in my chapter on 'Among School Children' I set this celebrated poem among some of its most notable critics (including Delmore Schwartz), making evaluative judgements of my own. Critical responsibility is maintained, or ignored, not only in relation to the primary text itself but to schools of criticism and to the institution of criticism; and, although critical consensus is a chimera and anyway probably undesirable, the act of criticism is a form of inter-generational conversation and is itself the establishing and extending of forms of cultural knowledge. Responsive and responsible literary criticism is the means by which the poem continues to generate meaning. In my chapter on Ted Hughes's prose, I examine some of the ways in which, for this poet who was also deeply responsive to Yeats, his literary criticism, notably that of his own work and of Sylvia Plath's, constitutes a peculiarly agonized form of responsibility, becoming both obligation and exacerbation. It is virtually axiomatic that poets writing critical prose will also be writing about themselves, creating or maintaining the taste by which they wish to be enjoyed; and there are ways in which this is true of Ted Hughes. But something else too, something much stranger and darker, seems to be going on in Hughes's prose, which makes it a revealingly peculiar, if also in some ways wholly characteristic, contribution to the study of a poet's responsibilities.

In defining my subject in this book, I have referred to several major modern elegies, which it considers at some length: Wilfred Owen's 'Futility', W. H. Auden's 'In Memory of W. B. Yeats', Seamus Heaney's 'Casualty', Zbigniew Herbert's 'Elegy of Fortinbras', Frank O'Hara's 'The Day Lady Died'. There is a sense in which Yeats's 'Among School Children' is an elegy too, and certainly the elegiac is one of the most intense of that poem's changing moods. If we allow the term some extension, we might even locate elegy as the major form taken by the modern lyric; and this might seem appropriate as a chastened if usually tacit or even unconscious response to Adorno's stricture, or to his friend Walter Benjamin's dictum, uttered in 1928, that 'the work is the death mask of its conception', or even to the melancholy that inheres in widely accepted contemporary understandings of the nature of language itself, in which, as Robert Hass expresses it in the beautiful poem 'Meditation at Lagunitas' in his defiantly entitled volume *Praise* (1979), 'a word is elegy to what it signifies'.[9] Elegy involves poets nevertheless in what might be considered a generic embarrassment: its narcissism. All elegy, that is, must mourn for the elegist as well as the elegized; and this embarrassment has been a matter of acute sensitivity among modern poets, for whom elegy has often been written in a spirit of anti-elegy too. Which is why I discuss in my final chapter Anne Carson's astonishing poem-artefact *Nox* (2010), in which the ethical issues inherent in elegy are put into circulation once more, but with kinds of formal and aesthetic novelty and command which are themselves the painful product of vulnerability. Addressing the subject of her dead brother, she enters into conversation with the ancient poetic dead, and notably with the Roman poet Ovid; and this conversation, happening as an act of movingly responsible elegiac witness, is projected forward into our future as readers.

That all acknowledgements of poetic tradition are themselves responsible conversations with the dead is one of the things Auden intends in his elegy for Yeats; and we should ourselves responsibly attend to his famous statement about poetry not in the form of extracted pseudo-aphorism but in its own permanently living context:

> Now Ireland has her madness and her weather still,
> For poetry makes nothing happen: it survives
> In the valley of its saying where executives
> Would never want to tamper; it flows south
> From ranches of isolation and the busy griefs,
> Raw towns that we believe and die in; it survives,
> A way of happening, a mouth.

True poetry survives as counter or oppositional, as language not to be made available to interest or betrayed into accommodation or appropriation. It survives as singularity, as utterly its own, but always touched too by obligation: by isolation, grief, community, faith and death. Poetry is the human mouth figured as the mouth of a river: flowing, purifying, making a place for itself, pressing on.

PART I

CHAPTER 1

The Price of Pity: Wilfred Owen among the Poets of the First World War

I

In 'The Owl', written in February 1915, three months before he enlisted, Edward Thomas characteristically sets himself on the open road: walking at night feeling hungry, cold and tired. When he enters an inn, though, the exterior world is 'quite barred out' except for 'An owl's cry, a most melancholy cry // Shaken out long and clear upon the hill' – and shaken out too across a stanza break, a formal prolongation which dramatizes the owl's effect on the poet. In fact, the cry is also shaken out across English literary history, since it is explicitly distinguished from the owl's 'merry note' in Shakespeare's song 'When icicles hang by the wall' in *Love's Labours Lost*. For this owl carries an echoing message 'telling me plain what I escaped / And others could not, that night, as in I went':

> And salted was my food, and my repose,
> Salted and sobered, too, by the bird's voice
> Speaking for all who lay under the stars,
> Soldiers and poor, unable to rejoice.[1]

'Salted', the word repeated: seasoned, but also rendered poignant or piquant. The bird's voice, the only voice we hear in this poem of human shelter and sustenance, transforms the poet's circumstances by its insistent reminder of all who lack such things, 'soldiers and poor'.

Where the owl is insistent, however, this poet is not. 'The Owl' is merely shadowed by the symbolic properties of its eponymous bird; but this voice is a wise one too, offering exemplary but disconsolate counsel, and doing so by 'speaking for' others. And, by taking their part, by speaking in their stead, the owl obviates the need for the poet to do likewise more directly. The owl is the means by which Edward Thomas both gives weight to, and avoids being weighed down by, the expectation that poets in wartime should speak for others, should take on representative status; and, avoiding that, Thomas manages also to avoid the pitfalls that might accompany such commitments: self-approval, presumption, the too easily earned satisfactions of indignation. Indeed, his co-ordination – 'soldiers and poor' – by omitting the definite article (not 'the poor') may insinuate that 'poor' is an adjective defining 'soldiers' rather than a separate category, and this may carry a political insinuation too: that soldiers might also be the poor, that poverty might have made them soldiers (as it appears to have made Isaac Rosenberg), even that war might be the continuation of state policy by other means. The poem's own 'most melancholy cry', in February 1915, is therefore an understated but politically charged undermining of its final rhyme. This poet's voice is unable to rejoice in the imperial wartime mode of Rupert Brooke's 'The Soldier' but is also wary of the authority of representative status about to be implied and occasionally made explicit in the poems of Siegfried Sassoon and Wilfred Owen.

Just over two years after writing 'The Owl', Edward Thomas, not after all escaping what others could not, was killed; and in the intervening period he in fact spent very little time in the trenches. Many of the over 140 poems he wrote then are war poems, therefore, in a rather different sense from those of the combatant poets. Such poems as 'Words', 'Roads' and 'Rain' – monosyllabic titles which seem almost casually unassertive but also hugely inclusive – are work in which the war is internalized not only as a context for consciousness and sensibility but as the very ground of these things. In 'Words' the English language must be 'worn new', an oxymoron in which 'worn' is both 'dressed in' and 'worked at': so the poem celebrates the virtue of linguistic renovation, implicitly challenging the language of a political journalism worn very old indeed – worn out – in jingoistic cliché. And 'Rain' transforms its exterior weather into an interior state of being which seems inseparable from the state of being at war, when a wrenching beatitude – 'Blessed are the dead that the rain rains upon' – introduces lines in which the unnamed war plunges thought into a form of trance. Here the language is worn new when something is worn out, in lines that waver between prayer, personal melancholia and universal lamentation, and do so in a limpidly fluent, self-possessed syntax and with a haunting assonantal music, at ironic odds with the desolation being given its consummate expression:

> But here I pray that none whom I once loved
> Is dying tonight or lying still awake
> Solitary, listening to the rain,
> Either in pain or thus in sympathy
> Helpless among the living and the dead,
> Like a cold water among broken reeds,

Myriads of broken reeds all still and stiff,
Like me who have no love which this wild rain
Has not dissolved except the love of death,
If love it be towards what is perfect and
Cannot, the tempest tells me, disappoint.

II

Such poems make Edward Thomas very definitely a war poet: but the combatant poetry of officers nevertheless seems a special case, since the poets' responses to this unasked-for material involved them in such radical self-questioning, both aesthetically and ethically. To be an officer in charge of troops – of the 'men', sometimes referred to in poems as 'boys' – was to be made directly responsible for the suffering and death of the young, this being the inevitable consequence of orders necessarily given and faithfully obeyed. For Wilfred Owen and Siegfried Sassoon this appears to have been supportable eventually only to the extent that the anxiety, guilt or self-reproach consequent upon it was the spur to the writing of poems engaging with it. Both felt acutely their poetic responsibility, and plight, as witnesses. Owen defines this in a letter of 1917 in which he tells his mother that he has become 'a poet's poet' – he means that he has earned the approval of Sassoon and Harold Monro – but that his poems must capture the 'look' of men at the Front, 'more terrible than terror, for it was a blindfold look, and without expression, like a dead rabbit's': 'It will never be painted, and no actor will ever seize it. And to describe it, I think I must go back and be with them.'[2] This is remarkable and unforgettable as evocation but it is also perhaps slightly self-approving, and Owen in his letters is always working for his mother's approval; but that element is wholly absent from 'The Calls', in which the thought in the letter becomes a promissory poem:

For leaning out last midnight on my sill,
I heard the sighs of men that have no skill
To speak of their distress, no nor the will!
 A voice I know. And this time I will go.[3]

Comparably, Siegfried Sassoon in 'Sick Leave' expresses the guilt of withdrawal from the field by imagining 'the noiseless dead' approaching his sickbed to reproach him: '"When are you going out to them again? / Are they not still your brothers through our blood?"'[4] The poem adds a self-recriminatory frisson to the trope of the revenant common in wartime poems (and made exceptional in Thomas's 'Roads', where 'the dead / Returning lightly dance'); and, by stopping at thirteen lines, it calls up too the ghost of the sonnet, that most typical of wartime poetic forms, to suggest unfinished business, as if the business of the poem might be completed only by a return to the business of battle.

Owen's 'Spring Offensive', however, complicates the call. It recreates the lull before battle and then the attack itself, before the final line of the penultimate stanza turns to the aftermath: 'Some say God caught them even before they fell'. This poem does not explicitly deny that, although the non-specificity suggests scepticism; but the final stanza asks what the survivors 'say': 'Why speak not they of comrades that went under?' The question contains bafflement, regret and even irritation, but also anxiety. This very poem, by speaking at all, is presuming to speak for those who either cannot, or who decide not to, speak for themselves. The question anxiously and honourably queries the whole undertaking of this poet's own work, implicitly recognizing that the officer in charge, the man who has given the orders for this 'offensive', is very dubiously positioned as a spokesman for those who stay silent subsequently. The war becomes his subject while he is literally making others subject to him. The poem appears to query its own right to 'speak for', perhaps even to acknowledge that this might seem 'offensive'; and this stress in the very undertaking is one of the several complications that enrich Owen's finest work. His poetry is the scene of his anguished examination of what it is to be a lieutenant, a *lieu-tenant*: one who holds, or stands in, the place of others. The place he holds on the battlefield is that of the commanding officer; the place he holds in the poem can only be very self-questioningly that of the private soldier.

But there are other ramifying complications in Owen's wartime poems too. An untitled, two-sentence poem brilliantly and disturbingly clarifies at least one of them:

> I saw his round mouth's crimson deepen as it fell,
>   Like a sun, in his last deep hour;
> Watched the magnificent recession of farewell,
>   Clouding, half gleam, half glower,
> And a last splendour burn the heavens of his cheek.
>   And in his eyes
> The cold stars lighting, very old and bleak,
>   In different skies.

This poem does what many of Owen's war poems do: it reconfigures almost allotropically a motif everywhere in his work, a homoerotic fantasizing about the faces and bodies of young men. Such continuities are apparent in Jon Stallworthy's edition, which reveals how, even in the *annus mirabilis*, 1917–18, in which Owen wrote most of his war poetry, he was still revising earlier work and drafting callow poems of unalloyed homoerotic fantasy, such as 'Page Eglantine' and 'The Rime of the Youthful Mariner'. These same continuities are written large in Dominic Hibberd's biography.[5] In 'I saw his round mouth's crimson', however, these tropes are both complicated and distressed. The feeling with which the 'mouth's crimson' is gazed at is certainly erotic; the repetition of 'deepen' and 'deep' is a form of pulsation; and the conjuration of that flush on the soldier's dying cheek carries into a sexually provoked register the frequent flushes of arousal which Owen would have noticed in his hugely admired and much imitated Keats. Along with this, the stellification or apotheosis of traditional masculine, self-involved English elegy – of Milton's 'Lycidas', for instance – is absorbed into the poem's imagery of sun, heaven, stars and skies. But the poem is charged with other sympathetic recognitions too, which raise sexual feeling to the power of a quasi-religious 'recession' of mourning.

Indeed, the recessional hymn of the Anglican liturgy is recalled by the word 'recession', and a form of displaced Anglicanism is never far from the tenderness of Owen's regard. It is as though his poem 'Maundy Thursday', probably drafted in 1915 and revised in late 1917 or early 1918, was a kind of paradigm or template for the war poems. When the crucifix is held out to the congregation for veneration in that poem, during the Roman Catholic ceremony known as 'the Veneration of the Cross' (which actually takes place on Good Friday), the poet kisses not the silver icon itself – although in fact this would have been to have kissed a virtually naked male image – but 'the warm live hand that held the thing', the 'brown' hand of 'a server-lad'. This is intended to represent a transferral of religious into humanist feeling; and so it does, very powerfully: but the feeling is also vibrantly erotic ('my lips did cling'), and the word 'lad' constitutes virtually a code in the homoerotic poetry of the late nineteenth and early twentieth century. 'I saw his round mouth's crimson' is also a poem of transferred or displaced veneration, deepening eroticism into mourning, while also disturbingly, but bravely, acknowledging the presence of such feeling in the context of gazing on a dying body.

'Maundy Thursday' risks blasphemy; 'I saw his round mouth's crimson' also takes risks, by striving for honest record and accurate emotion and by unflinchingly attempting to make language newly commensurate with horrific event. Refusing to sanitize response, it intertwines suffering and reaction, victimization and voyeurism, in a knot of intricate complexity. Welling out of Owen's psychosexual subjectivity, the poem thereby also meets the extreme demand of its historical moment. James Fenton has said of Owen's juvenilia that 'the realm of Eros was what he felt to be his great subject'.[6] In 'I saw his round mouth's crimson' and other war poems, Owen produces work in which what he felt to be his great subject, 'the realm of Eros', is forced into devastating confrontation with a subject he did not want at all, the realm of Thanatos; but this turns what he felt to be his great subject into his truly great subject, and the subject of great poems. The combination of the erotic and the representative is what makes poems such as 'Strange Meeting', 'Greater Love', 'Asleep' and 'Disabled' so emotionally complicated. In these poems the quality of yearning undermines the elegiac principle of assuagement, with the consequence that they revise the history of English elegy, in a way commensurate with the exceptionality of their occasions.

'I saw his round mouth's crimson' may also, however, briefly flicker with another element apparent in Owen's war poems, when it gazes into those withdrawing eyes and sees there 'The cold stars lighting, very old and bleak, / In different skies'. Peter Howarth discovers the word 'indifferent' here, reading it as Owen's awareness of the soldier's unresponsiveness to the poet's interest. However, it could also leave the man's eyes glazing over with what this poet takes to be the civilian reaction to such deaths: indifference.[7] Owen's poems are designed to shock readers out of indifference by confronting them with actuality; and some, much more obviously than 'I saw his round mouth's crimson', prominently include an element of the homiletic: notably 'Apologia pro Poemate Meo' ('These men are worth / Your tears. You are not worth their merriment'), 'Insensibility' and 'Dulce et Decorum Est'. This is one of the implications of the preface he drafted in May 1918 for a book he hoped to publish the following year:

> This book is not about heroes. English Poetry is not yet fit to speak of them. Nor is it about glory or honour or any might, majesty, dominion or power nor about anything except War. Above all I am not concerned with Poetry. My subject is War, and the pity of War. The Poetry is in the pity ... Yet these elegies are in no sense consolatory to this generation. They may be to the next ... All a poet can do today is warn. That is why the true Poet must be truthful.[8]

The capitalizations speak volumes: the usual motives for and prizes of war, those voiced by politicians and journalists – glory, honour and those words with strong Christian-liturgical associations, 'dominion' and 'power' – pale into lower case, and what stands upright is what the soldier must face, almost in the form of an apotheosized abstraction, 'War', and what the poet has to offer, 'Poetry'. There is a politics in this, as there is in Edward Thomas's reticence; there is a revisionary aesthetics; and, for all that it has a certain rhetorical inflation, there is a strong sense of the poem as an act of cautionary witness. In fact, Owen's list of contents for this putative volume itemizes not only the title of each poem but also its 'motive'; and one of the ways in which Owen was not Keatsian – as opposed to all the ways in which he was, in his youth – is his agitated certainty that poetry *should* have a palpable design upon us. From this poet endlessly concerned, as his letters constantly show, with poetry, it is a self-revising gesture of the profoundest kind to declare that the poetry lies somewhere other than in the poetry. Indeed, it is almost as though Owen can permit himself poetry, under these circumstances and out of this material, only when it has become something other than itself.

In an outstanding critical study, Douglas Kerr has shown how, in order to write these poems, Owen deliberately schooled himself in elegy, especially pastoral elegy; but he schools himself as a subversive.[9] Where the traditional English elegy is consolatory, assuaging grief in Christianized pastoral – 'Some say God caught them even before they fell' could almost be read as Owen's account of this tradition – the truthful elegy of this war is 'in no sense consolatory'. Merging the erotic with the homiletic to create poetry of scrupulously less deceived witness, poetry against itself, Owen resists consolation with a more deeply distressed melancholy. Jahan Ramazani, in a Freudian reading of Owen, makes less of the homoerotic than I do here, more of the poems' impulsion towards masochism, and nothing of the homiletic: but he also regards Owen as exemplifying the 'paradox' of modern elegies: that 'the best are frequently the most anti-elegiac'.[10]

'Futility' is exemplary in this way, and it is also a poem in which subverted elegy and homiletic intention modify and differently focus desire. The exacting intensity with which it manages this makes it, in my view, Owen's greatest poem:

> Move him into the sun –
> Gently its touch awoke him once,
> At home, whispering of fields half-sown.
> Always it woke him, even in France,
> Until this morning and this snow.
> If anything might rouse him now
> The kind old sun will know.
> Think how it wakes the seeds –
> Woke once the clays of a cold star.
> Are limbs, so dear-achieved, are sides
> Full-nerved, still warm, too hard to stir?
> Was it for this the clay grew tall?
> – O what made fatuous sunbeams toil
> To break earth's sleep at all?

This poem revises traditional elegy in several ways. It is a sonnet, and therefore a form conjuring a tradition of English lyric, notably of love lyric. But its three- and four-stress lines, refusing pentameter, make the form anxious, curtailed, self-resistant. Owen's characteristic pararhymes (sun/sown; once/France; and so on), that influential modern invention, add to the edge and unease, the irresolution of emotion. Pararhyme, Douglas Kerr memorably says, is 'a broken promise to return'.[11] Traditional elegies on the other hand, we might say, keep their promises, and return is what they promise. Some of the locations and properties characteristic of pastoral elegy – the half-sown fields, the personified rising sun, the waking from death into some form of new life – are warped in 'Futility' in the direction of dissent and disconsolation. Employing a standard rhetorical trope inherited from classical literature and, most famously in English poetry, from Wordsworth's *Prelude* ('Was it for this?'), Owen asks one of the largest of his rhetorical questions, 'Was it for this the clay grew tall?', collapsing elegiac solace into an ultimate insecurity desolately in harmony with the fact that by the time 'Futility' was written in May 1918 many, both on and off the battlefield, were asking whether there was any reason to continue.

'Futility' also brings to a point of pained self-revision the trope of the homoerotic gaze. The poem's opening instruction – 'Move him into the sun' – sounds like the initiation of a pastoral ritual, but it could equally well be that of an officer to his men, telling them what to do with a corpse; and so Owen represents himself as both officer and poet, caught between actuality and art. But the instruction at the opening of the second stanza – 'Think how it wakes the seeds' – seems much more deeply interiorized, an instruction from the self to the self; and this is a self situated once more in the role of artful voyeur, that relevant phrase coined in the poem 'Punishment' in his volume *North* (1975) by an admirer of Owen's, Seamus Heaney, defining his own relationship to another war and its dead. Those 'limbs' and 'sides', particularized in a succession of achingly poignant epithets, might well, in another kind of poem, have been the spur to further erotic reverie; and we might even remember, with a kind of discrepant appropriateness, the knowing jocularity with which Owen, in the trenches, writes punningly to Sassoon that he wants 'no more *exposed flanks* of any kind for a long time'.[12]

In 'Futility', however, the eroticism is also curtailed. The licence of kissing the warm live hand in 'Maundy Thursday' has become the anguish of watching the warmth disappear forever from limbs now, just, 'still warm'; and what might elsewhere stir this onlooker erotically is in the process of becoming 'too hard to stir', except to stir this poet to the desperation and bitterness of his concluding questions. These questions raise Owen's quarrel with the pieties of orthodox Christianity to a level of almost apocalyptic weariness; but this weariness is quite a different thing from resignation. 'Futility' offers, in its piercingly eloquent economy, the spectacle of a poet in whom, under the most extreme responsiveness of obligation, everything is organized into sympathetic coherence and brought to its highest pitch of concentrated utterance. It is the exemplary combatant poem of war by an officer poet.

III

'Pity' is a significant word in Siegfried Sassoon's poems, and Owen was undoubtedly aided in the formulation of his preface, and altogether confirmed in his competence as a poet and in the tractability of the war as a subject for poetry, by his relationship with Sassoon, whom he met when both were inmates of Craiglockhart Hospital in Edinburgh. Owen was there as a consequence of what was classified as 'neurasthenia' following front-line experience, and Sassoon as an alternative to standing trial for a 'declaration' against the running of the war, which he made in July 1917. Not a pacifist's declaration, but, its title proclaimed, 'A Soldier's Declaration', it expressed Sassoon's belief that the war had become one of 'aggression and conquest'; it made a stand against 'political errors and insincerities'; and it blamed 'the callous complacency with which the majority of those at home regard the continuance of agonies which they do not share, and which they have not sufficient imagination to realize'.[13] This indictment, with its characteristic quiver of intellectual disdain, was extremely brave of Sassoon, who was a quite extraordinarily impressive human being; and the fact that he also published satirical poems about the war provided Owen with a model for the way personal, non-pacifist bravery could be combined with poetic truth-telling.

Sassoon's poems inherit something from Hardy's *Satires of Circumstance* and comprise anecdote, reportage, invective and imitated demotic speech, and Owen learnt a great deal from work such as 'Base Details', 'The General' and '"They"'. In the last, a bishop – and Sassoon had the bishop of London specifically in mind – celebrates in the first verse the fact that the returning boys 'will not be the same', after heroic transformation in battle. The second verse, which is both counterpart and contradiction, then offers the boys' version of being 'none of us the same': one is legless, one blind, one lung-damaged and one syphilitic. The poem concludes with a characteristic satirical epigram: 'And the Bishop said: "The ways of God are strange!"' Sassoon's poems typically work by such reversals of expectation and explosions of cliché, and they are capable of corrosive ironies and invective. If they seem now sometimes a little pat in their reversals or peripeteia, they are historically highly significant, and should not be underestimated. However, to witness Owen in poems such as 'The Chances' assimilating and transforming the manner absorbed from Sassoon is to witness poetic genius in the process of self-discovery. That poem begins in satire, as it imitates the cockney speech of its soldier speaker who tells us that, the night before battle, he and four mates debate the 'five things as can happen' to them: 'You get knocked out; else wounded, bad or cushy; / Scuppered; or nowt except you're feelin' mushy.' The satire becomes less self-confident, more humanly wounded, more emotionally wrecked, though, than it ever does in Sassoon, as the sudden, devastatingly unpredictable conclusion has a perennial, rather than a propagandistic, desolation:

> But poor old Jim, he's livin' and he's not;
> He reckoned he'd five chances, and he had:
> He's wounded, killed, and pris'ner, all the lot,
> The flamin' lot all rolled in one. Jim's mad.

In those terrible and unforgettable lines, satire mutates into tragedy.

In fact, whereas Owen's letters soon after meeting Sassoon are effusions of hero worship – Dominic Hibberd believes that Owen was in love with him – he is, by December 1917, telling his cousin Leslie Gunston, in a letter, that 'Poetry with him [Sassoon] is become a mere vehicle of propaganda': and this harsh dismissal, authoritatively self-assured and even brutally ungrateful, seems a defining moment in Owen's astonishingly speedy acquisition of a sense of his own competence.[14] In 'The Chances' everything in Owen is alert and keyed to advantage; and similar effects of mastery and self-mastery are apparent in other poems too where, as Hibberd and others have shown, his early slavish indebtedness to Keats is pushed up against, and confronted by, such radically modifying influences as the French Decadents, the English Georgians (especially Harold Monro) and Baudelaire. In fact, you could almost claim of Owen what Ezra Pound famously claimed of T. S. Eliot in 1914: that 'he has actually trained himself *and* modernized himself *on his own.*'[15] And, given that he was in fact absorbing some of the same French influences as Eliot himself, it is tantalizing to think that the fractures between Modernism and what has sometimes been thought of as the 'native English tradition' may have looked very different had Owen survived the war; or, indeed, that Owen may have found a way different from Eliot's of bringing French decadence and symbolism into post-war English poetry.

But to think about the poets of the First World War who died so young, and with such attenuated poetic careers, is to be plunged, always, into the melancholy consideration of such alternative histories and literary histories.

IV

Owen may have modernized himself on his own; and certainly until he met Sassoon he had no one to help him. Isaac Rosenberg, from a far more poverty-stricken background than Owen's – in the working-class Jewish East End of London – nevertheless managed, by a form of short-lived patronage, to gain an acquaintance with pre-war avant-garde movements in the arts, and his poetry was supported, in a rather half-hearted way, by Ezra Pound, and by Harriet Monroe, who published him in her influential magazine *Poetry* (Chicago). Rosenberg's forms have, as a consequence, affiliations with both free verse and Imagism. Employing biblical and Jewish materials, and ambitiously attempting a kind of post-Blakean religio-prophetic poetry, he also had a much larger range of pre-war subject matter than Owen. For these reasons, among others, his war poetry appears less shocked into variant utterance, less alternatively galvanized, than Owen's, although the war does newly animate and sharpen what can seem a certain vatic vapidity in the earlier work. He also experiments with the same phrases and lines in different poems; and one letter poignantly promises further drafting in tranquillity: 'I will not leave a corner of my consciousness covered up, but saturate myself with the strange and extraordinary new conditions of this life, and it will all refine itself into poetry later on.'[16]

So it is a shock to learn from Vivien Noakes's edition that Rosenberg, a private soldier, actually wrote most of his war poems in the trenches, unlike Owen, who wrote his on leave, including the extended sick leave of his spell in Craiglockhart. Rosenberg enlisted in October 1915 and was killed on 1 April 1918; and during twenty-one months in France he had only ten days' leave. 'It is unusual,' Noakes says drily, 'for a manuscript not to be folded, torn and dirty'.[17] As a consequence, the editorial lot is more than usually unhappy, and many of Rosenberg's given texts must be regarded as provisional. Although this is one of the reasons why his reputation has never settled in the way Owen's has, reading him is sometimes to feel that an element of folded, torn and dirty provisionality inheres in his very aesthetic, which seems to honour, more than most, the improvisational. It may even be that he meant something of the kind when he wrote in a letter to Gordon Bottomley (who edited his first posthumous volume in 1922) that his ideal was one of 'Simple *poetry* – that is where an interesting complexity of thought is kept in tone and right value to the dominating idea so that it is understandable and still ungraspable'.[18] This seems to anticipate Wallace Stevens's much more famous contention that 'the poem must resist the intelligence almost successfully' and to harmonize with T. S. Eliot's conception of the destabilizing difficulties inevitably inherent in a genuinely modern poetry. Like these, it has a quality of almost truculently confrontational self-assurance; and it indicates that Rosenberg was modernized, perhaps with a little help, from a very early stage. It is remote indeed from Owen's guarded but still sometimes almost skinless affectivity.

As a consequence, Rosenberg's poems characteristically move by ellipsis and elision, by the melting or dripping of image into image, by abruptions of rhythm and cadence, by unsettling and not always easily 'graspable' syntactical transitions. His forms can jarringly convey, almost mimetically, the actualities of trench warfare, as in 'Dead Man's Dump', in which army 'limbers' (carts or gun-carriages) 'lurched over sprawled dead'. This poem itself lurches and jostles in its attempt to convey this exceptional gruesomeness in a fury of alliterative and assonantal linguistic wreckage ('The plunging limbers over the shattered track / Racketed with their rusty freight'), in biblical and other religious half-echo and allusion, in anguished questioning, and in sudden astonishing, quasi-metaphysical conceit, as in the likening of a bullet to a bee: 'When the swift iron burning bee / Drained the wild honey of their youth'; which is a motivating of the inanimate as luxuriously appalled as Owen's homoerotic anthropomorphizing in 'Arms and the

Boy': 'these blind, blunt bullet-leads / Which long to nuzzle in the hearts of lads.'

In contrast to such poems of driven physical representation, there are in Rosenberg much cooler poems of ironic mutedness. The greatest of these, and one of the greatest of the war, is 'Break of Day in the Trenches', a poem of eerily disquieting calm. Here simple *poetry*, poetry in a very pure distillation, is being written, and it is poetry in which complexity of thought, and tone and right value, are lucidly self-validating means and effects. D. W. Harding, one of Rosenberg's earliest critics and editors, says that suffering in Rosenberg is treated in such a way that 'no secondary distress [arises] from the sense that these things *ought not* to be. He was given up to realizing fully what *was*'; and this appears to be at least partly right about this poem.[19] Given that exactly such secondary distress impels all of Owen's war poems and that it is actually the primary, exacerbated distress of Sassoon's, this quality makes 'Break of Day in the Trenches' very much the poem of a private soldier, one that speaks for itself and not on behalf of others. In this sense, it may even be regarded as a kind of answer to Owen's anguished question in 'Spring Offensive', 'Why speak not they of comrades that went under?'

The poem imagines its speaker picking a poppy from the trench parapet to stick behind his ear, when a rat from No Man's Land 'leaps [his] hand'. The rat is anthropomorphically figured as 'sardonic' and 'droll', and the speaker himself drolly rebukes the rat's treacherous 'cosmopolitan sympathies' (it crosses the lines, but the phrase is also glossed by Rosenberg's Jewishness). So – almost unimaginable thing if Rosenberg had not managed it – drollery and wit are brought to the poetry of the trenches. Complexities of thought then combine with drollery, when the dead are said to be 'less chanced than you for life' and 'bonds to the whims of murder'. So the poem plots a politics into its drollery too. Soldiers in the trenches are worth less than rats; their deaths are 'murder', and not some other thing – 'sacrifice', for instance; and are governed by 'whim' and not by 'glory or honour', or even policy. So Harding is not wholly right about this poem. Although it makes no parade of its 'secondary distress', it certainly knows that these things ought not to be.

The poem moves towards conclusion with two of Rosenberg's characteristically vast rhetorical questions, asked of the rat, and so crossing drollery with desperation, and then astonishingly inflecting anguish with recovery in a way almost jaunty in its self-presentation:

> What do you see in our eyes
> At the shrieking iron and flame
> Hurl'd through still heavens?
> What quaver – what heart aghast?
> Poppies whose roots are in man's veins
> Drop, and are ever dropping,

> But mine in my ear is safe –
> Just a little white with the dust.

This nonchalance, a desperate composure, proffers an extraordinary image: that of the trench soldier as dandy; where, previously, the cosmopolitan rat is almost a kind of Baudelairean *flâneur*, out strolling in the early morning for – the speaker says – 'your pleasure'. Yet the out-of-tune, dissonant fall of 'aghast' against 'dust' insinuates the fate of this stylish respite, and unnervingly orients the figure of the dandy, which is usually, of course, comic, towards tragedy. Managing such a style and such a tone at such a time and in such a place, Rosenberg is validating the authority of the aesthetic: 'Break of Day in the Trenches' refuses to permit terror or despair to cramp, or dictate, a style. And, managing like this, Rosenberg is also displaying a very high form of courage.

V

Rosenberg and Owen died in the war; Ivor Gurney survived. But he survived by spending a great deal of his life in mental institutions, and constantly revisiting the war in his poems of the 1920s, permanently preoccupied by what, in the poem 'First Time In', he calls, with perspicaciously awkward understatement, as if damning it with a mildly euphemistic oath, 'the whole craft and business of bad occasion'.[20] Gurney's survival therefore offers one emblem for the way the First World War cannot be extirpated from cultural memory. This makes P. J. Kavanagh's devoted act of recovery of Gurney in his edition of 1982 a major moment in the history of the poetry of the war, giving us in their required contexts at least two of its outstanding poems.

'To His Love', written during the war, collapses a Virgilian pastoral eclogue of companionship into an urgent yearning to forget what can never be forgotten, and does so in the most jolting of enjambments, in a line-break like a headlong stumble:

> Cover him, cover him soon!
>   And with thick-set
> Masses of memoried flowers –
>   Hide that red wet
> Thing I must somehow forget.

Between 'red wet' and the next line's 'Thing' – those three funereally heavy stresses – falls the absolute knowledge that flowers will never be enough to hide this memory, and that there is only a no-how to supply for this 'somehow'. And 'The Silent One', written several years after the war, expresses one of the worst horrors of trench warfare: having to see your friends die on the wire of No Man's Land beyond the reach of succour. The dead man commemorated in the specificity of his language and accent may stand here as an emblem for what the poets of that war managed in their own languages and accents, wearing them new; and also, since Gurney pointedly remarks the folly of faithfulness, for the infinite waste of all the war's silent, and silenced, ones:

> Who died on the wires, and hung there, one of two –
> Who for his hours of life had chattered through
> Infinite lovely chatter of Bucks accent:
> Yet faced unbroken wires; stepped over, and went
> A noble fool, faithful to his stripes – and ended.

CHAPTER 2

Isaac Rosenberg's Possessives

I

'Break of Day in the Trenches', which I touched on briefly in the last chapter, is Isaac Rosenberg's most celebrated poem and one of the best of the poems he wrote at the Front; and as such it is one of the best poems of the War itself. For anyone who knows what preceded it in Rosenberg's short career but substantial poetic output, it also seems almost a miracle of emotional sensitivity, ironic self-awareness and technical subtlety. W. B. Yeats, although he had recommended Rosenberg to Ezra Pound, refused an invitation to introduce a collection by the poet in 1922, saying that he found it 'all windy rhetoric'.[1] This misjudgement is as crass as that with which Yeats dismisses all the war poets in his notorious introduction to his *Oxford Book of Modern Verse* in 1936: that 'passive suffering is not a theme for poetry'. However, while even of the pre-war work Yeats's judgement would be indiscriminately harsh, it would probably not be altogether too harsh. For the fact is that 'Break of Day in the Trenches' and others of Rosenberg's outstanding war poems follow on a body of work in which large ambition often almost poignantly outruns technical capacity and sureness of allusive touch.

The intensely difficult circumstances of Rosenberg's youth – his origins, that is, in a penurious Jewish East End family, which had made his formal education nugatory – also provoked in him a high degree of partly defensive but seemingly arrogant self-assurance. Under the circumstances, this may appear admirable; but Jean Moorcroft Wilson's biography catalogues the ways in which it often hardened into an almost impenetrable self-absorption.[2] This made Rosenberg a sometimes very difficult companion, tutee and even object of well-meaning if occasionally condescending patronage, and it can also be felt to diminish poetic force. Large social sympathy or even interest are not essential to the production of arresting poetry, but such things do need to be more adequately supplied for than they are in pre-war Rosenberg if the work is not to seem sustained by little more than an effortful, exhausting and ultimately self-undermining form of determination and self-determination.

The human sympathies and ironies of 'Break of Day in the Trenches' and their unpredictable line-by-line flux are therefore one of the most breathtaking instances of the truism about the poetry of the First World War: that the war itself rapidly, urgently and originally charged the work of its young poets in a way that it is almost impossible to believe anything else ever would have. In fact, the poem opening with Rosenberg's first truly unforgettable line – 'Snow is a strange white word' – demonstrates this with almost diagrammatic neatness: it is the poem entitled 'On Receiving News of the War: Cape Town'. 'Break of Day in the Trenches' therefore manifests achievement as the sudden precipitate of strength from hitherto inchoate ambition. It is a poem in which rhetorical strain is purified into poetic necessity; in which formal and even, on occasion, grammatical incoherence are electrified into sheer steadiness of articulation; and in which unbendingly self-assertive will, which can be poetically inhibiting, melts into the true power of imagination. It is therefore an exemplary poem of Rosenberg's speedy maturation, and we may read his contribution through it:

> The darkness crumbles away.
> It is the same old druid Time as ever.
> Only a live thing leaps my hand,
> A queer sardonic rat,
> As I pull the parapet's poppy
> To stick behind my ear.
> Droll rat, they would shoot you if they knew
> Your cosmopolitan sympathies.
> Now you have touched this English hand
> You will do the same to a German
> Soon, no doubt, if it be your pleasure
> To cross the sleeping green between.
> It seems, odd thing, you grin as you pass
> Strong eyes, fine limbs, haughty athletes,
> Less chanced than you for life,
> Bonds to the whims of murder,
> Sprawled in the bowels of the earth,
> The torn fields of France.
> What do you see in our eyes
> At the shrieking iron and flame
> Hurl'd through still heavens?
> What quaver – what heart aghast?
> Poppies whose roots are in man's veins
> Drop, and are ever dropping,
> But mine in my ear is safe –
> Just a little white with the dust.

When Rosenberg sent 'Break of Day in the Trenches' in a letter to Edward Marsh in 1916 he recommended it as 'surely as simple as ordinary talk'.[3] As it opens, we do seem to overhear a mode of introspective rumination or meditation. This tone is a function of both the opening declarativeness and of Rosenberg's insidious rhythm and cadence. 'Regular rhythms I do not like much,' he wrote, again to Marsh, saying he would have preferred it if Andrew Marvell 'had broken up his rhythms more'.[4] 'Break of Day in the Trenches' constantly breaks up an iambic pulse with trochaic, spondaic and anapaestic measures, making for an intense liveliness of felt vocal presence and pressure. The opening trochee and the following four strong stresses, distributed among only eight syllables, of the line which introduces the poet's addressee, the rat, for instance – 'Only a live thing leaps my hand' – are mimetic of the surprise and urgency of the event, as the poem's voice is startled out of meditation into perturbed apprehension and recognition. We therefore need to modify what Rosenberg says to Marsh: the poem is only as simple as ordinary talk *in poetry*; and that is not simple, but the fixing into memorable cadence on the page of what a finely tuned ear has apprehended as the music of human speech. The poem's ensuing cadences and rhythms, which include rhetorical elements (and rhetorical questions) not at all like 'ordinary talk', could be described to reveal similar subtleties of response and effect.

Donne's 'The Flea' has been adduced in relation to Rosenberg's rat. However, in Donne the addressee of the poet is the woman, not the flea itself. By addressing the rat, and more specifically by addressing it with the ambiguous compliment of 'droll', Rosenberg is himself drolly inheriting and revising – downwards – a romantic tradition of apostrophe to the non-human, which reaches its apogee in Shelley's 'To a Skylark' and Keats's 'Ode to a Nightingale'. Skylark and nightingale undergo an implicit metamorphosis in Rosenberg, of the kind David Jones makes explicit in Part 3 of *In Parenthesis*, where, remembering the Anglo-Saxon poem *The Battle of Maldon*, and alluding to Darwin, he says that 'the speckled kite of Maldon / and the crow / have naturally selected to be un-winged / to go on the belly, to / sap sap sap / with festered spines, arched under the moon'; to exchange their nature as birds, that is, for that of trench rats. Both Keats and Shelley are influential but largely unassimilated presences in pre-war Rosenberg; and it is an irony of more than just literary history that his proper absorption of them should be so revisionist.

If drollness is an attribute shared by rat and poet, the rat's other epithets may seem applicable too. This poem also has its 'sardonic' aspect, and other war poems of Rosenberg's have that more strongly. 'Queer', in its sense of 'odd' or 'peculiar', has relevance to a poet who often, even before the war and absolutely during it, as a private soldier, felt at odds and incapable, or – worse – was made to feel so by others. And 'cosmopolitan' is a word prominently associated with Jews, notably in the derogatory phrase in which it is accompanied by the adjective 'rootless' (the rat is also, disgustingly, a feature of anti-Semitic discourse). This rat, travelling indiscriminately between English and Germans, has no national attachments; and in wartime that may be thought to involve the potential for disloyalty. In a letter to Marsh, Rosenberg makes it plain that he 'never joined the army from patriotic reasons. Nothing can justify war.'[5] In fact, his motives were predominantly financial, as he sought a way to avoid poverty and dependency on his family, whose pacifism he appears fundamentally to have shared. The apparently ironic, witty use of the word 'cosmopolitan' therefore has extensive ethical and political ramifications. Further, the evocation of the potential consequences of cosmopolitan behaviour ('they would shoot you if they knew ...') is underwritten dreadfully by a letter to Sydney Schiff in 1916 in which, referring to a mutiny of private soldiers, Rosenberg says that 'some men got bayoneted'.[6]

These implications are all subtly muted in the poem, which maintains under extraordinary circumstances an extraordinary decorum. Just as the epithets applied to the rat appear sophisticatedly self-referential or poetically self-reflexive too, the poem's decorum is almost itself advertised by the slightly parodic element of its address: 'if it be your pleasure / To cross the sleeping green between'. This weird fastidiousness is a little like Alice's unnerving composure as she addresses the anthropomorphized creatures down the rabbit hole in *Alice in Wonderland*. Such courtliness is sardonically discrepant, of course, since the pastoral 'green' is actually the desolation of No Man's Land where human corpses lie rotting beyond retrieval; and the rat's elective affinities are in reality dependent on nothing more fastidious than an opportunistic hunt for food.

In the phrase 'sleeping green' the epithet may be transferred. It may be the bodies of both English and German soldiers that lie 'sleeping', that common euphemism for death. And as this poet contemplates these bodies, one of which may well soon be his own, the sardonic element of his poem sharpens into something more angrily political. That soldiers slain in war are 'bonds to the whims of murder' undermines a great deal of the powerful political rhetoric, or cant, of the First World War. 'Bonds' makes the soldiers slaves (and in a letter to Lascelles Abercrombie in 1916 Rosenberg says that 'nobody but a private in the army knows what it is to be a slave'); 'whims' implies a negative judgement on the potential efficacy of any military strategy under these conditions; and 'murder' makes all military killing morally reprehensible.[7] But calling these deaths murder now provokes a rhetoric of Rosenberg's own; provokes rhetorical questions, in fact, in which the rat is asked what he reads in the eyes of those still living. The second of these questions suggests abject terror: 'What quaver – what heart aghast?', which introduces a further faint allusion to Romantic apostrophe: to Blake's 'The Tyger' ('What immortal hand or eye ... ?'). Blake ascribes 'fearful symmetry' to his tiger. 'Break of Day in the Trenches' is a poem about fearful asymmetry, the dispro-portion between the frail bodies of men and 'the shrieking iron and flame' of mechanized warfare. The poem's companion piece or early version, 'In the Trenches', which immediately precedes it in Vivien Noakes's edition, is much less successful but inevitably casts a dire shadow over it. In that poem the speaker picks not one but two poppies, sticking one behind his ear and giving the other to a companion. At the poem's end a shell bursts, killing the companion and smashing his poppy to pieces.

In his use of rhetoric in 'Break of Day in the Trenches' Rosenberg is as warm or as heated as Wilfred Owen in the perturbed erotic tenderness of 'I saw his round mouth's crimson' or as Ivor Gurney in the anguished, obsessive recoil of 'To His Love': but 'Break of Day in the Trenches' is exceptional in the way it finally disciplines the heat of agitation, composing itself – in both senses – to a kind of cool. 'Cool' as in a lowering of the temperature, certainly, as the poem returns to the poppy of its opening lines. There, the poet has stuck it behind his ear. Now, the flower is first generalized, in the common fantasy or myth that poppies are stained red by human blood, and then personalized:

> Poppies whose roots are in man's veins
> Drop, and are ever dropping,
> But mine in my ear is safe –
> Just a little white with the dust.

'Man's veins', not 'men's veins', with a reminder that mortality is the general condition: but then 'man's' cedes to 'mine', the frail individual resistance to the common fate. Rosenberg manages this transition with a studied but tactful grace: casual, off-hand, throwaway, with a combative whimsy of his own. Behaving like this, 'Break of Day in the Trenches' also becomes cool in the idiomatic contemporary sense. The poet sticking the poppy behind his ear and then adverting to it again, after everything his poem has confronted, is playing the dandy, maintaining an elegant gesture and a pose in the face of the insupportable.

In a curious pre-war prose fragment called 'On Noses' Rosenberg considers how what he calls 'noise projectivity and ostentation' – he means, I think, simply a lot of it – may seem useless and superficial but can still act as 'echoes and heralds of the great, the useful and substantial'. His examples form an odd threesome: 'If we take religion as an instance, or a great cause like dandyism or women's suffrage, is not the spouting, the shouting, the foppishness but the effervescence, the first dribblings of a solid and profound idea, of an earnest soul-enthralling basis?'[8] It is hard to know what irony, if any, inheres in Rosenberg's making the politics of dandyism equivalent to those of women's suffrage: but the passage does reveal his clear understanding that provocation of a Wildean kind forms an oppositional political position.

A photograph of Rosenberg with a group of fellow art students at the Slade in 1912 shows him kneeling apart from the others, dressed quite soberly, almost certainly in what his biographer tells us was 'the one family suit'. Others of the students, however, notably Rosenberg's friend David Bomberg and his acquaintance Mark Gertler, are distinctly dandyish, even foppish, with flowing neckties and huge, soft, bucket-shaped hats (Bomberg painted himself several times wearing one). In 'Break of Day in the Trenches' Isaac Rosenberg, who did not wish, or could not manage, to cut such a figure in life, does figure himself as a dandyish exquisite. This is now truly the dandyism of a great cause, the solid and profound idea that permits this private soldier to revise a fin-de-siècle style into the ability, at least in spirit and imagination, to confront the ostentation of shrieking iron and flame. The poem, learning a style from a despair, offers us the figure of the private soldier as dandy and the figure of the dandy as hero: defiantly, even jauntily resilient as he makes his cool refusal, and framing his gesture as a grimly off-hand, ironic joke: for of course we ask, even without the aid of 'In the Trenches', how 'safe' a poppy is in a front-line trench.

The coolness of 'Break of Day in the Trenches' is powerfully aided also by its quasi-imagist poetic, which had affinities with the aesthetics of the plastic arts in the opening decade of the century. Rosenberg's letters reveal a distrust of Imagism, just as he showed a suspicion of Vorticism in the plastic arts, although Bomberg had embraced the movement. Even so, Rosenberg admired some of the work of the imagist F. S. Flint, and had contact with Ezra Pound, who recommended him to Harriet Monroe, the editor of the little magazine *Poetry* (Chicago), in which imagist poems appeared, and in which 'Break of Day in the Trenches' was first published in 1916. We could even consider the poem a kind of exploded imagist poem, with its opening two and its closing four quiet, quasi-imagist lines of mise-en-scène disrupted by the intervention of the unmannerly wartime rat. Despite Rosenberg's reserve about the avant-garde, it is clear that his war poetry gains from his knowledge of it. Geoffrey Hill, in fact, makes an arresting case for considering Rosenberg's experimental way of 'thinking through the phrase or image', which is signalled partly by his propensity to repeat phrases and images across different poems, an equivalent of what Bomberg later called the 'sense of mass' in painting. The ideas canvassed in the many conversations shared by painter and poet, Hill thinks, may well have contributed to the production of both.[9]

II

'Break of Day in the Trenches', then, concentrates three elements essential to an understanding of this poet's significance: his mythologizing; his voicing the experience of the private soldier; and his Jewishness.

The poem's second line, 'It is the same old Druid Time as ever', personifies time as a pre-historic priest for whom dawn had high religious import but who also, ominously, engaged in human sacrifice, at least according to hostile Roman sources. The trope registers both the poet's surprise that time continues as it always has, even in the apparently unique circumstances of the trenches, and also an undeceived acceptance of such continuity. The quasi-mythologizing personification is consistent with a great deal in Rosenberg's pre-war poetry, in which he moves among the vast shadows of classical, biblical and Hebraic mythology, aiming at a synthesis whose primary avatar is probably Blake in his prophetic books. These poems are almost wholly unsuccessful, but they do make it clear that something deep in Rosenberg's imagination is compelled by the scope and economy of myth, by its apparent capacity to resolve human complexity into symbolic or emblematic opposition and resolution. Such compulsions are more successfully actualized in some of the war poetry, notably 'Daughters of War' and 'A Worm Fed On the Heart of Corinth'.

The former makes something compellingly strange out of a rather incoherent element in the pre-war poetry: a powerful, terrifying female deity, a savage god, synthesized from such sources as the Amazons, the Valkyries and the Babylonian-Talmudic figure of the demonic Lilith (who appears as a character in Rosenberg's play *The Unicorn*). Rosenberg admired Whitman, particularly his poems of the American Civil War. 'Daughters of War' therefore appropriately deploys a quasi-Whitmanian free verse, apparently improvisatory in its rhythms, reiterations and intermittent rhymes, and a quasi-Whitmanian visionary ego ('I saw in prophetic gleams ...'), to convey the image of a hideous afterlife in which soldiers' corpses are violated – both the sexual and sacrilegious connotations of the word are apt – by the rampaging figures of the poem's title.

The rhythms of 'Daughters of War' imitate, in their careering momentum, the naked dances of the eponymous 'maidens' in their perverse 'blood-heat'. These 'daughters' corrode the corpses until 'the soul can leap out / Into their huge embraces'. Doing so, these daughters share another sibling in the similarly mythological figure of 'sweet sister death' in Part 7 of *In Parenthesis*, who 'has gone debauched today and stalks on this high ground with strumpet confidence, makes no coy veiling of her appetite but leers from you to me with all her parts discovered'. 'Howsoever they may howl for their virginity', writes David Jones, 'she holds them'. Jones and Rosenberg are at these moments extravagantly disruptive and confrontational, melding the world of trench warfare with that turn-of-the-century male iconology and iconography which had strong elements of both misogyny and the fear of castration. These daughters of war share something in common with both Picasso's *Les Demoiselles d'Avignon* (1907) and Baudelaire's *femmes damnées*; and we know that Rosenberg had, like Wilfred Owen, read Baudelaire. Just as

'Break of Day in the Trenches' brings the late nineteenth-century figure and motif of the dandy to entirely unpredictable topographical and poetic locations, 'Daughters of War' revises fin-de-siècle decadence by figuring a perverse wartime apocalypse in which, as the representative sister who voices the poem's final lines boasts, as if advertising sexual conquest, 'My sisters have their males / Clean of the dust of old days'.

Although he was suspicious of the contemporary avant-garde, Rosenberg still had a defiant sense of what he wished his own work to advance forward from: and, although he in fact admired several of his poems, Rupert Brooke was one of his names for that. Rosenberg castigates Brooke's 'begloried sonnets', believing, in one of the sharply analytical, self-defining formulations that constantly enliven his letters and make them a necessary adjunct to the poetry, that the war 'should be approached in a colder way, more abstract, with less of the million feelings everybody feels; or all these should be concentrated in one distinguished emotion'.[10] When the savage goddesses of the battlefield strip the heroes 'clean' of their souls and of the dust of the old days in 'Daughters of War', therefore, we may regard this as a desacralizing or 'deglorying' revision, won from catastrophic experience, of the famous, or notorious, trope Brooke adapted on the outbreak of war in his sonnet 'Peace', which imagines the young entering war 'like swimmers into cleanness leaping'.

The rhythmic and syntactical energies of 'Daughters of War' are only insecurely, sometimes even crudely, disciplined to satisfactory poetic form, even if this has its mimetic point. 'A Worm Fed on the Heart of Corinth' has altogether greater command and compaction:

> A worm fed on the heart of Corinth,
> Babylon and Rome.
> Not Paris raped tall Helen,
> But this incestuous worm
> Who lured her vivid beauty
> To his amorphous sleep.
> England! Famous as Helen
> Is thy betrothal sung.
> To him the shadowless,
> More amorous than Solomon.

Cut this worm in two and one half would writhe back, instinct with origin, to Blake's 'The Sick Rose', where, 'invisible', its 'dark secret love' is a negative agent of disintegration. Perhaps the poem's exclamatory apostrophe to 'England' remembers the word's appearances in Blake too (most famously, 'And did those feet in ancient time / Walk upon England's mountains green?' in 'Jerusalem'), and the phrase 'amorphous sleep' may pick up Blake's famous castigation of anti-imaginative 'single vision and Newton's sleep'. The poem is also haunted by Marvell's 'To

His Coy Mistress', where the most chilling motive for sexual submission ever offered in poetry is phrased as the threat of a submission eventually to be made inevitable by the very fact of mortality itself ('Then worms shall try / That long-preserved virginity').

Rosenberg's amalgamation of his sources is also richly transformative. The story of Paris and Helen that supplies the origin of Homer's *Iliad* is revised with an astonishing declarative boldness, making this worm the agent of the destruction of four ancient civilizations and not only of Troy. The figuring of the rape of a woman by a worm perceived as male, a figure almost certainly inherited from Marvell, is starkly repulsive in its horror; and the worm is 'incestuous', I think, where Blake's is 'secret', because Germans and English might be considered members of the same racial 'family' if one subscribes to certain racial theories. The invocation of England as at least potentially the fifth in the poem's corrupted series – since a 'betrothal' is not yet, quite, a marriage – is an unnervingly devastating condemnation, even as it is also a brilliantly subtle revision of the ancient and enduring trope of war as amatory embrace.

The poem's verbal compaction, its 'sense of mass', is clearest here in the way the worm's 'amorphous sleep' almost luridly tightens into his 'amorous' outranking even of Solomon with Sheba, the word 'amorphous' shedding its medial consonants, which happen to be the initial letters of the word 'phallic', to expose the word 'amorous'. This is no real amorousness at all, though, since the worm is bound on rape, not love, and therefore on the perversion of sex by power; and it is appropriate, then, that the word 'amorous', vilely hatched out of 'amorphous', should itself rhyme assonantally and trisyllabically with the mysterious epithet for the worm, 'shadowless'. The worm is that presumably because he works underground, out of the light, in the way secret incest may need to operate too. However, because something like human agency and motive are being ascribed to the worm, there seems something diabolic too in his having no shadow. In Book IX of *Paradise Lost* the poet addresses Eve to tell her that 'in evil hour thou didst give ear / To that false worm, of whomsoever taught / To counterfeit man's voice; true in our fall, / False in our promised rising'. Rosenberg's worm is the serpent of Eden too; and it is hardly surprising that the trenches of the First World War should draw him out, together with the human consequences of his actions, from the imagination of a poet formed so deeply by the Old Testament and other Hebraic scriptures as well as by Milton himself.

The word 'shadowless' still retains, though, an air of mystery and an irresolvability wholly fitting to the strange mythological shape that Rosenberg has invented in this poem. Brief, clenched, bitten off and battened down, absorbed in and intent on its own making, 'A Worm Fed on the Heart of Corinth' moves in the mind as a node of trapped energy, a permanent invitation to explication. It is appropriate funeral music.

III

Both 'Daughters of War' and 'A Worm Fed on the Heart of Corinth' are the myths of a poet who has seen too much but has been stunned into speech rather than silence. If the mythical is one essential pole of Rosenberg's hectic wartime imagination, though, the harrowingly experiential is the other. With their accounts of the ordinary privations and terrors of the private soldier, his letters make the grimmest reading. They describe the disgustingly inadequate food given to the men, compared to that of the officers; and this was also, of course, for Rosenberg to feel the sharpest edges of the class system. They reveal how he constantly went in fear of having his possessions stolen, and had to maintain permanent vigilance; how his boots ruined his feet; and how he suffered draconian punishments for minor misdemeanours. He seems, indeed, to have endured these more often than most, referring frequently in his letters to his chronic absent-mindedness. It could be that the poetry itself was in large part responsible for this. Rosenberg was able to write only in the trenches themselves, permitted just ten days' leave in the whole period of 22 months which he served before his death; and Vivien Noakes piercingly tells us that 'dustings of mud' fell from the creases of some of his manuscripts when they were being rehoused.[11] With insightful empathy, Geoffrey Hill thinks that such forgetfulness 'is not actually a sign of weakness but of strength – the immense strength of other priorities, such as working on massive and complex poems in your head amid the manifold terrors and routine hard labour of the trenches'.[12] It is not hard to understand how being absorbed by and intent on a poem like 'A Worm Fed On The Heart of Corinth' may well have proved a distraction from trench routine. Poetry, therefore, may have disabled Rosenberg as a soldier, even while it enabled him as a poet.

Many of the private soldier's experiences feed Rosenberg's work, making it an exceptional anthology of deprivation and endurance. The private soldier's perspective is explicit in the very title 'Marching – As Seen From the Left File'; but the poem concerns itself with another kind of perspective too, as the poet's viewpoint has an almost futurist or Vorticist dimension, in which this routine march seems like a Wyndham Lewis drawing or an early David Bomberg painting. The file is 'All a red brick moving glint', and human agency is read as disciplined to mechanical measure: the soldiers' hands are 'Like flaming pendulums' and their feet are 'automatic'. The epithet expresses the industrialized modernization of human will just as T. S. Eliot's use of it in *The Waste Land* does, where the lovely woman who stoops to folly 'smoothes her hair with automatic hand'; and the reduction of human mobility to abstract image and simile resembles the comparable geometric reduction in Bomberg's extraordinary painting *The Mud Bath* of 1914 which it is hard to believe Rosenberg had never seen, given what appear the almost identical modernist perceptions and efforts involved.

Many of Rosenberg's poems depend on such dual perspectives of lived experience and a coolly, if not coldly, abstracted art, and are never mere reportage: but within these privileged perspectives of the soldier-poet – perhaps the only privileges permitted him – we gain access to such things as the distressed insomnia of being conveyed to war 'Grotesque and queerly huddled' in 'The Troop Ship'; the unendurable irritation of being lousy and flea-riddled, which is outstandingly defined in 'Louse Hunting' (Rosenberg at least once slept naked in the rain rather than endure his lousy clothing any longer); and the queasy disgust and self-disgust of being a stretcher-bearer or a member of a burying-party in 'Dead Man's Dump'. That poem makes its raw report ('A man's brain's splattered on / A stretcher-bearer's face') even as it discovers an enduring conceit for being killed by a bullet: 'conceit' in the sense in which it is used of seventeenth-century English poetry, which is often also the poetry of the charnel house, as Rosenberg brings a Donnean metaphysical wit into No Man's Land, yoking together the mortally wounding bullet and the busily questing insect: 'When the swift iron burning bee / Drained the wild honey of their youth'.

IV

Beyond these usual perturbations of the private soldier at the Front, Rosenberg had to endure a further exceptional one: anti-Semitism. Some of his letters, especially to Jewish correspondents, are explicit about what he had to put up with. In 'The Jew' he is articulate about this in the poetry itself, writing in wounded affront and baffled outrage:

> The blonde, the bronze, the ruddy,
> With the same heaving blood,
> Keep tide to the moon of Moses,
> Then why do they sneer at me?

Insisting that Christians and Jews share so much of a common heritage, Rosenberg is here nevertheless making it plain, with the opposed pronouns 'they' and 'me', that no possessive pronoun of his could ever wholly include him along with the majority of those he fought with.

Early in 1918 Rosenberg wrote to John Rodker that he would 'like to read Elliott's work'.[13] Rosenberg is here misspelling the name of the poet who, the previous year, had published his first volume, *Prufrock and Other Observations*. Rosenberg never got the chance to read Eliot; but Eliot read and admired Rosenberg, calling him in 1953 'the most remarkable of the British poets killed in that war'.[14] Some years earlier, in 1935, Eliot had made a judgement which has since been the source of controversy: 'The poetry of Isaac Rosenberg does not only owe its distinction to being Hebraic: but because it is Hebraic it is a contribution to English literature. For a Jewish poet to be able to write like a Jew, in western Europe and in a western European language, is almost a miracle'.[15] Anthony Julius in *T. S. Eliot, Anti-Semitism and Literary Form* reads this as an anti-Semitic 'libel', asking, in exasperated outrage, 'What is it to write like a Jew?'[16] In a spirited defence of Eliot, however, James Wood thinks that his observation 'quite clearly means that Rosenberg was a distinguished English poet, but his particular addition to English literature was that he retained a Jewishness that was not assimilated; and that this retention, within the pressure that the English poetic tradition exerts to surrender one's literary Jewishness, was almost miraculous'.[17]

Although he has never been as well known as some other poets of the First World War, and his 'particular addition' to English literature has been very little regarded, the debate at least suggests that Rosenberg's work continues to carry insinuations and provocations a long way beyond the immediate, dreadful context of its origin. Eliot and anti-Semitism will persist as a topic of investigation, and properly so. In this case, however, it seems to me that Rosenberg would have appreciated Eliot's assessment as the insightful recognition of realized ambition: because, with genuinely admiring discrimination, Eliot regards Jewishness as an outstanding attribute of this poet's distinction but does not limit his distinction to his Jewishness; and that makes all the difference.

So: what is it for Isaac Rosenberg to write like a Jew? It is to write a poem like 'The Jew' about the experience of wartime anti-Semitism and to notice, with pained wit, the 'cosmopolitan sympathies' of a trench rat; it is to write – *in the trenches* – poetic drama like 'Moses' and 'The Unicorn' based on biblical and Talmudic material; and it is to refer in a letter to Sydney Schiff, who was also Jewish, to the nineteenth-century German poet as 'Heine, our own Heine', making the intensified possessive now simply, pleasurably inclusive: 'I admire him more for always being a Jew at heart than anything else'.[18] This is ambiguous: did Rosenberg admire Heine more for being a Jew at heart than for anything else he might have admired him for; or, did he admire him more for always being a Jew at heart than for being anything else he might have been at heart? Nevertheless, it suggests that, had he lived, Rosenberg may well have written with more obvious recourse to a wide European tradition, and not only to literature in English; and in fact his first language was not English but Yiddish.

The dual exceptionality Eliot recognizes in Rosenberg, however, sharpens the pain of loss; and sharpens too the perspective in which Rosenberg himself perceives loss when, in 'August 1914', with the slow gravity of trochaic and spondaic rhythms, he uses a plural possessive to suggest that what his generation may actually in the end have shared in common is only that they were so cruelly and pointlessly wasted:

> Iron are our lives
> Molten right through our youth.
> A burnt space through ripe fields,
> A fair mouth's broken tooth.

CHAPTER 3

A Politics of Translation: Some Modern Hamlets

I

It is almost certainly now a truism that *Hamlet* is an intensely political play, although it took the twentieth century fully to discover that; and it is also a truism that, at least since 15 June 1827, when Coleridge discovered Hamlet in himself ('I have a smack of Hamlet myself, if I may say so'), Hamlet the character, Hamlet the prince, has acted as a self-representation for poets.[1] Hamlet, who not only speaks poetry but lets us know that he is capable of penning an additional speech for the play of Gonzago, is, in Romantic and post-Romantic conceptions, an honorary or co-opted poet. T. S. Eliot's famous figuration in 'The Love Song of J. Alfred Prufrock' in 1917, where the poem's smartingly self-conscious persona says, 'No! I am not Prince Hamlet, nor was meant to be', may be read as both a knowing inheritance from, and a telling critique of, a tradition of poetic fascination and self-identification which had culminated in the nineteenth-century French poetry avidly read and, some of it, stolen by the young Eliot: such poems as Baudelaire's 'La Béatrice', for instance, Rimbaud's 'Ophélie', Mallarmé's 'Le Pitre Chatié', and 'Hamlet; ou les Suites de la Piété Filiale' in Laforgue's *Moralités Légendaires*.

In this chapter I want to think about three figurations of Hamlet, latecomers after so many interventions, by poets reading themselves and their contemporary culture into, through and out of the play and its hero, and now at moments of peculiarly modern political stress. Two of these are translations, versions, or imitations in English of poems already existing in other languages, Russian and Polish; and the third is an original poem by a renowned poet-translator, which may also be comprehended by an idea of translation.

Robert Lowell's 'Hamlet in Russia, A Soliloquy' is the penultimate poem in his collection of versions or translations published as *Imitations* in 1961; 'imitation' is a term used by Dryden in his 1680 preface to *Ovid's Epistles. Translated*. Lowell's poem is an 'imitation' of Boris Pasternak's poem 'Hamlet', the first of the poems published as 'The Poems of Yuri Zhivago' at the end of the novel *Doctor Zhivago*. This had been published first not in Russia but by Feltrinelli in Milan in Italian translation in 1957, with the Russian original following there shortly afterwards. It was published therefore just four years before Lowell's book, during what was probably the sharpest period of the Cold War. Pasternak's 'Hamlet' had actually been written, however, in 1946, when he had first begun work on the novel.

Zbigniew Herbert's 'Elegy of Fortinbras', published in his volume *Study of the Object*, in 1961, first appeared in English translation by Herbert's fellow Polish poet (and eventual winner of the Nobel Prize), Czesław Miłosz, in the English journal *Encounter* the same year. It was given greater currency in Miłosz's anthology *Polish Post-War Poetry*, first published in the US by Doubleday in 1965 and by Penguin in Britain in 1970. It also appeared in 1968 in the extensive Penguin *Selected Poems*, translated by Miłosz and Peter Dale Scott, a volume in the ground-breaking Penguin *Modern European Poets* series, of which A. Alvarez was general editor.

Ciaran Carson's 'Hamlet' first appeared as the final poem in his volume of 1989, *Belfast Confetti*. This book and Carson's previous one, *The Irish for No* (1987), are generally regarded as amongst the outstanding achievements of the contemporary poetry of Northern Ireland.

The Pasternak–Lowell and the Herbert–Miłosz poems are monologues; dramatic monologues, if we allow the term sufficient elasticity. Pasternak's poem is the monologue of an actor playing Hamlet who appears to be terrified by stage-fright before a performance. Lowell emphasizes the element of monologue in his imitation by newly entitling the poem 'Hamlet in Russia, A Soliloquy' and by setting the whole in inverted commas, as if direct speech. This also effects a kind of continuity with the volume of Lowell's which immediately preceded *Imitations*, *Life Studies*, published in 1959, a revolutionary book in the history of modern poetry, and the volume responsible for introducing the controversial idea of poetic 'confessionalism' into American verse. In its poems of personal anecdote and reportage inverted commas are used frequently to signal the quoted speech of others. 'Elegy of Fortinbras' is an address to the dead Hamlet by the man who inherits the throne of Denmark by military fiat, at the moment the prince's body is being removed for burial. Ciaran Carson's poem is not a monologue in this technical sense, but his long-line ruminations, meditations and collocations in *Belfast Confetti* all have the aspect of monologue, since his sophisticated use of popular forms of narrative and reportage imply vocally characterized narrators. In Carson's 'Hamlet', allusions to the play, with its 'strange eruption to our state', are woven into, or counterpointed with, a digressive tale about the state of Belfast, or the statelet of Northern Ireland, in the 1970s and 1980s.

These are my texts, then. I have some specific questions to ask of each of them but my general questions are: what might a modern political poetic translation of *Hamlet* be like? What uses does the play appear to serve for poets at times of political crisis and anxiety? Why *Hamlet*?

II

Robert Lowell's *Imitations*, versions of European poems from Homer to Pasternak, is still a controversial book. To some, it seems overly permissive, even licentious, in its apparent refusal of the kinds of tact customarily thought necessary to translation. To others, it appears a milestone in Lowell's career and in modern contributions to the art of translation, given permission by the way its unorthodox methods bring significant new Lowell poems into the language and reveal an exceptional modern American poet engaging fruitfully with a European tradition. Lowell's biographer Ian Hamilton probably gives the greatest permission when he approvingly coins the verb 'to Lowell' of this translator's peculiar procedures.[2]

The history of this text's reception is therefore virtually a history of the possibilities of modern verse translation itself. It includes Elizabeth Bishop's partly admiring, partly sceptical anxiety in letters to Lowell himself; the acerbic hostility of Vladimir Nabokov and George Steiner; and the wholehearted approval of Edmund Wilson, A. Alvarez and Nadezhda Mandelstam, Osip's widow, and a powerful writer herself, author of the outstanding memoirs *Hope Against Hope* (1970) and *Hope Abandoned* (1974). She actually sent Lowell a congratulatory letter, which touches on a theme I intend to pursue. Of translator and translated in 'Hamlet in Russia, A Soliloquy', she says, 'There is sudden recognition between them, as if the poet and his translator had struck up a close friendship. In such translations everything is unexpected, and only they belong to literature as such.'[3] Her implication is that translation is always only predictable, a second-order necessity, whereas literature is unforeseeable, the thing worth obtaining by any necessary means, and the thing that is, in the end, the only thing worth having.

This lengthy history of antagonistic views has culminated recently in books by well-known poet-translators: Paul Muldoon's *The End of the Poem: Oxford Lectures on Poetry* (2006) and Peter Robinson's *Poetry & Translation: The Art of the Impossible* (2010). This is not the place to take up these arguments with any thoroughness, although I shall return briefly to them. The context needs to be sketched in relation to Lowell's Pasternak though, since this version does something exceptional not only for a poetic translation but even for a Lowell imitation. It juxtaposes under a single title separate poems by the writer in question. 'Hamlet in Russia, A Soliloquy' joins together Pasternak's 'Hamlet' poem with parts of two early poems, the title poem of his first book, *My Sister, Life*, published in 1917, and another translated by Peter France and Jon Stallworthy as 'Oars Crossed'. These poems are markedly different in tone, mood, setting and atmosphere from the Hamlet poem: so Lowell appears to be proposing a juncture between disjunctions, and this is clearly crucial to an understanding of what he has in mind.

Pasternak's 'Hamlet', as it appears in *Doctor Zhivago*, is a double translation or transposition of himself: into Yuri Zhivago first of all, the hero of this novel whose work this purports to be, who shares many biographical characteristics and circumstances with his author; and then into the actor playing Hamlet, whose voice we may regard as ventriloquized by both Zhivago and Pasternak himself. In the poem's brief, intense, highly charged four quatrains, the actor figures himself stepping out on to the stage with his ears attuned to 'the echoes from far off / Of what my age is bringing'.[4] Knowing himself the focus of 'thousands of opera glasses', he calls, as Christ does on the cross, on 'Abba Father' to 'Let this cup pass me by'. Accepting the Father's will for himself, he nevertheless believes that 'a different drama' from the one he has agreed to act in is now taking place and asks, again, to be spared the role. Finally, however, he realizes that the order of the play is preordained and 'leads to just one end'. Lamenting his complete isolation, he rails against the 'pharisaism' of his time and concludes, apparently accepting his lot, by quoting a well-known Russian proverb, 'Life is no stroll through a field'.

Pasternak's own identification with Hamlet was close. The play was the first in his sequence of eight translations of Shakespeare's plays. It was made in 1938; and a revision of the 'To be or not to be' soliloquy in 1947 signalled clear affinities, in its new linguistic decisions, between the rotten state of Hamlet's Denmark and the plight of artists and intellectuals in the Soviet Union. As such, of course, it constituted a coded political message to any audience of this translation. Pasternak had a high Romantic, quasi-religious sense of Hamlet as a self-sacrificial hero fulfilling a destiny in service to the future. This may be a strained, and is certainly not a 'modern', or at least modern Western European, reading of Shakespeare, but it also informs various references to Hamlet in the text of *Doctor Zhivago*, which, after the hero's dreadful solitary trek across Siberia, explodes into an abjectly anguished address to God, as Pasternak's Hamlet does in his poem. When the poem voices Christ's wracked petition on the cross to his Father, an original resistance to preordination combines, as it were, theatrical and divine stage fright. It also breathtakingly makes Hamlet a kind of 'figura Christi', a figure of Christ. When such ordination is finally accepted it is also, for both Christ and Hamlet, the acceptance of death.

Yet, crucially, despite the fact that Pasternak's Hamlet has quoted Christ's anguished words to his father that the cup might pass from him, this acceptance of his destined lot is not signalled in the poem by the quotation of Christ's equally well-known final words in Luke's gospel: 'Into thy hands I commend my spirit'. Although those words inevitably ghost the end of Pasternak's poem, the Russian proverb actually quoted, with its sense of stoical endurance, appears to offer the lonely hero not the relative relief of entrustment but a kind of solidarity: that of the hard-won experience of a people enduring immense suffering. This should be read as the consolatory evocation of an alternative audience to the one actually about to witness this actor's performance. We are at liberty to identify this pharisaical crowd behind terrifyingly judgemental opera glasses with the censors or spies of a police state. Pasternak's history in Soviet Russia between the 1930s and 1950s included both public denunciation and private anxiety and self-rebuke and culminated in his more or less compelled rejection of the Nobel Prize in 1958. The poem he wrote about that, called simply 'Nobel Prize', offers a direct parallel to the Hamlet poem, although the poet's desperate voice is now raised without the irony or obliquity of monologue: 'But the hunters are gaining ground. / I've nowhere else to run.'[5]

It seems wholly fitting, then, given all the ramifications of Pasternak's relationship with this Shakespearean tragedy and its hero, that 'Hamlet' should be the first of the poems in *Doctor Zhivago*, his major prose work and the one by which he is best known in the West, even though it was not of course fitting – even if inevitable – that the book appeared first in Italian translation, forbidden in the author's own country. It was fitting also that Pasternak's 'Hamlet' was recited over the grave at his funeral in 1960.

III

Robert Lowell's keen interest in, and high regard for, *Doctor Zhivago* are manifest in his letters of the late 1950s, notably when he tells Elizabeth Bishop in the year of its publication that the novel is 'really an earthquake ... and something that alters both the old Russia and the new for us – alters our own world too'.[6] Lowell's introduction to *Imitations* praises Pasternak as 'a very great poet' and makes admiring reference to the Russian poet's own principles of translation:

> Boris Pasternak has said that the usual reliable translator gets the literal meaning but misses the tone, and that in poetry tone is of course everything. I have been reckless with literal meaning, and labored hard to get the tone. Most often this has been *a* tone, for *the* tone is something that will always more or less escape transference to another language and cultural moment. I have tried to write live English and to do what my authors might have done if they were writing their poems now and in America.[7]

During the Cold War *Doctor Zhivago* was a powerful cultural weapon for the West. It was regarded as a great novel too bravely dangerous to be published in the author's own (Communist) country, and one that brought upon its author huge psychological and political difficulties, including his refusal of the most internationally renowned literary prize. As such, it seemed a paradigmatic case of Soviet cultural repression. Some critics have read Western democratic triumphalism in the last sentence of Lowell just quoted: 'I have tried to write live English and to do what my authors might have done if they were writing their poems now and in America.' Peter Robinson thinks that Lowell is here implying that 'European poetry is to be saved from the Communist threat by being rendered into the style of the free world. The freedoms that Lowell claims may be thought, then, to oppose the restrictions upon what writers may be allowed to do, or not do, by Warsaw Pact states'; and Paul Muldoon, who, as I have said, is diametrically opposed to Robinson in his sense of the value of Lowell's mode of imitation, holds a comparable opinion, although he expresses it with more reserve.[8] 'There's more than a faint air of cultural imperialism, not to speak of personal imperiousness, hanging over that last sentence', he says, especially since he senses within it the presence of what he understands as 'the haughty note' of the speaker in T. S. Eliot's 'Little Gidding': 'History is now and England'.[9]

These poet-translator-critics may be right in their identifications: but Muldoon, although he suggestively relates Lowell's phrasing and cadence to Eliot's, fails to notice that Dryden is a much more immediate source when, in his Ovid preface, he says, 'I take imitation of an author ... to be ... to write as he supposes that author would have done had he lived in our age, and in our country'.[10] I would also set in tandem with Lowell's introduction the apparent linking of East and West in the observation to Elizabeth Bishop that *Zhivago* 'alters our own world too', which he reinforces in a letter to Harriet Winslow when he says of the novel that 'For a moment the stone facades of the new Russia blow away like gauze, much of our own too'.[11] These relatively casual remarks in letters may suggest that Lowell perceives an alignment or rapprochement between the two poets in their conceptions of, and attitudes to, their own nations or states; and this may lie behind his decision to write a version of Pasternak's poem. It may also be woven into the texture of the imitation he actually produced.

There can be no doubt that Lowell 'Lowellizes' Pasternak. His letters, in fact, suggest that he was doing this deliberately in opposition to other ways of doing it. He tells Stephen Spender that in Lydia Pasternak Slater's versions 'she grinds [Pasternak] down to a pretty and innocent neatness and in remaining perhaps true to his spirit, falsifies and extinguishes his powers'.[12] Prettiness and innocence and neatness are manifestly not Lowell's way; and his imitation is undoubtedly powerful. Pasternak's earlier poems now form an introduction of eighteen lines to the seventeen of Lowell's imitation of Pasternak's 'Hamlet' proper: the transition is effected by two lines ending in characteristically Lowellian trailing ellipses. The opening of the poem therefore presents a contrastive pastoral scene of a boat on the water in high summer, which also acts ambivalently as a kind of correlative for a state of mind or being, since the boat said to have 'throbbed' on the water is also a simile for the motion of the speaker's heart.[13] Lowell repeats twice the famous Pasternakian apostrophe to 'My sister, life!', which entitled his first volume, but in a way that introduces into the scene of pastoral idyll the note of menace which is of course sounded more harshly in the 'Hamlet' section of the poem: 'the world has too many people for us, / the sycophant, the spineless – / silently, like snakes in the grass, they sting'. The final verse of the opening section then makes reference to Hercules 'who holds the world up forever' and to the crying of nightingales. The line which then introduces the 'Hamlet' section of the poem seems ominously to bring one world to a decisive end, repeating the image and the verb of Lowell's opening line: 'The boat stops throbbing on the water ...'. Lowell's account of the poem then begins by explicitly drawing out what is only an implication in the original, that the speaker of this monologue is an actor playing Hamlet: 'The clapping stops. I walk into the lights / as Hamlet'.

Reading Lowell on Lydia Pasternak Slater's version of the poem, we may well find something condescendingly gendered in his categories. This may make us more likely to find that the greater 'power' of his own version derives partly from an almost clichéd masculinism of rhetorical inflation. His version resounds with the verbs and participles 'throbbed', 'dragged', 'thrilled', 'throbbing', 'clapping' and 'hammering', for instance. The excitement, or occasional over-excitement, of the unresolved or irresolute participle is a strong Lowellian trait in his original poems. In addition, 'throbbing' used of the heart likened to a boat on the water seems to bring Pasternak into the radius of the Eliotic mode of *The Waste Land*, which features, in the scene between the typist and 'the young man carbuncular' in Part III, 'the human engine like a taxi throbbing, waiting' in sexual arousal. One implication of this is that if Pasternak had been writing now and in America he would, like Lowell, have been unable to avoid Eliot and, like Lowell too, would have had to employ strategies of negotiation. A deeper implication of such surface echo and allusion may even be that the very effort Lowell is making in *Imitations* is a consequence of Eliot's concept, writ large in the essay 'Tradition and the Individual Talent', that true poetic individuality in a modern poet – even, or especially, an American modern poet – involves a self-conscious relation to a European tradition. Lowell is busy, in this very volume, making manifest such a traditional relation and orientation on his own part; and *Imitations*, for all its originality of method, may therefore have been intended as the necessary complement to the influential American radicalism of *Life Studies*.

The penultimate line of Lowell's version of 'Hamlet' takes rhetorical inflation to the point of the grotesque. 'All's drowned in the sperm and spittle of the Pharisee' is a version of what Pevear and Volokhonsky translate simply as 'all drowns in pharisaism'. Lowell's bodily emissions are given no sanction by the original. The Pharisees appear in Pasternak, I have suggested, as the dead weight of cultural and political censorship pressing down on the poet who stands forsakenly alone and terrified, subject to the excruciating scrutiny of a thousand opera glasses. Lowell's having them simultaneously ejaculate and expectorate to the point of an almost apocalyptic universal drowning certainly makes the point, but makes it with disconcertingly relished hyperbole.

IV

Robinson and Muldoon are clearly right, then, to identify an imperiousness of appropriation, a will to power, in Lowell's poetic. But, as often in Lowell's original work, this is accompanied, savingly, by both vulnerability and gratitude. The former makes him one of the greatest testifiers to distressed subjectivity in modern poetry; and the latter makes him one of the great poetic acknowledgers of the power of others. The *Imitations* introduction witnesses this, in a small way, with its tacit allusion to Dryden. This combination of emotions and moods, rather than any mere cultural appropriation or expropriation, seems to me the point of Lowell's joining together early and late Pasternak in his version of 'Hamlet'.

Olga Carlisle, who edited the anthology *Poets on Street Corners* (1968), in which various of Lowell's revised translations from the Russian appeared, said of 'Hamlet in Russia, A Soliloquy' that it is 'as much a poem *about* Boris Pasternak as an adaptation *from* Boris Pasternak' and regarded the addition of the earlier poems as a kind of imagist biography of the Russian poet.[14] This is an insightful and fruitful way of conceiving it. The natural world of Pasternak's culturally privileged childhood and youth is evoked in those early poems almost as a languid erotics of reverie. Lowell's version introduces a faint, appropriate echo of Wordsworth with 'the world has too many people for us' and, just possibly, of Mallarmé, when the 'hint of blue' that 'dotted a point offshore' suggests the French symbolist's 'azur'. The world that has too many people for us is also too much with us because it conceals snakes in the grass, waiting with the sting of the sycophant and the spineless. The apparently delightful pastoral of Pasternak's first world becomes, therefore, in Lowell's poem, the place for those who bide their time, before erupting as the Pharisees of the Soviet state. Lowell's original pastoral eroticism is eventually elided into a world where Hercules, the powerful man of action, no longer sleeps at ease or holds the world up.

'The clapping stops' may signal the transition between, or merging of, the two worlds, as the noise of the water against the boat merges into the sound of the theatre audience. In this new world the pleasurably erotic gives way to a politics of scrutiny, fear, panic and finally stoic resolution.

Robert Lowell himself, the scion of a famous New England family, had a childhood privileged in ways comparable to Pasternak's: and, although he certainly never suffered at the hands of the state in the way Pasternak did, and lived as a comfortable, even wealthy, Westerner for most of his life, despite periods in mental hospitals, he still had his problems with the US state. A conscientious objector during the Second World War, he made what he later called, in a poem, his 'manic statement' to President Roosevelt, a public letter refusing the draft. There was no doubt a certain sense of entitlement in his assumption that a New England Lowell should make a public, not a private, declaration, but there was also risk; and the consequence was a period of imprisonment. Some time after the publication of *Imitations*, in 1965, Lowell was to offer a comparable public rebuff to President Johnson, refusing an invitation to the White House because of his objection to American foreign policy. He attended the anti-Vietnam march on the Pentagon in October 1967 and is famously captured there by Norman Mailer in his account of that event in his 'nonfiction novel', *The Armies of the Night* (1968).

So Lowell is a poet who, like Pasternak, made a significant stand against the state. I think we should read into the various ellipses of 'Hamlet in Russia, A Soliloquy' another ellipsis too: a stretching out of the hand from an American poet with considerable public presence and authority to a Russian poet similarly but much more excruciatingly positioned. The poem thereby voices a profound awareness of the universality of political crisis in the Cold War of the late 1950s and early 1960s, in which both Western and Eastern European poets are ideologically entrapped. The soliloquy or monologue of Lowell's imitation becomes a form of political colloquy. The poem is Robert Lowell's self-aware testimonial meditation on Boris Pasternak's predicament and the companionable sharing of solitude. And who might better enable such solidarity than Hamlet? Perhaps the loneliest of Shakespeare's tragic heroes, he shows himself capable nevertheless of true friendship, even while also able to recognize false friends, those snakes in the grass of sycophancy and spinelessness, the pharisaical agents of the state, Rosencrantz and Guildenstern.

V

Thinking about the politics of translation in Lowell's Pasternak poem, then, is also inevitably to think about the politics of the Cold War. Czesław Miłosz's translation of Zbigniew Herbert's 'Elegy of Fortinbras' was, as I have said, first published in the London-based journal *Encounter*. In 1967 it was revealed that the main backer of *Encounter*, the anti-Communist Congress for Cultural Freedom, was covertly funded by the American Central Intelligence Agency, the CIA. The scandal consequent on this revelation resulted in the resignation of the journal's editors Stephen Spender and Frank Kermode. Although the involvement of the CIA was uncovered only in 1967, it appears that the journal had been willing to pay the price exacted by its backers: that is, at least tacit support for American foreign policy. In 1967, the time of the Vietnam War, this was increasingly under Western liberal and leftist attack. The journal's tacit or clandestine political negotiations need not impugn its literary policy, of course. *Encounter* published superb work, and no odium attaches to Herbert or Miłosz for publishing there. It does reveal though the extent to which, during the cultural Cold War, apparent neutrality was frequently facade or charade. This publishing history may, I think, be thematically as well as circumstantially relevant to this great poem, and may even in some sense be included in, or comprehended by, it.

'Elegy of Fortinbras' is dedicated 'To C. M.'. The initials are those of its translator, and the dedication appears in the form of initials because in the Poland of 1961 Czesław Miłosz's name was unprintable. Before we even reach the poem, then, our attention is drawn to the reality of censorship in the Warsaw Pact culture its poet inhabits. The dedication by the poet to his translator also suggests a deftly courteous mutual acknowledgement. This has its poignancy now, given the subsequent severe rupturing of their relationship which prompted a truly vicious, if coded, denunciatory poem from Herbert, 'Khodasevich', in his penultimate volume *Rovigo* (1992): but it may still be allowed to shadow the relationship which the poem figures, that between Fortinbras, the elegist, and Hamlet, the elegized.

The poem, which opens, 'Now that we're alone we can talk prince man to man / though you lie on the stairs and see no more than a dead ant / nothing but black sun with broken rays', figures an unpredictably empathetic tenderness that even contains an element of rueful envy from the active Fortinbras towards the reflective Hamlet.[15] A. Alvarez is accurate in his introduction to the Penguin *Selected Poems* when he calls it 'a kind of love poem'. The discrepancy in the natures of these princes is the focus of a sort of humbled admiration from Fortinbras rather than the kind of reproof a reader might have initially expected. Even with his knowledge that Hamlet's radically alternative way of being in the world can end only in death, Fortinbras is still ambivalently caught between derogation of and appreciative fascination with Hamlet's 'crystal notions', with the fact that he has 'hunted chimeras', and with the way he has known 'no human thing': 'you did not know even how to breathe'.[16]

Fortinbras is certain of his own motivation and justification. He can make a wry but terrifying joke out of Hamlet's bitter observation that

Denmark is a prison ('I must also elaborate a better system of prisons / since as you justly said Denmark is a prison'); he is capable of cynically opportunistic propaganda, if that is the implication of his granting Hamlet a military funeral and making him a 'star' ('This night is born / a star named Hamlet'); and he knows he can also manage 'eternal watching', a phrase whose disabused knowledge tells us that if the price of freedom is eternal vigilance, then so is the price of constraint. But there is genuine regret in Fortinbras's regard for Hamlet too. It is there in the exquisite tenderness of the surreal simile in which he sees Hamlet's hands lying on the stone 'like fallen nests', which makes it clear that Fortinbras does not know himself at all well enough when he says he knows 'nothing exquisite'; it is there in the courtly courteousness of his final valediction, 'Adieu prince', which echoes Horatio's 'Good night, sweet prince' in the original play, although Fortinbras is not yet on stage when the line is spoken; it is there in the recognition that Hamlet is at 'peace', a word enviously repeated; and it is there in the almost self-pitying knowledge that his own life 'will not be worth a tragedy'.

It is there above all in Fortinbras's final question, with its melancholy falling cadence and its absence of punctuation, which makes it at least as ruminative as it is interrogative. It is a question that recognizes the abject fact of incommensurability:

> It is not for us to greet each other or bid farewell we live on
>   archipelagos
> and that water these words what can they do what can they
>   do prince

The absence of punctuation here consorts with Herbert's lack of punctuation in the rest of the poem and, indeed, in his work as a whole. As in T. S. Eliot, from whom Herbert almost certainly learnt how to absent punctuation, the absence of punctuation is itself a form of punctuation. In 'Elegy of Fortinbras' the absence makes us, most appropriately, read backwards as well as forwards, constantly negotiating syntactical fluidity in order to establish or untangle meaning. It is as though we, as readers, must work alongside Fortinbras to decipher what must seem even to him the surprise of his own responses.

In its elaboration of the empathetic dichotomy between Fortinbras and Hamlet, the poem appears to require, as many of Herbert's do, that we read it under the rubric of allegory. If Pasternak's monologue uses *Hamlet* as a code for his own relationship with the Soviet state, Herbert's proposes, in the relationship of Fortinbras to Hamlet, that of the commissar to the poet, or the censor to the writer, in a Warsaw Pact state; and we may well think that Herbert has Pasternak in mind as a model. Even so, I think it is C. P. Cavafy who stands most immediately behind 'Elegy of Fortinbras', Cavafy the melancholy historical commentator and ventriloquist. As allegory, Herbert's poem is organized as a brilliantly emblematical antinomy, like Cavafy's 'Waiting for the Barbarians', in which immense political perturbation is ironically rendered down into an apparently almost placid but still unnerving *im*perturbability.

In addition to Shakespeare, Pasternak and Cavafy, Eliot is also himself a presence in this profoundly intertextual poem. Some of its imagery – of stairs, dead ant, clock's dial – has the minatory quality of some almost surreally specific images in early Eliot; and the run of nouns in the second verse paragraph ('helmets boots artillery horses drums drums') recalls similar runs in Eliot's 'Gerontion' ('Rocks, moss, stonecrop, iron, merds') and 'Coriolan', which also features a comparable repetition ('Stone, bronze, stone, steel, stone, oakleaves, horses' heels'). Above all, though, the poem's final lines – 'and that water these words what can they do what can they / do prince' – which are suffused with both longing and self-doubt, have the cadence of the opening lines of Eliot's 'Marina', which also originates in a Shakespearean play, *Pericles*: 'What seas what shores what grey rocks and what islands / What water lapping the bow'. In 'Marina' the cadence as it reappears at the end of the poem figures the reconciliation between father and daughter; in 'Elegy of Fortinbras' it signals the eternal, archipelagic divorce between comparably placed people who might, in a different dispensation, have been friends; or even, if we allow Alvarez's 'kind of love poem' its fullest implication, lovers. (A Polish friend, the poet and translator Jerzy Jarniewicz, tells me that in his translation of the line Miłosz faithfully represents a cadence in Herbert's original.)

In his own *Hamlet* poem, then, Herbert may well be acknowledging a precursor in the Eliot who wrote a famous essay on the play and who, in 'The Love Song of J. Alfred Prufrock', makes what is almost certainly the best-known allusion to *Hamlet* in modern poetry. But Herbert is also, I think, registering a debt at what is in effect a political level too. In the poem 'To Ryszard Krynicki – A Letter', published in *Report from a Besieged City* in 1983, Herbert identifies the work of Eliot and Rilke as almost all that 'will remain ... of the poetry of our mad century'. In this same poem he laments the fact that so much of his own work, as he perceives it, has had to keep the quest for aesthetic perfection secondary because of the more urgent necessity of articulating the dreadful contemporary moment. Eliot therefore becomes implicitly one of the good forces required by this poem 'to whisper a good night in treason's garden'. That Zbigniew Herbert, writing out of catastrophic Polish experience in the early 1980s, should find T. S. Eliot exceptionally equal to the realities of his time is a testimony that may surprise some contemporary Western European readers: but, apart from the fact that such a provocation might persuade readers so minded to read and think again, it is precisely such unpredictable allegiances and co-options that create the genuinely new and radical work of poetic art; and 'Elegy of Fortinbras' is certainly that.

VI

In an essay on Herbert in his book about censorship, *Giving Offense* (1996), the great South African novelist J. M. Coetzee does not discuss 'Elegy of Fortinbras' but he does relevantly take up the question of Herbert's irony. This is, he accurately says, something quite different from the ironies and ambiguities of the New Criticism and its successors: it is 'ontologically more fundamental'. In his most remarkable poems, Coetzee observes, 'Herbert is an allusive and ironic poet not because he uses allusiveness and irony as devices to evade the censor's red pencil, not even because the history of his times has made him wary and indirect by temperament, but because allusiveness is for him a mode of humanistic affirmation, and irony an ethical value.' This makes the question of allegory in his work more problematic than it is usually considered; and in Coetzee's reading of another historical encounter in Herbert, in the poem 'To Marcus Aurelius', he judges that

> to propose that uncloaking the allegory constitutes a reading, does far less than justice to it. For, in the same motion that it invites uncloaking, the poem invites a question: In the face of the pressure for an allegorical reading created by the realities of Poland's historical situation and indeed by the paranoia of censorship itself – which, constitutionally opposed to innocent readings, spreads its habits of overreading through the whole of the reading community – how would it be possible to write a poem genuinely about Marcus Aurelius?

Responding to his own question, he approves Stanislaw Baranczak's account of the 'dynamic equilibrium' of Herbert's poems: their 'basic structural pattern ... is not only ... incessant confrontation ... but the *mutual unmasking* of the two sets of antinomical values and two types of reality: the reality of heritage and the reality of disinheritance'. Hence, Herbert's 'fables of interpretation' are resolutely set against both absolutism and the reading of the censor.[17]

I want to attempt to transpose Coetzee's question to 'Elegy of Fortinbras', particularly since the categories of heritage and disinheritance are so clearly appropriate to it, both to what we might call its plot and to its assimilations of, and variations on, literary history. How would it be possible to write a poem genuinely about *Hamlet* in the political situation in which Zbigniew Herbert finds himself at the time of writing? Do we too quickly leap to the judgement that Denmark 'is' Warsaw Pact Poland; that Hamlet 'is' the liberal incompetent of the old exhausted order, forever succeeded by a Fortinbras who 'is' the new order, a regretfully empathetic but still entirely persuaded commissar of the new regime? Does the allegorical reading, which is of course utterly inevitable and deeply informative of the poem's actual operations, does it nevertheless distract us from anything the poem might profitably be saying not about its own moment but about Shakespeare's play?

The question might prompt us to think a little further about Fortinbras, or to notice that Herbert has thought a little further. It could well be that 'Elegy of Fortinbras' attends to, or originates in, that odd moment during Hamlet's soliloquy in Act 4 scene iv, 'How all occasions do inform against me', when, calling him 'a delicate and tender prince', Hamlet appears envious of Fortinbras's eager expedition 'even for an eggshell' and of his 'divine ambition' in finding 'quarrel in a straw / When honour's at the stake'. The editors of the current (2006) Arden edition find these epithets 'inappropriate'. The 'problem,' they say, 'is that Hamlet insists on admiring Fortinbras while at the same time acknowledging the absurdity of his actions'.[18] In Shakespeare's play, then, Hamlet admires or envies Fortinbras as a man of action, in contradistinction to himself, even if this has illogic and absurdity in it, since Fortinbras's action is farcically inappropriate to any system of ethics to which we can imagine Hamlet more generally subscribing. In Zbigniew Herbert, Fortinbras admires or envies Hamlet not as the potentially capable monarch Shakespeare's Fortinbras pragmatically affects to suggest in his envoy – 'he was likely, had he been put on, / To have proved most royal' – but as, precisely, the ineffectual aesthete, the Coleridgean believer in 'crystal notions'.

Fortinbras has the last word in the play *Hamlet*, and Zbigniew Herbert's poem, as it were, stretches that word out into an intimation of contemporary psychic and political oppositions. But the poem deconstructively suggests too that these oppositions are never total, even that to propose thinking them total – to totalize them or render them absolute – would be a form of sentimentality, perhaps of the kind that has sometimes led Western critics, and poets, virtually to canonize, admiringly or enviously, their Eastern European counterparts. This might well be to do to them what Herbert, in his essay 'Delta' in *Still Life with a Bridle*, castigates in an unnamed art historian. When, Herbert says, 'more inspired than lucid', he writes about Jacob Ruysdael, this 'illustrious though unrestrained art historian' raises him 'to the rank of cherubim': 'the painter becomes an archangel'.[19] The double focus of 'Elegy of Fortinbras' – on *Hamlet* and on its own contemporaneity – works to unsettle any too comforting illusion about the relationship between aesthetics and politics, principle and pragmatism, poetry and power; which was also the lesson which had to be learned by those scandalized by discovering the CIA's funding of *Encounter*, the first place of this poem's publication in English.

The poem's own power – which is possibly all the greater for anyone who discovered it, as I did, in my teens, when I was reading *Hamlet* for the first time, and discovered it as revelation – tends to confirm what might initially seem Walter Benjamin's perverse view of translation in his classic essay 'The Task of the Translator': that 'in its afterlife – which could not be called that if it were not a transformation and a renewal of something living – the original undergoes a change'.[20] Czesław Miłosz has originally Englished Zbigniew Herbert; Zbigniew Herbert has originally translated Hamlet and Fortinbras into his contemporary Poland, and Polish; and these living transformations newly, originally and with profound political inflection, read the provocative and provoking 'original' that is William Shakespeare's *Hamlet*; which is, in several senses, no 'original' at all and which exists in three variant textual redactions.

VII

To read Paul Muldoon writing with such authoritative originality about the art of translation in *The End of the Poem* is to be reminded of how central translation in various senses has been to the contemporary poetry of Northern Ireland. Ciaran Carson has made notable translations, including versions of Dante's *Inferno* (2002) and of the ancient Irish epic poem *The Tain* (2007). *Hamlet* has also been variously translated into Northern Irish poetry, notably in Seamus Heaney's *North* (1975), in which, in the poem 'Viking Dublin: Trial Pieces', the poet ineffectual before political circumstance figures himself as 'Hamlet the Dane, / skull-handler, parablist, / smeller of rot / in the state ... / jumping into graves, / dithering, blathering'. In a later volume of Heaney's, *Station Island* (1984), the poem 'Sandstone Keepsake' comparably figures the poet 'not about to set times wrong or right, / stooping along, one of the venerators'. Carson's poem 'Hamlet' undoubtedly has such instances in mind, since a questioning, sometimes even querulous, conversation with Heaney is endemic in the poetry of the Northern Irish generation immediately succeeding him.

Carson's poem is not a translation in any of the usual senses, but it does move the play into a kind of congruence with the Belfast of the Troubles. *Hamlet*, by means of reference and allusion, is made to traverse the topography of this twentieth-century rotten state, contaminating it with its own poisons. The poem's interrupted narrative of checkpoint, interrogation and surveillance also maintains a kind of congruence with the play. Prominent in it, for instance, is a much-loved father figure and a son; and a ghost appears in the form of the superstition that just before catastrophic events a terrifyingly prophetic tin can is to be heard rattling down the affected streets.

The poem's extraordinary conclusion offers an almost visionary sense of literary potential, a kind of apotheosis of translation, of the way the voices of the past calling to us across vast temporal chasms can help us understand and interpret our successive contemporary historical presents. The implication, I take it, is that memory itself – human memory as it is preserved in literary texts, in poems, in classics – may offer forms of stoically bleak consolation. In addition to *Hamlet*, this passage alludes to the Shakespeare of sonnet 86, 'Was it the proud full sail of his great verse', often interpreted as Shakespeare's own acknowledgement of literary indebtedness, the summoning of his own ghosts. The passage also refers to the Spanish Armada, many of whose ships sank around the coast of Northern Ireland. It returns too to the poem's own beginning by referring to a 'hedge', a word whose etymology of boundary and division set this whole aberrant narrative in motion; and to a pub clock permanently set some minutes later than the actual time, which has been one of the poem's recurring motifs.

Translation, Henry Gifford once wisely and wittily said, 'is Resurrection, but not of the body'.[21] Ciaran Carson discovers in the ghost of *Hamlet* a telling metaphor for exactly that. It may stand over the translations that I have brought into their own congruence, I hope, in this chapter:

For the voice from the grave reverberates in others' mouths, as the sails
Of the whitethorn hedge swell up in a little breeze, and tremble
Like the spiral blossom of Andromeda: so suddenly are shrouds and
    branches
Hung with street-lights, celebrating all that's lost, as fields are reclaimed
By the Starry Plough. So we name the constellations, to put a shape
On what was there; so, the storyteller picks his way between the isolated
stars.

But, *Was it really like that?* And, *Is the story true?*
You might as well tear off the iron mask, and find that no one, after all,
Is there: nothing but a cry, a summons, clanking out from the smoke
Of demolition. Like some son looking for his father, or the father for his
    son,
We try to piece together the exploded fragments. Let these broken spars
Stand for the Armada and its proud full sails, for even if
The clock is put to rights, everyone will still believe it's fast:
The barman's shouts of *time* will be ignored in any case, since time
Is conversation; it is the hedge that flits incessantly into the present,
As words blossom from the speakers' mouths, and the flotilla returns to
    harbour,
Long after hours.

Coda

In 2009 Daniel Mendelsohn published his translation of C. P. Cavafy's *Collected Poems*.[22] One of the poems in the section of the book entitled 'Unpublished Poems' is called 'King Claudius' and dated 1899. It is of course of interest, particularly given that Cavafy's work seems to have influenced Herbert's 'Elegy of Fortinbras', that Cavafy too should have written his *Hamlet* poem. Mendelsohn's note tells us that Cavafy actually wrote two further poems based on the play, of which only the titles remain: 'Lights, Lights, Lights' (1893) and 'The Downfall of Denmark' (1899). 'King Claudius', the longest extant poem in Cavafy's corpus, turns out though to be of more than merely passing interest.

The monologue's anonymous speaker, in cool recollection and from the perspective of geographical and temporal distance, thinks back on events at Elsinore. He has nothing but admiration for the sanity, wisdom and good governmental judgement of Claudius and regards Hamlet as a lunatic, influenced by an incredible ghost, who ruined a perfectly peaceful kingdom by his despicable act of regicide. The poor people of Elsinore, the speaker says, wept for Claudius's death; but in secret, for fear of Fortinbras. Horatio's evidence is regarded as that of a duplicitous political manipulator.

This ironic counter-reading, wholly characteristic of Cavafy's way with the plots of history too, disturbs the original with persuasive force, and reminds us in particular how much our view of Hamlet in Shakespeare's play is based on what we know of him from his soliloquies. Cavafy's is not a unique reading – what would a unique reading of *Hamlet* look like? – and has affinities with, for instance, the views of G. Wilson Knight in a famous essay in his book *The Wheel of Fire*. But at the end of 'King Claudius' Cavafy points up, as Wilson Knight does not, the political implications of such counter-reading. These focus once again on Fortinbras and make it seem astonishing that Zbigniew Herbert did not actually know this poem:

> But Fortinbras, who had profited
> and had so easily acquired the throne,
> gave great weight and serious attention
> to everything that Horatio said.

PART II

CHAPTER 4

W. B. Yeats's 'Among School Children': The Poem and its Critics

I

W. H. Auden's 'In Memory of W. B. Yeats' famously says that on his death 'the poet became his admirers'. 'Among School Children' is one of Yeats's greatest poems, and it is also one of his most written-about. So it is possible with this poem to consider in some depth the way Yeats has become his admirers, to test the air he breathes in his afterlife. I want to follow the poem from its inception to one of its most recent critiques. This may tell us something useful about Yeats, and it may also tell us something interesting about the nature of literary criticism.

In 1922 Yeats became a senator of the newly created Irish Free State, and in 1923 he won the Nobel Prize. He had become therefore what he calls himself in the poem's opening stanza, 'a sixty-year-old smiling public man'. Yeats took his duties as a senator seriously; and they included sitting on a committee investigating Irish schools, most of which came under the direct control of the Irish Catholic Church. Yeats found them seriously lacking, materially, intellectually and spiritually; and his speeches and writings on the topic seemed almost to court the ferocious response they met from Irish Catholic opinion. One of the schools he visited, in 1926, however, St Otteran's in Waterford, which was run by the Sisters of Mercy, operated according to the recently formulated Montessori system, and Yeats admired it.

In March 1926 he made a note headed 'Topic for poem': 'School children, and the thought that life will waste them, perhaps that no possible life can fulfill their own dreams or even their teacher's hope. Bring in the old thought that life prepares for what never happens'.[1] That is 'the old thought' for Yeats because he had already expressed it in both *Reveries over Childhood and Youth* in 1914 and in *At the Hawk's Well*

59

in 1917. In another note shortly after this, Yeats rehearses the haunting thought once more, but now with a more stingingly personal application:

> I think of my grandfather and grandmother, to whom I was so much, and as I look in the glass, as I look at old age coming, I wonder if they would [have] thought it worth the bother. What have I that they value? I think of my father and mother, and of my first coming to their house. What have I that they value, what would have seemed sufficient at the moment? My thought would have seemed superstition to the one and to the other a denial of God.[2]

This gives the old thought a profoundly melancholy cast, the depth of Yeats's filial affection acting as the measure of his regret. It is evidence therefore of his almost skinless honesty, which may run counter to a great deal else in him, but always impresses. It is one of the places the poetry comes from; and 'Among School Children' came between May and September 1926. It was first published in August 1927 and appeared in book form in *The Tower* in 1928.

II

I shall begin by reading my way through the poem, stanza by stanza, accumulating the details that would structure any interpretation of my own.

The opening stanza establishes the schoolroom setting and introduces the figure of the poet. Although his admiration seems straightforward, a flicker of irony surely perturbs his use of the word 'modern' when he tells us that the children's education is conducted in 'the best modern way'; this poet who elsewhere, in his poem 'The Statues', refers damningly to 'the filthy modern tide'. Yeats is almost certainly, however, not being ironic in his treatment of the 'kind old nun in a white hood' who responds to the questions he asks as school inspector. This is noteworthy, since it suggests an ability in Yeats to differentiate this nun in her dutiful individuality from her function as a representative of the Church with which he was contemporaneously engaged in furious public battles; and in fact we know that during Yeats's visit to St Otteran's his wife George, who accompanied him, was witheringly unappreciative of these nuns, reading their apparently sacrificial lives as in fact evidence of 'supreme egotism'.[3]

If Yeats does not ironize the nun, however, he does operate ironically in relation to his self-representation, by splitting the 'I' of his first-person self-conception, with which the poem opens ('I walk through the long schoolroom questioning'), from the 'sixty-year-old smiling public man', which is the way he represents the children perceiving him, staring not merely *at* him but 'upon' him, as though he constitutes a specimen rather than a self. This fracturing of self-perception, however, is also an acknowledgement of the self Yeats performs in the classroom and, no doubt, elsewhere in his public life too, an exposure of his act as 'public man'. One of the strengths of 'Among School Children' is the way the poem's tone is constantly varied as it progresses; and these initial deft ironies open it in something close to the humorous.

In the second stanza the poet abstracts himself from the scene and from his public, moving his opening 'I' into a form of reverie ('I dream'). 'Reverie' is a frequent and significant word in Yeats, and he will actually use it, in the plural, in stanza VII of this poem. Here, in reverie, the memory of a woman telling him a story consumes his attention. The woman is not identified other than as 'a Ledaean body', and it is common in Yeats for identity to be registered by gesture and deictics rather than specification ('that man'; 'this woman'), in a way that contributes to both the quasi-aristocratic *hauteur* of some of his writing, and to its mythologizing of contemporary history. You do not have to be a particularly well-practised reader of Yeats, however, to know that Maud Gonne is the person meant.

Reverie is often erotic, its images coming unbidden and unignorable. Maud Gonne's certainly erotic representation as a 'Ledaean body' reminds us that Helen of Troy, Leda's daughter by Zeus, forms a strikingly hyperbolic analogy for Gonne in other Yeats poems ('Was there no second Troy for her to burn?'). It also carries an echo, for readers working their way through *The Tower*, of the sonnet two poems earlier in the book entitled 'Leda and the Swan', which takes as subject the divine rape itself, by Zeus in the form of a swan, and its consequences. That dangerous (even scandalous) poem's first publication in Dublin in 1923 had brought Catholic wrath on Yeats's head. We know pretty clearly therefore what implications 'a Ledaean body' has for this poet: in 'Leda and the Swan' we witness 'the staggering girl' having 'her thighs caressed' as the divine raptor 'holds her helpless breast upon his breast'. The body itself is to become crucially important in 'Among School Children'; it could hardly have been introduced more powerfully than by the way the poem's opening stanzas implicitly contrast the dedicated celibacy of Catholic nuns and the plundered virginity of classical myth.

I have said that Maud Gonne is not identified. Nor is the tale she told to the poet itself recounted, even though it is clearly of some moment, since it brought 'tragedy' to her early life, even if this was a form of tragedy dependent only on its being early. The fact that Maud Gonne has conveyed this intimacy to the poet, however, produces the stanza's astonishing image of interdependency – the blending of two natures, male and female, into a single sphere – which Yeats creates by adapting a figure of fantastic anthropology from Plato's *Symposium*. The fact that this stanza itself tells us that this is what the poet is doing – 'to alter

61

Plato's parable' – makes it clear both that this is to be a poem deeply preoccupied with the mind as well as the body, with the claims of the intellect as well as those of the senses, and that Yeats's own shaping spirit, as he foregrounds the act of his poetic creativity in an almost meta-textual manner, is an underwriting of whatever claims about art itself the poem is eventually to assert or propose.

The refusal to identify Gonne or to tell us, as readers of this poem, the story she has told the poet, preserves a tactful privacy important to what we might think of as the poem's ethics. Yeats may be a smiling public man but he is a poet who, at least in this poem, brings intimate privacies to the public language of poetry only with forethought and scruple. In fact, shortly after writing 'Among School Children', Yeats sent it to Gonne with a letter hoping it would not 'offend' her. In an answering letter she tells him that she in fact finds it 'very kind'.[4] This makes her the first of the poem's critics; and very appropriately so. We may wish, however, to dispute her judgement. It argues an exceptional equanimity in Gonne that she can find a poem 'kind' that portrays her in the way the fourth stanza of this one does.

The third stanza superimposes the reverie on the classroom. As the poet has what amounts virtually to a vision of Maud Gonne as a child – 'she stands before me' – Yeats evinces a certain characteristic hauteur in which the schoolchildren become 'paddlers' – ugly ducklings – to Gonne's now glamorously mythological projection as one of the 'daughters of the swan'. The poet's reaction to his vision is startlingly naked in its emotion: 'And thereupon my heart is driven wild'. The extremity of this is explained by the following stanza, in which Gonne in youth is contrasted with her 'present image' in age. It has been persuasively argued that the phrase 'Quattrocento finger' is a reference to Leonardo's unflattering caricature drawings of old people; and Gonne's photographs do indeed confirm that she did not age well: imprisonment and hunger strike no doubt played their part in that.[5]

In this fourth stanza, thoughts of Gonne's age prompt thoughts of the poet's own; and again there's surely an element of humour in the almost coquettish vanity of Yeats's observation that he too 'had pretty plumage once'. This phrase appeared only very late in the poem's composition, having begun lamely as 'And I, though never of Ledaean kind, / Had certain points', which then became the much more arresting 'And I, though never of Ledean kind, / Have wrong to brood upon'. An embittered self-pity lurks here, which, had it stood, would have to have taken the poem in a direction quite different from the one it actually pursues. What we have in the published version is a potential narcissism brusquely dismissed by the curt 'enough of that'. I think there is a glimmer of *Hamlet* here, a play often on Yeats's mind. 'Enough of that,' says Hamlet when he has recounted the sorry story of Rosencrantz and Guildenstern; and when Yeats then writes in this stanza 'Better to smile on all that smile', he may be echoing what Hamlet says of Claudius:

that 'One may smile and smile and be a villain'. In any case, the draft's self-pity is replaced in the published poem by impatient self-mockery. The irony, contrasting with what can be stridency elsewhere in late Yeats, is part of this poem's persuasive power. 'Among School Children' draws authority from its ruefulness.

Stanza V, the drafts show, was where Yeats began the poem, with just a scribble of single words: 'lap'; 'shape'; 'fears'; 'made'; 'escape'; and so on. Looking at this draft now, we may be reminded that Yeats admired Aubrey Beardsley's unromantic conception of creativity: 'I make a blot & shove it about till something comes'.[6] We also sense the way poetic thought in Yeats discovers itself in the play of language and rhyme, or the way the play of language itself brings thought to birth. You can feel this with an almost giddy vertigo sometimes when you read Yeats's drafts; and in fact the occasionally extreme difficulty or even near-impossibility of parsing his syntax suggests that in some poems thought is not wholly disclosed even in the published version.

With the fifth stanza of 'Among School Children', in its final version, the poem turns decisively from evocation to rumination by means of a stanza-length question that has prompted acres of explication. But the question is in essence a simple one: would any mother able to see her son at sixty think the pain of childbirth and the anxieties of child-rearing worth the effort? Yeats imports into the question the Platonic theory that a child is aware of pre-existence and horrified by the fall into the pain of human nature. This is what 'Honey of generation had betrayed' means; that is, that the sexual act itself produces the treachery of the fall into the pain of incarnate nature. This tacitly reintroduces Plato, who then opens stanza VI. What Yeats really wants from this reference though, I think, is the phrase 'honey of generation' itself, which his note tells us is taken from the Neoplatonist philosopher Porphyry. Yeats appropriates it with a poet's rapaciousness rather than a philosopher's precision; and in fact he *makes* it as well as takes it, since in the drafts it was originally 'the oblivious honey' and 'the generative honey'. Its final compacted, genitive form intensively figures the act of generative sex: its sweet viscosity, its busily compelled energy, its striving for product which still seems almost gratuitous gain.

Stanza VI, a densely compacted one, offers various philosophical understandings of the 'nature' into which the child is born, and in which he must age and die, as Yeats finds original images for Platonic idealism, Aristotelian substantiality and Pythagorean mathematics and music. He does so in what Helen Vendler justly calls 'the briefest of all histories of ideas, by its brevity made ironic'; ironic, because its brevity suggests the extreme brevity of human life too, and also the hopelessness of the intellect's attempts to account for it.[7] Irony inheres too in the way the brilliant, hermeneutically comprehensive systems of philosophy quickly suffer that horribly, almost Beckettianly reduced image for the philosophers themselves in age, which brings the stanza to conclusion: 'Old clothes upon old sticks to scare a bird.'

This prompts thoughts of the alternative interpretative system of religion, which occupies stanza VII: the religion of Catholicism that worships images, and what is virtually the religion of maternity that worships images of children. Yeats arrestingly accords these images equivalent value. The images of Catholicism are not of course those Yeats himself worships, but this poem respectfully acknowledges them. 'And yet they too break hearts' is as richly invested emotionally as 'my heart is driven wild'; more richly, even, because of this poet's intuitive, empathetic understanding of how things of little importance to him can be ultimately important to others. ('So get you gone, von Hugel, though with blessings on your head,' is, we remember, the concessive instruction Yeats gives to the Catholic philosopher in 'Vacillation'.) The poem thereby also convinces us that Yeats's empathy is provoked by the images that break his own heart: the woundingly contrastive images of Maud Gonne in youth and age.

And then 'Among School Children' moves towards its majestic conclusion with an apostrophe to capitalized but unidentified 'Presences', who appear to be some apotheosized form of the images worshipped by nuns and mothers. The apostrophe's syntax is, uniquely in the poem, energetically enjambed across two stanzas in a cumulatively swelling rhythm and rhetoric. Yeats's panache here is extraordinary. We cannot have much idea what exactly these suddenly introduced 'Presences' are, but they are indisputably present to the poet and the poem, nevertheless, in the almost affronting command of Yeats's adjuration, and in the way this inherits a tradition of apostrophe and personification in romantic ode. The Presences are not merely symbolic. They serve to make mental or imaginative images virtually existent; and Yeats makes absence presence by the sheer verve of rhythmic and rhetorical gesture.

And then he goes a step further. He does not listen to anything the Presences may have come to tell him: why should he, after all, since he has invented them? Instead, *he* tells *them* the poem's truth, articulated in the final stanza's opening lines and then intensified syntactically, imagistically and rhythmically in the further two apostrophes of its conclusion:

> Labour is blossoming or dancing where
> The body is not bruised to pleasure soul,
> Nor beauty born out of its own despair,
> Nor blear-eyed wisdom out of midnight oil.
> O chestnut tree, great-rooted blossomer,
> Are you the leaf, the blossom or the bole?
> O body swayed to music, O brightening glance,
> How can we know the dancer from the dance?

These lines seem to me a distillate of what a certain kind of poetic utterance might be at its greatest. I think of Samuel Johnson aghast in his *Life of Pope* at poems 'influenced by causes wholly out of the performer's power ... by sudden elevations of mind ... which sometimes rise when he expects them least'. The end of 'Among School Children' is utterly unexpected; and unexpected *every time I read the poem*. Great poetry goes on creating its own new surprise; which is why it demands and rewards so much rereading. The end of this poem comes out of nowhere, and ramifies everywhere.

So much in the poem has tended to disintegration: the contemplation of human ageing; the pain of childbirth and the pain for the child finding existence so loathsome that he will shriek and struggle to escape; the burden of parenting a child through youth and adolescence; the pain experienced by that child-become-an-elderly-man feeling that the life he has made for himself might seem repulsive to his parents; the pain of the process of education, whose promise may never be fulfilled; and the pain of Yeats's relationship with Maud Gonne, which could only for a very brief span be figured adequately by an image of inter-dependency. As a consequence, there's wrenching outcry in Yeats's cadences. And then this conclusion suddenly transforms all of that into another shape altogether when 'labour' is figured as fruition, burgeoning, simultaneity and identity.

The magnificence of Yeats's final stanza, though, also has everything to do with the labour of its own composition and revision, as Yeats manipulates syntax over the metre and rhyme scheme of his form, *ottava rima*, which he uses for the first time in *The Tower* and then subsequently in great poems in later volumes, including 'The Municipal Gallery Revisited' and 'The Circus Animals' Desertion'. The drafts of 'Among School Children' show how intensive this labour was, displaying a frenzy of cancellation and rewriting from stanza V on. The chestnut tree, for instance, flourished eventually from the near-banality of lines about a hawthorn tree, and the statement 'Labour is blossoming' was originally 'All is blossoming'. Yeats therefore had to labour for the word 'labour' itself.

III

The poem's critical reception includes notable peculiarities. Harold Bloom thinks it is overrated. He rejects as 'eloquent idolatry' a reading by a critic he admires, Thomas Whitaker, and refers instead to 'the darkened ecstasy of the famous last stanza', saying that '"Among School Children" may well be esteemed for the wrong reasons (as I think it is) but it is a poem in which ... Yeats knows his own limitations and the limitations of poetry, and of thought'.[8] Writing on Yeats in 1970, Bloom is well on the way to his hugely influential theory of the 'anxiety of influence' – his book of that title was published just a few years later, in 1973 – and any simply ecstatic reading would have ill consorted with his view of Yeats as a poet in whom consciousness is permanently unresolved conflict, in whom consciousness is contestation.

We have to assume, therefore, that Bloom would say of Seamus Heaney what he says of Thomas Whitaker. In 1983 Heaney delivered a lecture at Queen's University, Belfast in memory of the educationist John Malone and spoke about the politics of Northern Ireland and 'the bewilderments and attempts at resolution the sensibility can undergo in this country as it tries to grow into a coherent personality'. In this context, the last stanza of 'Among School Children' becomes a ringingly oppositional affirmation. It is, Heaney says, 'a guarantee of our human capacity to outstrip the routine world, the borders of ideology and the conditionings of history. It is a vision of harmony and fulfillment, of a natural and effortless richness of being, a vision, in fact, of the paradisal place'.[9]

Nothing darkens Heaney's quasi-Dantean ecstasy here. Another poet, however, Delmore Schwartz, had had his doubts in an essay first published in 1942. Schwartz is an excellent critic, and this essay is worth reading for many reasons: but even if it were not it could not be disregarded here because it makes one of the most bizarre statements ever made not only about 'Among School Children' but about any poem, ever. Taken aback by stanza V, Schwartz says that it 'becomes ... very much better *when it is misunderstood*'; and the italics are his. This is provocative, even outrageous, in the way of an ambitious young critic making a loud noise in order to be noticed, but Schwartz puts his money where his mouth is in a reading whose brilliant perversity brings to mind nothing so much as Charles Kinbote's commentary on John Shade's poem in Vladimir Nabokov's novel *Pale Fire*, which has nothing whatever to do with the poem and everything to do with the (mad) critic's state of mind.

The 'king of kings', says Schwartz, is Aristotle's Prime Mover or God; the taws are marbles representing the concentric spheres to which the Prime Mover gives impetus; they are played on the Prime Mover's bottom because he is 'turned away from all nature and wholly engaged in eternal thought about himself'; and so on, as Schwartz proceeds to draw Ptolemaic cosmology and Dante's *Commedia* into his genuinely compelling but demented reading before gracefully conceding that 'It seems fairly certain ... that Yeats intended nothing of the sort.' Schwartz's perfectly sane point though is that 'the historical-biographical interpretations' are 'obviously inferior', and he refers to the brilliant critical displays of William Empson in his famous book *Seven Types of Ambiguity*.[10]

Delmore Schwartz, that is to say, was of the generation profoundly affected by the New Criticism, and he is making his almost recklessly hyperbolic case for that method in this essay. The piece was first published in an issue of the *Southern Review* which also contained work by R. P. Blackmur, John Crowe Ransom, Allen Tate, T. S. Eliot and Cleanth Brooks; and these were collected in 1950 in a book called *The Persistence of Yeats*, which smoothed Yeats's path into the American New Critical academy. Many of these critics, either in this volume or elsewhere, wrote about 'Among School Children' so frequently that it became virtually the signature poem of the New Criticism. Eliot and Empson are usually regarded as the major theoretical presences behind this work; but Yeats, and 'Among School Children' in particular, is manifest within it.

In Cleanth Brooks, the poem becomes both exemplar and allegory. In the extremely influential anthology *Understanding Poetry*, which he edited with Robert Penn Warren in 1938, Yeats's essay 'The Symbolism of Poetry' is cited as authority for the doctrine of the organic relations between parts of a poem; and in Brooks's classic critical text *The Well-Wrought Urn* (1947), 'Among School Children' supplies the climactic reading. In the poem, Brooks says, Yeats commits 'the development of his theme to his imagery' and displays a strict 'inner logic' and 'an absolute economy of symbol'. Brooks's reading is explicitly anti-biographical, to the bizarre extent of claiming that the woman evoked in the poem need not be Maud Gonne, or even old. Such critical insistences, Brooks thinks, are a consequence of 'the perils of biographical bias'; and this critic satisfactorily demonstrates his own fastidious immunity to any such peril by actually misspelling Maud Gonne's name.

As the essay advances, though, 'Among School Children' turns into something more than an exemplar of New Critical method. The poem's final lines become, self-reflexively, images for the critical act itself. 'We must examine,' says Brooks, the 'bole, and the roots, and most of all, their organic inter-relations'. And from this it is a short step to adopting 'Among School Children' as an allegory of critical-methodological possibility:

> One staple study of literature consists in investigations of the root system (the study of literary sources) or … in questioning the dancer about her life history (the study of the poet's biography). But we cannot question her as dancer without stopping the dance or waiting until the dance has been completed. And in so far as our interest is in poetry, the dance must be primary for us.

The dance is of course the words on the page, and nothing outside them. It is easy to see how attractive this might be as critical method, especially since Brooks ends by demonstrating how 'Among School Children' 'is finally a poem "about" the nature of the human imagination itself'.[11] The inverted commas around the word 'about' there suggest both that this is by now so obviously the case, even a truism, that it is a bit embarrassing to have to be so explicit, and also that poems may not, in truth, ever be said to be in any conventional sense 'about' anything but themselves. The word 'about' in inverted commas, or implied inverted commas, is endemic to New Criticism; and so indeed is the word 'finally', as though, for all its eschewal of any rational logic in a poem and its recognition of an alternative symbolic logic, the critical essay itself is indisputably rational argument. The word 'finally' clicks it shut with the flourish of a QED at the end of a geometrical theorem. But it is hard now, despite its many local insights and felicities, to relish a method in which poems become their own allegories and in which what they 'finally' demonstrate is something so close to tautology.

Literary criticism demonstrates no Whiggish advancement of learning. On occasion it may actually demonstrate a progress in error. For instance, Delmore Schwartz's reading has been recounted by at least one later critic in a (good) book on Yeats as though it was intended unironically; and, unsurprisingly, it is regarded as preposterous. Brooks in the 1940s derogates 'the study of literary sources', and he has in mind some rather unsophisticated if nevertheless useful source-hunting studies. But Frank Kermode in 1957, in his book *Romantic Image*, engages in a hugely sophisticated version of exactly that: so sophisticated that we need to find a new term for it, and to call it not 'source study' but 'genealogical criticism.' The 'Image', with a capital 'I', is Kermode's term for what is passed on from Romanticism to Modernism by way of late nineteenth-century French symbolism and decadence. Crucial to this heritage is the figure of the dancer; and crucial to representations of that figure is Yeats's dancer. Kermode's book brilliantly traces a genealogy of the figure.

Mallarmé comes into the reckoning, and also such writers and painters as Huysmans, Wilde, Flaubert, Moreau and Toulouse-Lautrec. So too do actual dancers like Louie Fuller, who excited both Mallarmé and Yeats. So also do the poems of Arthur Symons, whom Yeats included in his *Oxford Book of Modern Verse* in 1936. These actual and poetic dancers are all women, and Kermode says that 'The beauty of a woman, and particularly of a woman in movement, is the emblem of the work of art or Image'.[12] Kermode does understand and make explicit the complicity between such an image, or 'Image', and Yeats's sense – 'important to him' – that 'girls are like poems' to the degree that intellectual labours would render them shapeless and graceless.[13] Kermode's use of the word 'girls' rather than 'women' might, however, suggest a certain blindness to the full implications of Yeats's own intellectual practice; and a later feminist critic, Elizabeth Butler Cullingford, in her book *Gender and Identity in Yeats's Love Poetry* (1993), returns the poem from genealogy to politics with, you might say, a historicizing vengeance, when she reads it as a work intimately entangled in Yeats's tormented relationship with Irish Catholicism, in the Irish Free State's attitude to divorce (in the context of Maud Gonne's traumatic marriage), and in the implications of the School Attendance Bill of 1925.[14] Cullingford's reading is fascinating but threatens to collapse the poem completely back into the tissue of circumstance and contingency in which, it is true, it may well have had its birth. With great poems, however, origin is never end; and criticism that concentrates too exclusively on derivation and aetiology runs the risk of losing sight of the true prize of creativity.

For Kermode, though, it is by an original amalgamation of his sources that Yeats fashions the dancer who appears at the end of 'Among School Children' as one of his 'great reconciling images'. As such, it bears a meaning crucial to Yeats's whole sense of the fruitful relationship between art and life: 'No static image will serve; there must be movement, the different sort of life that a dancer has by comparison with the most perfect object of art'. And the tree at the end of the poem shares this meaning, it is congruent with it and equivalent to it, 'since it so powerfully reinforces the idea of integrity'. It becomes 'fitting' therefore, Kermode says, that 'the two emblems should have been fused in "Among School Children", where the cost to the artist is also so wonderfully expressed'.[15] Kermode's sense of these concluding images not only *as* images of reconciliation but as themselves reconciled is, in my experience, the way most readers conceive of them and receive them, with strong emotions of release, even catharsis. But, as we shall see, not everyone understands them in this way.

Paul de Man is a name it has become difficult for some people to utter at all in the wake of revelations about his wartime Nazi associations. Some also think that his critical practice proceeds from forms of repression or mendacity similar to those that structure his biography. In thinking about the critical reception of 'Among School Children', though, it is impossible to omit de Man, since the 100-page-long essay 'Image and Emblem in Yeats' in his book *The Rhetoric of Romanticism* (1984), is centrally preoccupied with the poem. De Man was indeed centrally preoccupied with Yeats, and the essay is excerpted from his PhD thesis, 'Mallarmé, Yeats, and the Post-Romantic Predicament', presented at Harvard as early as 1960.

I shall not attempt to summarize de Man's involved argument. Most relevant for my purposes is the way he takes issue with Kermode by opposing a concept of 'emblem' to that of 'image'. 'Image' for de Man is the natural object; 'emblem' something drained of the natural, taking its authority only from traditional agreement. As we have seen, Kermode actually uses the words interchangeably, and this is not unnatural for a critic. However, like many practitioners of deconstructive kinds of criticism, de Man permits himself a rather specialized terminological inflection which is never very explicitly accounted for or justified.

His essay emphasizes the preoccupation in late Yeats with violence, apocalypse and death, and it consequently finds the 'dazzling imagery of unity' at the end of 'Among School Children' 'reductive'. Kermode's reconciliatory reading does injustice, de Man thinks, to the 'cold terror and strident dissonance' of late Yeats. Feeding such things back into the poem, de Man reads its rhetorical figures against themselves. 'Assuming', he says that a difference exists between what is represented by the dancer and what is represented by the dance ... the question would just as well express the bewilderment of someone who ... does not know what choice to make. In that case the question would not be rhetorical at all, but urgently addressed to the 'presences' in the hope of receiving an answer.

The answer would be momentous, for 'to choose the dancer means to fall into the transient world of matter for the sake of a few moments of illusive pleasure; to choose the dance means to renounce all natural joys for the sake of divine revelation'.

The poem's final lesson is therefore that

the ways of the image and of the emblem are ... opposed; the final line is not a rhetorical statement of reconciliation but an anguished question; it is our perilous fate not to know if the glimpses of unity which we perceive at times can be made more permanent by natural ways or by ... renunciation, by images or by emblem.[16]

Even if we find the high seriousness of this, with its impressive sense of what is at stake in a great Yeats poem, impressively in tune with at least an element of 'Among School Children', it is still hard not to remember de Man's own 'perilous fate' when we read that phrase now. Nor is it inconceivable, I suppose, that he may have been remembering, when he wrote it, his own perilous existence as the hoarder of dangerous secrets; to which the denaturing of imagery by the traditional conventions of emblem, the opposing of the category of the 'natural' with the category of the culturally accredited, may not be wholly irrelevant.

De Man's reading, though, imports into 'Among School Children', without authority, concerns from other late poems, as though poems from the same phase of a career must be identical, or at least congruent with one another. I cannot understand, though, how such formulae as 'cold terror and strident dissonance' would accommodate poems such as 'Man and the Echo', with its guilty regret and vulnerable rhetoric of aposiopesis, in which the cry of a wounded hare puts an end to thought, and to the poem itself, or 'Cuchulain Comforted', Yeats's sole poem in Dantean *terza rima*, which Seamus Heaney admires – not at all idolatrously – as 'full of a motherly kindness towards life'.[17] Even so, this destabilizing reading does coincide with those dissatisfactions felt by Bloom and Schwartz too, their sense that this poem is not as resolved as it appears to be, or as it appears to want to be. After you have read de Man, you are less likely to fall into idolatry, eloquent or otherwise, about the poem's final stanza.

The renowned formalist critic Helen Vendler could hardly be expected to agree with Paul de Man, and it is unsurprising that she nowhere mentions him in her study of Yeats, *Our Secret Discipline* (2007). But in the whole of this long book she refers to hardly any previous critic of Yeats, offering as justification at the outset the fact that it would be impossible to debate the vast number of readings that Yeats's poems have received. The book is a study of a shamefully neglected topic, lyric form, in Yeats; and it is an excellent book. In one of her finest ever critical performances, Vendler is outstanding on the effects of *ottava rima* in 'Among School Children': on the way sense-units play against form, for instance, to create 'a contrapuntal variety which confers on the poem its air of spontaneous musing, inner hesitation, recalcitrance, and emotionality'.[18] This is discriminatingly empathetic criticism of the necessary means of poetry, and it sings with revelatory intelligence and sensibility, even if it makes severe demands of the reader's concentration over the length at which Vendler employs it. Even so, this critic interprets the final stanza of Yeats's poem in, to my mind, an unlikely way and thereby produces a reading in effect as 'deconstructive' as de Man's.

The images of tree and dancer are not harmoniously reconciled or equivalent, she thinks: they are, on the contrary, distinct and even progressive. The tree lacks free will, and its capacity for sexual generation in age is not that of human beings, so it cannot act as the rehabilitation of the poem's hideous representations of ageing. The image of the dancer therefore corrects the image of the tree, in what Helen Vendler calls 'a counterspell to the poem's despair'. She notes that in a draft Yeats has a 'dancing couple' and a 'glance that mirrors glance': but this reciprocity fails to take into account 'the brevity of the span of sexuality for some human beings'. So, in 'his most radical revision', Yeats correctively 'chooses to make the dancer solitary, ungendered, unmirrored by a responsive human look'; and for Vendler this carries autobiographical freight, since 'Yeats himself is, at sixty, far distant in time from the sexual ecstasy and mirroring of gaze represented by the image of the dancing couple'.

Formalism here has an ethical as well as an aesthetic end; and the moral of the critique is proposed in an expansive generalizing question of Vendler's own about human identity, together with two responsive statements: 'Who are we? We are the dance we go on creating from birth to death. Yeats has found something to say for life: it is a solitary but endlessly satisfying set of creative inventions.' Yeats has written a philosophical poem for everyone: 'Among School Children' 'offers as its example of an art-work the self-choreographed articulation of a life over time – an enterprise that every conscious creature must in some way undertake': 'self-choreographed' because the dance needs no training, unlike other art forms – sculpture, for instance – that figure in Yeats's late poems.[19]

This is thrillingly inclusive and consolatory, and its contrarian reading of the way the poem's final images relate to each other supplies solace where de Man's provokes despair. So I rather resent my doubt: but

Vendler's view of Yeats seems to me a little complaisant. To think him interested in 'everyone' is to find him more democratically inclined, or even just more *interested*, than I do; and to think him distant from thoughts of sexual ecstasy simply because he is sixty is strangely to ignore the agonized sexuality of some of the late poems, whose paradigm is 'Politics', where the final lines – 'But O that I were young again / And held her in my arms' – constitute a sigh or gasp of impossible, incommensurable sexual yearning. To diagnose in Yeats a species of charity responsive to people with a brief span of sexuality is also more than I can manage: I cannot conceive of him caring.

In addition, I cannot see why Vendler thinks that the image of the dancer in its final form is 'ungendered'. Gender is inexplicit, it is true: but has anyone ever conceived of Yeats's dancer as male? The word 'swayed' would tend to make any such male distractingly epicene: but in any case most readers surely *sense* something of Frank Kermode's genealogy, even if they have not read his book, since the genealogy has so many cultural roots as to be more generic than specific. Although Vendler thinks that Yeats's figure is not to be perceived as a 'specific "trained" dancer (such as one of Loie Fuller's "Chinese dancers")', she does not say why not; and we may well think that any dancer needs some training, even if it is no more than the self-training of copying and imitation.

The dancing that Kermode has in mind required extensive training and great physical skill. It was exceptional, well beyond the capacity of 'everyone'. If everyone can do it *without training*, does that not also fatally compromise a stanza proposing that 'labour' can be so managed as to constitute a mode of being in which 'body is not bruised to pleasure soul'? Vendler nowhere mentions Kermode, however, or the tradition of genealogical criticism that he exploits and refines. Her reading of 'Among School Children' happens in a kind of critical vacuum, as though no one has ever read the poem before. Even if we are obliged to agree with her about the impossibility of debating all the readings Yeats's poem has received, in a book which after all has a great deal of illuminating work of its own busily to get on with, this does seem to reduce the efficacy of the demonstration.

It is always an anxiety in writing literary criticism to know how much previous criticism to take into account: since, as Henry James said, in the preface to *Roderick Hudson*, 'really, universally, relations stop nowhere'. To pay previous criticism too much attention may well be either to embarrass one's own prose with references, or to be blocked from writing it in the first place. On the other hand, simply to ignore the history of a text's reception can seem solipsistic in its refusal to recognize the institutional and historical nature of the activity of literary criticism; it can seem a disconcerting form of intellectual amnesia. The dialogic cannot but be enlivening, and the concessive is not merely a necessary courtesy and tribute to labour but itself an essential aid or spur to the arrival at true judgement, or – if such a thing has been placed under radical suspicion by modern theory – at least to the production of significant new readings which may themselves reintroduce great literary texts to their always altering cultural moments and contexts and, by effecting such introductions, may alter or modify these moments and contexts too.

IV

Oscar Wilde says that criticism is the only civilized form of autobiography. It is also a civilized form of conversation, and of conversation across the generations. It is actually moving to read others coming to terms with poems you love, even if the terms are not your terms and even if you want to argue with the results; and you can read yourself into these continuities in clarifying ways. Ted Hughes, generously allowing for all possibilities of critical method, once proposed a metaphor and a relationship that seem to me both enlivening and workable. 'Everything we associate with a poem,' he says, 'is its shadowy tenant and part of its meaning'.[20] Even Delmore Schwartz's Ptolemaic marbles are given their permission by this: and it is just true that once you have read about them you cannot get them out of your mind. Finally, when you read a great deal of literary criticism about a single work of art, in many modes and styles, you quickly discover the simple truth of T. S. Eliot's apothegm in 'The Perfect Critic' that 'there is no method except to be very intelligent'. It is not method that matters; it is the way method is managed.

These, then, are some of the ways in which this poet, W. B. Yeats, has become his admirers. The poem itself goes on surviving its admirers, including the poet, even if it appears to change shape depending on who is looking at it, and when. Reviewing some of the most interesting criticism of 'Among School Children', we discover no consensus: but this may well itself be a discovery about this poem. Although consensus may prove not to be an attribute of any review of the criticism of any major poem, the almost exacerbated lack of consensus about this one is, I think, revealing about its nature. It tells us that there is something inherently unstable in it; that it is drawn in opposed directions by antithetical forces; and that these are never satisfactorily resolved, even by the heroic will to resolution magnificently manifest in the final stanza.

This also tells us though why this poem goes on engaging so many people so deeply and, as it were, viscerally. Everything in Yeats pitches in, in that last stanza, to find in the art of poetry an image or an emblem that will help in a full facing of the worst. Witnessing Yeats doing this is to be fortified, and to feel accompanied. Nevertheless, so much in Yeats also fails to find succour, anywhere: which is why so many of his late poems are rancorous with outrage. 'Among School Children' scandalously houses and earths both the truth of human desire and the desolating truth that such desire can never find adequate reciprocation.

Coda

In 1990 the *Yeats Annual* edited by Warwick Gould published a brief article entitled 'The Paddler's Heritage: Yeats's Visit to St Otteran's School, 1926' by Sister Marybride Ryan OP. Sister Ryan had been a pupil at the school, aged 12, at the time of Yeats's visit. She had, indeed, presented him with one of her poems, about a cat, which he, the poet of 'The Cat and the Moon', one of the greatest cat poems ever, admired. Even so, there was not much sympathetic contact: 'He was seeing a school-age Maud Gonne,' she says, 'and I was seeing a strange man who briefly interrupted my day'.[21] She has little more than this to say about the visit, but the epithet and the note of irritation possibly reinforce a criticism implicit in the surely ironic title of her article: for, who would willingly accept the title of paddler when that of the daughter of the swan is available? Sister Ryan's own 'heritage', though, has clearly been in part a literary one, since her article concludes with a poem, an able and striking sonnet entitled 'Shadow and Substance'. It is a poem about the Christian Annunciation, and its trope bravely revises Yeats's scandalous scene of divine rape in 'Leda and the Swan': 'Here is no blow, no shrinking flesh to yield. / The God, more courteous, sends a deputation'.

This poem makes Sister Marybride Ryan one of the critics of 'Among School Children' as well as of 'Leda and the Swan' too; hers a poem that continues the conversation in an unpredictable way: for in 'Shadow and Substance', we might say, the convent has the temerity to write back.[22]

Question Me Again: Reflections on W. B. Yeats and Seamus Heaney

I

In 1967 Richard Ellmann, who had already written extensively on Yeats, published a book called *Eminent Domain*, which, its subtitle tells us, is a study of Yeats 'among' a number of other writers, including Joyce, Eliot and Pound. It is a book about literary inter-relationship and influence, what most of us now would call 'intertextuality'. The metaphor of Ellmann's title, drawn from the sovereignty of property rights, suggests the view of literary community that the book advances; and its opening paragraph tells us that 'influence' is a term that 'conceals and mitigates the guilty acquisitiveness of talent':

> That writers flow into each other like waves, gently rather than tidally, is one of those decorous myths we impose upon a high-handed, even brutal procedure. The behaviour, while not invariably marked by bad temper, is less polite. Writers move upon other writers not as genial successors but as violent expropriators, knocking down established boundaries to seize by the force of youth, or of age, what they require. They do not borrow, they override.[1]

This may itself derive from T. S. Eliot's well-known contention in his essay on Philip Massenger that 'Immature poets imitate; mature poets steal', even as it adds to it an apparent readiness to be impressed by the manners of the jungle. So Ellmann's observation may be thought to practise what it preaches, by performing its own act of over-riding.

Eminent Domain is cited in the preface to the book Harold Bloom published on Yeats in 1970, and Ellmann is one of its dedicatees.[2]

Bloom's book is taken up largely with the poet not among his peers and successors but among his Romantic forerunners, notably Blake and Shelley. It was while writing this book that Bloom began to construct his theory of what he called, now famously, 'the anxiety of influence'. Even though Bloom's stated preoccupation is not with psyche but with pneuma – with the spirit of poetry that bloweth where it listeth – this is essentially Ellmann's conception of writerly inter-relationship as a kind of ferocious rapacity, but now immensely and arcanely complicated. Bloom's neo-Freudianism, as we know, reads literary history as Oedipal struggle and stress, a revisionary battle in which the successor poet accrues strength by contesting a precursor poet and swerving away from him according to what can be drawn as a 'map of misreading'.

This theory has of course been enormously influential, even among those who dislike what they perceive as its congruity with certain kinds of corporatist or masculinist competitiveness. I have referred to it myself as the 'Promotions Board' theory of poetry; and Naomi Segal speaks of Bloom's 'waste land of reading' – taking a kind of feminist issue with Bloom's own issue with Eliot – in which 'poetry is begot by a just war between fathers and sons, strength passed on by the resolute refusal to inherit meaning; these texts have no mothers and no sisters'.[3] In his book on literary allusion Christopher Ricks has observed that 'we are all both beneficiaries and victims' of Bloom's 'energies': 'Beneficiaries, granted his passion, his learning, and his so giving salience to the impulse or spirit of allusion. Victims, because of his melodramatic sub-Freudian parricidal scenario, his sentimental discrediting of gratitude, and his explicit repudiation of all interest in allusion as a matter of the very words.'[4] This makes it clear enough that Ricks is in fact antagonized by being Bloom's victim far more than he is delighted by being his beneficiary. However, despite such objections, it is not hard to account for the success of Bloom's theory. He is a busily efficient cartographer who does indeed provide a map for difficult terrain. Yet his efficiency is often apologetic, shadowed by a palpable and mitigating melancholy. In his most arresting work he makes you aware of the weighty personal sadness that attends, for him, the responsibility of bringing us the bad news that poetry is the sublimation of aggression. I think of this combination of efficiency and a melancholy rebuke to efficiency as a kind of Woody Allen effect, and a very potent one; and, indeed, it is sometimes not without its rather lugubrious humour: as when, for instance, Bloom says of 'The Witch of Atlas' that Shelley had been reading far too much late Yeats when he wrote it.[5]

It is of great interest, though, that Bloom's theory was developed in relation to Yeats, a poet in whom violent acts of appropriation and contestation figure largely at the level of subject matter. There is his poetry of Anglo-Irish virtue and decay, in particular, poetry immersed in that late-nineteenth and early twentieth-century history of Ireland in which antagonism was not merely a literary trope but an all too literal revolutionary war of independence succeeded by an appallingly bitter civil war. This resulted in the creation of a political state that Yeats found increasingly antipathetic, even though it was generous, or pragmatic, enough to make him a senator in its parliament; and his hostility provokes some of his most rancorous later works. But such antagonisms figure even in Yeats's poems of love and sexuality – in those magnificent and terrifying poems 'Solomon and the Witch' and 'Leda and the Swan', for instance – as they do also in his speculations on the 'gyres' of human history. Yeats is the poet to go to, in other words, if you want a view of creativity as contestation.

Perhaps because it was developed in relation to this particular, and peculiar, poet, the only thing wrong with Bloom's theory, successful as it has been, is that it is not, actually, true – or at least, not universally true. It would be sentimental to think that there are not truths in it, to believe that poets move upon one another as harmonious reconcilers; but it is a sort of inverted sentimentality to believe that it is the sole or whole truth. I want to defend an alternative model of literary history, one I think appropriate to the relationship I am about to consider here, and one which also proposes that any purely psychoanalytic theory of literary history is likely to be deficient if it ignores, as Bloom's almost entirely does, the category of history itself. In the relationship between these two poets of modern Ireland that category is inescapable.

II

Terence Brown ends his excellent critical biography of Yeats with a chapter on his 'afterlife', an account of the various ways in which his work survives in the valley of others' saying. He says that Seamus Heaney 'has engaged as critic with the poetic achievement of Yeats more fully than any other Irish poet since MacNeice', who published the first full-length critical book on Yeats in 1941.[6] In fact, Heaney's writings on Yeats to date would almost make a book too – a relatively slim one, but intellectually substantial. These are also, in the main, instances of Heaney at his best as a critic. Elsewhere, on occasion, his critical prose can be prone to a certain reflexivity or even orotundity, in which the work in question is not so much analysed as celebrated or even flattered; but Yeats always proves much less compliant to such procedures, provoking Heaney into some of his most alert and challenged acts of attention.

A collection of Heaney on Yeats would begin with two essays of 1978. One, 'The Makings of a Music: Reflections on Wordsworth and Yeats', sustains a contrast between the different kinds of poetry represented by the names of these two poets, a poetry of 'surrender' and a poetry of 'discipline'; a contrast which, it may be, would not survive a confrontation with poems of Wordsworth's different from those cited by Heaney. The other, 'Yeats as an Example?', adds a question mark to the title of an essay by W. H. Auden to suggest how deeply problematic a figure Yeats is for Heaney. 'Yeats as an Example?' is central to my sense of this relationship, and I shall return to it shortly.[7] Other essays would include the uncollected 'A tale of two islands: reflections on the Irish Literary Revival', published in 1980, in which the Protestant Anglo-Irish Yeats is compared with the nineteenth-century Catholic apostate novelist William Carleton; and the comparison introduces the denominational element which even then bristled in some modern Irish literary and cultural criticism.[8] Then there is an essay of 1988, 'The Place of Writing: W. B. Yeats and Thoor Ballylee', in which Heaney meditates on the various meanings of the Norman tower in the West of Ireland in which Yeats lived for a few years, and which he figured extensively in his poetry. The essay is one of three – the others are frequently allusive to Yeats too – which made a short book, also called *The Place of Writing*, published in the USA in 1988, excerpts from which were reprinted in the prose collection *Finders Keepers* in 2002.[9]

This putative collection of Heaney on Yeats would continue with an essay of 1990 called 'Joy or Night', which compares attitudes to death in Yeats and Philip Larkin, decisively favouring Yeats as 'more vital and undaunted', and proposing, in its affirmation of a persisting value in Romantic transcendence, that Larkin's rejection of Yeats may have been 'too long and too readily approved of'.[10] It would include the lengthy essay on Yeats written for *The Field Day Anthology of Irish Writing* in 1991, a revised version of which forms the introduction to the Faber selection of Yeats which Heaney published in 2000.[11] And it would end with the Nobel Prize acceptance speech delivered in Stockholm in 1995 entitled 'Crediting Poetry', which he subsequently reprinted at the end of his not-quite-collected volume *Opened Ground: Poems 1966-1996* in 1998.[12] An account of his own career as a poet in relation to the circumstances of Northern Ireland since 1969, this lecture is also much taken up with Yeats, that earlier Irish winner of this same prize – with Yeats's own Nobel speech, and with some of the poems he wrote out of the political turmoil of Ireland in the 1920s. Peter McDonald has said that 'this feels like the last word on a topic Heaney knows must now be dropped'.[13] This may be so: but, given that Yeats remains a supreme model for poetic persistence into old age, it may be wise not to agree too readily.

Yeats has been, then, a constant presence in Heaney's criticism since the late 1970s, and a central figure in his consideration of poetic influence. Auden, in his elegy for Yeats on his death in 1939, famously said that 'The poet became his admirers'. One of the admirers Yeats has most crucially become is Seamus Heaney.

III

The strenuousness of Heaney's ongoing engagement with Yeats is of keen interest not least because it sets him in the midst of one of the most fraught and contentious debates in recent Irish literary and cultural criticism. In this debate the voice of the critic Seamus Deane has been particularly penetrating, with its articulation of Yeats's later career as an exercise in 'the pathology of literary Unionism', and with its inveighing against a criticism complaisantly tolerant of certain presumptively Yeatsian formal procedures in contemporary Northern Irish poetry, in which 'The literature – autonomous, ordered – stands over against the political system in its savage disorder'.[14] But it is of keen interest also because Heaney's place in contemporary Irish national life has been of a kind that no Irish poet since Yeats has enjoyed, or endured. One consequence of this has been that, as early as the mid-1970s, Yeats was adduced in critical discussions of Heaney with the clear implication that he was to inherit the mantle. This must have been at least as daunting as it was encouraging; and it certainly put him in the way of the scepticism of his younger contemporary Paul Muldoon, who, in a prominently placed review of *Station Island* in 1984, said tartly that 'a truly uninvited shade' to the title poem's purgatorial setting would advise this poet 'that he should resist more firmly the idea that he must be the best Irish poet since Yeats, which arose from rather casual remarks by the power-crazed Robert Lowell and the craze-powered Clive James, who seem to have forgotten both MacNeice and Kavanagh'.[15] That advice may not have been entirely innocent of this reviewer's jostling at the time for his own place in the firmament, not least because it would be hard to credit it that these power-crazed and craze-powered international luminaries would ever, in the first place, have remembered Patrick Kavanagh sufficiently to have forgotten him; and I have written elsewhere of the complexities of the Heaney-Muldoon entanglements, to which I do, in fact, find the Bloomian categories in some ways appropriate.[16] But Muldoon's review certainly makes it plain that the relationship between Heaney and Yeats which I am discussing here is an affair of peculiar delicacy, in which the bold but wary subtleties of Heaney's negotiations over the years may have been almost matched by the subtleties of suspicious scrutiny to which they have been subjected.

But I am interested here in the way Yeats figures in Heaney's poems as well as in his critical prose. Any full treatment of this would prominently consider the sequence 'Singing School' in *North* in 1975, whose title derives from 'Sailing to Byzantium', and whose epigraphs set a quotation from the *Autobiographies* against another from Wordsworth's *Prelude* in a way that makes, of itself, an ironic political point; and it would examine many other poems in that volume too. It would think about the poem 'The Master' in the sequence 'Sweeney Redivivus' in *Station Island*, published in 1984, where the anonymous figure of authority is dressed in very Yeatsian imagery; and it might think about that poem all the more because Heaney in fact identifies the master in an interview as the Polish poet Czesław Miłosz.[17] It would consider the poem 'A Peacock's Feather', published in *The Haw Lantern* in 1987, but punctiliously dated 1972 – an extremely significant date in Irish history, about which I shall have more to say shortly. This is an apparently occasional poem written for the christening of a niece, but its ironically Marvellian octosyllabics offer a consideration of Anglo-Irish and class resentments in which prominent reference is made to Yeats's poems of Coole Park, the Irish house owned by his patron, Lady Gregory. A full treatment of the topic would also examine the references to Yeats in the sequence 'Squarings', published in the volume *Seeing Things* in 1991, in some of which we would discover a poet learning from Yeats's astonishing poem 'The Cold Heaven' one way of registering a religious sensibility without using the terms of religious orthodoxy. However, I want here to focus the relationship between Heaney and Yeats by bringing three texts together: the essay of Heaney's to which I have already referred, 'Yeats as an Example?', written in 1978 and published in his critical book *Preoccupations* in 1980; Yeats's poem 'The Fisherman', published in *The Wild Swans at Coole* in 1919; and Heaney's poem 'Casualty', published in his volume *Field Work* exactly sixty years later, in 1979.

IV

'Yeats as an Example?' is one of the most spirited of Heaney's earlier essays. We witness in it his approach to another writer with the clear awareness that this is going to be a significant phase of self-development. The essay notices, as much criticism has, something cold, violent and implacable in Yeats's art, and asks if this can be regarded as in any way exemplary. Heaney does admire, he tells us, what he calls Yeats's 'intransigence', and admires too the way 'his vision did not confine itself to rhetorics, but issued in actions'.[18] He respects, that is to say, the inextricability of the life and the work in this poet who nevertheless maintained a theory of their separation. He then offers a quite unpredictable reading of a couple of moments from the life. One is from the 1890s, in the first flush of Yeats's enthusiasm for spiritualism, and the other from 1913, when he spoke in outrage against Irish middle-class philistinism. Yeats did so on this occasion because Dublin Corporation had refused to fund a gallery for a collection of Impressionist paintings offered to the city by Lady Gregory's nephew, Hugh Lane: this episode also lies behind such poems as 'To a Wealthy Man', 'Paudeen' and 'September 1913'. Where others have found only Yeats's silliness or snobbery in these episodes, and have ridiculed him, Heaney reads them as moments in which Yeats admirably 'took on the world on his own terms, defined the areas where he would negotiate and where he would not'. Heaney assumes that 'this peremptoriness, this apparent arrogance, is exemplary in an artist, that it is proper and even necessary for him to insist on his own language, his own vision, his own terms of reference'.[19] Such admiration is in fact tempered in the essay as a whole by a concerted attempt to find in Yeats moments not peremptory or arrogant at all, but instinct with a kind of saving humanitarianism. The end of the essay, for instance, finds Yeats's poem 'Under Ben Bulben' unfortunate, even ethically obnoxious, in itself – this is not hard to do – and particularly so as the intended final poem of his *Collected Poems*. Heaney would, he says, 'put a kinder poem last' – and he believes that he has found such a thing in 'Cuchulain Comforted'. (In fact, as Warwick Gould has demonstrated, the decision to place 'Under Ben Bulben' last was not Yeats's but George Yeats's, after his death.)[20]

But, to understand why, nevertheless, Heaney might approve of Yeatsian 'arrogance', I want to quote the second of his two instances from the life. His comment on it then leads into a quotation from 'The Fisherman'. The passage is a piece of raillery taken from George Moore's autobiography, *Hail and Farewell*. Moore has given an account of the Lane controversy and of a lecture of his own on the Impressionists, which Yeats attended. And then Yeats appears, the victim of Moore's mocking and arrestingly engaging prose:

> As soon as the applause died away, Yeats who had lately returned to us from the States with a paunch, a huge stride, and an immense fur overcoat, rose to speak. We were surprised at the change in his appearance, and could hardly believe our ears when, instead of talking to us as he used to do about the old stories come down from generation to generation he began to thunder ... against the middle classes, stamping his feet, working himself into a temper, and all because the middle classes did not dip their hands into their pockets and give Lane the money he wanted for his exhibition. When he spoke the words, the middle classes, one would have thought that he was speaking against a personal foe, and we looked round asking each other with our eyes where on earth our Willie Yeats had picked up the strange belief that none but titled and carriage folk could appreciate pictures ...
>
> We have sacrificed our lives for art; but you, what have you done? What sacrifices have you made? he asked, and everybody began to search his memory for the sacrifices Yeats had made, asking himself in what prison Yeats had languished, what rags he had worn, what broken victuals he had eaten. As far as anybody could remember, he had always lived very comfortably, sitting down invariably to regular meals, and the old green cloak that was in keeping with his profession of romantic poet he had

exchanged for the magnificent fur coat which distracted our attention from what he was saying, so opulently did it cover the back of the chair out of which he had risen.[21]

This passage has the confidence, and perhaps the condescension, of Moore's own certain knowledge that he is himself, as the scion of a (Catholic) Big House far grander than Lady Gregory's, socially several cuts above 'our Willie Yeats'. (Possibly because it would distract attention from his argument here, Heaney omits a sentence from the passage in which Moore makes the specifically directed social point: 'And we asked ourselves why Willie Yeats should feel himself called upon to denounce his own class, millers and shipowners on one side, and on the other a portrait-painter of distinction'.)[22] Nevertheless, the critique of Yeats's aristocratic pretensions hits its target. Animated by animosity, Moore deflates Yeats in a rhetoric of bathos. And one might expect Seamus Heaney to have some sympathy with this, since he seems congenitally incapable of any such behaviour himself. He does of course note the 'theatricality' of Yeats's performance, but he regards it as deliberate. Yeats is busy creating out of himself, he says, 'a character who was almost as much a work of imagination' as James Joyce's Stephen Dedalus. And, Heaney thinks, for the same reason: the exercise of intransigence is a protection, he says, of 'his imaginative springs, so that the gift would survive' – by which he means, of course, the gift of poetry.[23]

I suppose that most poets dread the departure of the gift. There are, after all, many precedents in literary history for that, including Wordsworth, who is probably the most deeply and originally informing presence in Heaney, despite his far more extensive critical engagement with Yeats. A lot is made in this essay of the fact that Yeats is particularly exemplary for a poet 'approaching middle age', as Heaney may well have considered himself in 1978, when he was nearing forty. Yeats is of course, paradigmatically, the post-Romantic poet who managed to go on writing and, indeed, produced some of his greatest work in, and about, old age. It is in this context of writerly survival that Heaney then quotes the ending of 'The Fisherman' and comments:

> The solitude, the will towards excellence, the courage, the self-conscious turning away from that in which he no longer believes, which is Dublin life, and turning towards that which he trusts, which is an image or dream – all the drama and integrity of ... 'The Fisherman' depend to a large extent upon that other drama which George Moore so delightedly observed and reported.[24]

The apparent silliness or snobbery of the behaviour, that is to say, is a way of making possible new developments in the art. The drama of the life and the drama of the art, which must superficially seem almost destabilizingly discontinuous, are in fact continuous at the deepest creative level.

'The Fisherman' is written in iambic trimeters: three-stress lines, occasionally varied to two-stress ones by Yeats. The form is stately but also taut, even nervous. It seems to permit the possibility of a heightened tone while at the same time preventing any such thing from being too easily achieved; and this tonal hesitation is underlined by the irresolution of the poem's pararhymes. In its first verse paragraph Yeats has disdained the urban middle classes – 'The craven man in his seat, / The insolent unreproved' – and then he turns to the West of Ireland fisherman of the poem's title. Such a person must seem, on the face of it, an unlikely recipient of the work of William Butler Yeats, but he is celebrated here as the work's ideal, and ideally demanding, audience:

> Maybe a twelvemonth since
> Suddenly I began,
> In scorn of this audience,
> Imagining a man,
> And his sun-freckled face,
> And grey Connemara cloth,
> Climbing up to a place
> Where stone is dark under froth,
> And the down-turn of his wrist
> When the flies drop in the stream;
> A man who does not exist,
> A man who is but a dream;
> And cried, 'Before I am old
> I shall have written him one
> Poem maybe as cold
> And passionate as the dawn.'

V

What exercises Heaney throughout 'Yeats as an Example?' and what 'The Fisherman' explicitly considers too is the relationship between poet and audience. The questions raised by this encounter between one Irish poet and another concern the way a relationship with an audience may become a worrying element in the attempt to survive properly as a poet; the desirability of remaking yourself, at a point in your life when you have become a public person as well as a private poet, in order to resist certain expectations; the necessity of refusing certain kinds of invitation or co-option. Heaney's poem 'Casualty', published in *Field Work* in 1979, just a year after this essay was written, makes it clear why such issues should be the focus of his attention when writing about Yeats in the

1970s; and the poem is in some significant ways the acknowledgement of debts.

'Casualty', one of several personal elegies in this volume, is Heaney's sole poem 'about' Bloody Sunday, one of the crucially defining moments in the history of Northern Ireland since 1969. Heaney's attitude to the killings then, and to the judgement of the Widgery tribunal which followed them, has never, I think, been much in doubt. My assumption is that he shares the view of Catholic nationalists, and others, that the finding represented a fundamental injustice, and his Nobel Prize speech is explicit about how 'the "mere Irish" in oneself was appalled by the ruthlessness of the British Army on occasions like Bloody Sunday in Derry in 1972'.[25] He also published, for the first time, in the *Sunday Times* on 2 February 1997, to commemorate the twenty-fifth anniversary of the event, some of the lyrics of a broadside ballad called 'The Road to Derry', which he had written in 1972 to be sung by the Irish singer Luke Kelly of The Dubliners folk group.[26] These read, in part, 'In the dirt lay justice / Like an acorn in the winter / Till its oak would sprout in Derry / Where the thirteen men lay dead' – where the metaphor, drawing on the Irish etymology of the word 'Derry' (from 'doire', the oakwood), carries minatory implications of both resentment and the necessity for reparation. It is also relevant that it was later in 1972 that Heaney resigned his lectureship at Queen's University, Belfast and moved with his family to the Republic. What bearing, if any, the events of Bloody Sunday and their aftermath had on this move I am not in a position to say, but it was the material of considerable media speculation at the time, and the figure of the poet as 'inner emigré' in 'Exposure' in *North*, published in 1975, may be thought to reflect this political and topographical move from North to South, just as one significance of that poem's title is undoubtedly the media 'exposure' which accompanied it.

Whatever the reactions of Heaney as a man and as the composer of a song lyric, however, his reactions as a poet are much more complex, and their complexity resides in, precisely, his sense of audience. 'Casualty' is, among other things, the register of that complexity. It is also, in a way insufficiently realized, I think, an affront to nationalist sentiment, since it is an elegy not for the thirteen dead of Bloody Sunday, but for one man, a fisherman, killed by the IRA in the reprisal bombing of a pub shortly afterwards: the word 'Casualty' of the poem's title is the rendering anonymous of this person in the usual neutrally exculpating way of the military, or paramilitary, strategist who also, of course, conventionally 'regrets' such casualties. That this is Heaney's only explicit consideration of Bloody Sunday, and that he waited seven years before he published it, is in itself very revealing, particularly when you remember that the much admired poet Thomas Kinsella published an outraged satire called *Butcher's Dozen* within a week of the publication of the Widgery report. In concentrating on the individual death, Heaney is honouring, first of all, a personal rather than a political obligation:

the poem seems initiated by the commemorative and preservative desire to give a character back to this man who would otherwise be only an anonymous statistic. This is, that is to say, a real as opposed to Yeats's ideal, fisherman: he is 'dole-kept' indeed, even though 'a natural for work', because Northern Ireland in the 1970s had one of the highest unemployment rates in Europe.

There is no doubt that Heaney intends an allusion to Yeats's poem, since not only do both involve fishermen, but they share a metre (the iambic trimeter) and the subtle and tactical deployment of pararhyme, even though Heaney does vary the rhyme scheme itself. The connection between the two poems was pointed out, in fact, by Blake Morrison in the first critical book on Heaney, in which Yeats, along with Joyce, is read as a 'governing spirit' of the poem, although not much more than this is made of the relationship there.[27] Heaney's revision of Yeats's ideal into a real man in a socially particularized Northern Ireland – rather than, as in Yeats, in an idealized Connemara – is managed deftly and uninsistently, but it carries a large cultural freight. Some of this is explicated in one of the critical essays I referred to earlier, 'A tale of two islands', published in 1980. There, Yeats's vision of the West and its noble peasantry and hard-riding country gentlemen is read as 'not ennobling but disabling'.[28] Yeats's image of the fisherman is found to share with other such images and symbols in his work a mystificatory quality which offers the Irish a self-image which, if accepted, could only prove sentimentalizing, nostalgic or fey, an image deriving from the cultural condescensions of a post-Arnoldian Celticity and a more recent Celtic Twilightery. That essay, and this element of the poem 'Casualty', are in complete harmony with the revisionist criticism of Yeats which has dominated the study of his work since the early 1970s.

But there is also in the poem a vivid evocation of the amiably masculine relationship between fisherman and poet – an evocation that nevertheless includes a strong sense of constraint in a way that may critique, or may be allowed to critique, even as it evokes, the norms of Irish masculinity. Where Yeats's fisherman – coldly isolated from all the appurtenances of modernity in an idealized, aristocratic West of Ireland – is unambiguously the poet's ideal first audience, Heaney's, the poet tells us, finds his 'other life' – the life of poetry, that is – 'Incomprehensible'. Yet it is the fisherman who raises the subject, seeking understanding, and the poet who refuses to pursue it, even if, understandably, 'shy of condescension' – because to speak at all would be to speak about all they do not share. Arguably, however, this refusal is in fact the greater condescension, the committing by silence or elision of precisely the offence that the poet claims to wish to avoid; and a readerly unease at this point matches the deep social unease that attends the encounter. The poet of 'Casualty' falters where the poet of 'Digging', the first poem in Heaney's first book, bridges a comparable gap with the metaphor of the pen as spade, and does so with apparent confidence ('I'll dig with it'), but perhaps with a certain stridency that is itself a register of vulnerability.

And when the word 'educated' does finally figure in 'Casualty', it does so almost as rebuke or taunt to, and certainly as challenge from, fisherman to poet: 'Now you're supposed to be / An educated man. / Puzzle me the right answer / To that one.' In subsequent poems of Heaney's, such as 'Casting and Gathering' in *Seeing Things* (1991), as if in apology for such actual condescension, poetry and fishing are in fact soldered metaphorically together; and 'The Daylight Art' in *The Haw Lantern* (1987) runs a conceit on the conjunction when it figures 'a natural gift' for practising the art closest to one's nature as 'poetry, say, or fishing; whose nights are dreamless; / whose deep-sunk panoramas rise and pass // like daylight through the rod's eye or the needle's eye'.

In 'Casualty' the question to which the fisherman asks the poet to 'puzzle the answer' is: 'How culpable was he / That last night when he broke / Our tribe's complicity?' and it occurs after the poem's description of the funerals of the thirteen dead in its second section, where the fisherman's refusal of 'complicity' is opposed by that peculiarly ambivalent imagery used of the mourners, the 'swaddling band, / Lapping, tightening / Till we were braced and bound / Like brothers in a ring'. In fact, the word 'braced' does occur occasionally in Heaney's prose, where it is always a term of approbation. Here, however, when combined with 'bound' and 'swaddling', it suggests something both constricting and infantile in the kinds of complicity that the tribe may demand. The complexity of this poem's sense of complicity is that it is the fisherman's refusal of it – specifically, his refusal to honour the IRA's curfew, those 'threats [that] were phoned' – that is paradoxically, but causally, both his freedom and his death: the fisherman has become the fish, 'Swimming towards the lure / Of warm, lit-up places' and, by doing so, lured to his death. And so the final part of the poem sets him as the object of this poet's agonized self-enquiry, as it commemorates a shared moment –

> that morning
> When he took me in his boat,
> The screw purling, turning
> Indolent fathoms white,
> I tasted freedom with him.
> To get out early, haul
> Steadily off the bottom,
> Dispraise the catch, and smile
> As you find a rhythm
> Working you, slow mile by mile,
> Into your proper haunt
> Somewhere, well out, beyond ...
>
> Dawn-sniffing revenant,
> Plodder through midnight rain,
> Question me again.

In this respect, however – and this is a kind of allusive irony in 'Casualty' – this fisherman turns back into something much more like Yeats's ideal. In his ghosthood, Heaney's fisherman too is a man who does not exist, a man who is but a dream.

And actually this staging of the encounter as a dialogue within the poem – which does not happen in Yeats – may represent a crossing of Yeats with Wordsworth, the poets also joined in 'The Makings of a Music'. The moment might be compared with the one in 'Resolution and Independence', for instance, where the poet says of the leech-gatherer that

> ... the whole body of the man did seem
> Like one whom I had met with in a dream;
> Or like a man from some far region sent,
> To give me human strength, by apt admonishment.

No longer the socially realized character of his first appearance in the poem, but the symbolically challenging and questioning 'revenant', this fisherman cannot supply any actual answers, but only those the poet chooses to ventriloquize on his behalf and to draw from his example or admonishment: 'How culpable was he / That last night when he broke / Our tribe's complicity?' – where the word 'tribe', inflected with the demotic, also has the harshness of judgement.

I have just said that the fisherman 'turns back' into something more like Yeats's fisherman; and in doing so I am using the language of the poem itself, where the image of the turned back is prominent, and so too is an imagery of the specular. 'Casualty' is a poem preoccupied with watching, observing, seeing and being seen, and with how, in these processes of scrutiny, you might choose to turn, to turn your back, to turn back.[29] It is a poem, that is to say, about how a poet, or a poem, might discover his, or its, own appropriate or 'proper' audience – this dead fisherman – and might do so by resisting another audience's – the 'tribe's' – expectations or assumptions. 'Casualty' is a refusal of instrumentality, an insistence on the virtue of reflection. Far from being what he has sometimes been accused of being – a poet who, whatever he says, says nothing – Heaney is here, schooled by the Yeatsian example in self-protective intransigence, insisting on the poet's right to do otherwise. We might assume behind the poem actual confrontations between poet and audience in Irish, and probably Irish-American, public spaces; and Heaney would have been newly returned from the USA in the mid-1970s, as Yeats was in Moore's unflattering reminiscence. But rising through the mists of the ellipsis, or aposiopesis, of the ending of Heaney's penultimate stanza – 'Somewhere, well out, beyond ...' – we can also surely just about perceive some other Yeatsian questions, those which end his best-known poem of all, and one also written in iambic trimeter, 'Easter 1916', that elegy for the dead, or the casualties, of an earlier phase of Irish political violence, a poem which Yeats also waited some time – until 1920 – to publish in its definitive form:

> Too long a sacrifice
> Can make a stone of the heart.
> O when may it suffice?
> That is Heaven's part, our part
> To murmur name upon name
> As a mother names her child
> When sleep at last has come
> On limbs that had run wild.
> What is it but nightfall?
> No, no, not night but death;
> Was it needless death after all?
> For England may keep faith
> For all that is done and said.
> We know their dream; enough
> To know they dreamed and are dead;
> And what if excess of love
> Bewildered them till they died?
> I write it out in a verse –
> MacDonagh and MacBride
> And Connolly and Pearse
> Now and in time to be,
> Wherever green is worn,
> Are changed, changed utterly:
> A terrible beauty is born.

Yeats's poem, which, as I said earlier, is sometimes popularly read – or misread, or even unread – as though it approves or celebrates the tragic destiny of the fifteen executed leaders of the rebellion of 1916, a destiny in which banality and routine are transformed into the aesthetics of self-sacrificial tragic fulfilment, is in fact elaborately self-questioning. When may it suffice? What is it but nightfall? Was it needless death after all? What if excess of love / Bewildered them till they died? These naggingly insistent anxieties undermine the magisterial balladic inevitability of the refrain, with its apparent assurance about transformative historical and political metamorphosis. That the poem is the place for such self-questioning, a self-questioning which is that of the individual poet first of all, certainly, but which might also be that of a culture, a community or even a 'tribe' too, is a lesson which 'Casualty' may well have inherited from 'Easter 1916' – even if, as Terence Brown has pointed out, when Yeats did finally publish his poem, on 23 October 1920, in the English journal *The New Statesman*, the lines 'For England may keep faith / For all that is done and said' would have sounded out with 'corrosive irony' in the context of the contemporary war of independence.[30]

But if, in the end, it is Yeats who is looking at Heaney in 'Casualty', and the ghosts of Yeats's metres and rhetorical inflections which haunt Heaney's, the ethic of 'Casualty' is in fact the emulation not of Yeatsian arrogance or intransigence, such as Heaney found in the performing self of George Moore's anecdote, but rather of the urge to decison, singularity, authoritative independence. The mood of this in Yeats's 'The Fisherman' is passionately indicative and promissory, voicing itself in a cry; in Heaney it is still mutedly interrogative, although the poem's final use of the verb 'Question' is itself voiced in the imperative. The result is that 'Casualty' could never be accused, as Kinsella's *Butcher's Dozen* – however justified its anger – perhaps could, of being itself complicit with military action or reaction. The poem's ellipsis and its self-questionings are a deeply meditated and a profoundly considered stepping to one side of the ethic of revenge. Even so, the questions about poetic responsibility in relation to public atrocity which are raised here, in the context of Bloody Sunday, with a painful, even piercing, intensity remain unanswered in the poem, only to be raised again and again in the work of this much-haunted and endlessly self-questioning poet. The encounter with Yeats in 'Casualty' and the formal indebtedness that it manifests also surely mark a crucial stage in the creative processes which inspire and then underwrite some of the theoretical formulations of Heaney's critical prose, with, first, its rather forbiddingly forensic concept of the 'jurisdiction of achieved form' in *The Government of the Tongue* (1988) and then with the more benignly humane concept of poetry's 'redress', a 'total adequacy' that will prove 'strong enough to help' in *The Redress of Poetry* (1995).[31]

VI

What does the relationship between Yeats and Heaney tell us, then, about the nature of poetic inheritance; what does it say about the way literary history happens and can be described? Certainly Heaney, *pace* Harold Bloom, revises Yeats in this encounter by, as it were, putting 'a kinder poem last', since 'Casualty' is 'kinder' than 'The Fisherman', more obviously humanitarian in its emphases and empathies, even if it needs the supreme assurance of that coldly passionate 'precursor poem' to come into being. It could be, of course, that Heaney has to misread Yeats as kinder than he is in order to read him at all, has to transform him into a poet more manageably like himself. But an adjustment in the direction of kindness is hardly what Bloom has in mind, or would permit, in his theory of misprision. I hope that I have shown too, though, that Heaney means it, and means it deeply in relation to his own practice, when he admires Yeats's intransigence: and this is reading, not misreading. Sometimes too, reading Bloom, you can feel that the contest between poets is conducted at an extraordinarily remote level of abstraction that does not leave much scope for the consideration of something essential in the relationship I have discussed here: poetic form. 'Casualty' is initiated by what it calls, self-referentially, 'finding a rhythm', and the rhythm is, characteristically, although not exclusively, Yeats's, just as the poem's progress is towards the realization of a quasi-Yeatsian figure. 'Casualty', in my view, does a richly inventive and surprising thing with this rhythm and this figure. Behaving like this, Heaney is, arguably, following that famous, magisterially arrogant instruction that Yeats gave his contemporaries in 'Under Ben Bulben': 'Irish poets, learn your trade, / Sing whatever is well made, / Scorn the sort now growing up / All out of shape / From toe to top.' But if he follows the instruction it is in no spirit of aridly prescriptive formalism, but in the art and scope of his recognition, made in the teeth of certain antagonisms both political and literary-theoretical, that 'Yeats's essential gift is his ability ... to make a vaulted space in language through the firmness, in-placeness and undislodgeableness of stanzaic form'.[32]

'Casualty' suggests powerfully that the relationship between successor poets need not be, or need not be only, a matter of contestation. It may also be a difficult education in the exemplary, and an education found where you might least expect it: in Yeats, a haughty Anglo-Irish Protestant kowtowing to the aristocracy and sometimes venting anti-Catholic spleen, for instance, when you are Heaney, an apparently genial Northern Irish Catholic from a farming background who was subjected in youth to some of the political consequences of the venting of anti-Catholic spleen. Form, which involves inter-relationship as well as self-limitation, is a kind of society; and, if you are an exceptional poet, it is where you encounter the only true society of your peers, your only true first audience. As in all well-regulated societies, contractual relationships of obligation, indebtedness and responsibility obtain. But so too, and at the most intimate level, do relationships of challenge, inquiry, scrutiny and self-advancement obtain. Relationships between poets, that is to say, may be corroborative as well as competitive, but only when they are bravely entered into; and this is a conclusion also reached by Fiona Stafford, as part of an argument against the singularity or monodrama of Bloom's view of poetic influence, in her book *Starting Lines in Scottish, Irish, and English Poetry*, where, during her reading of one of the 'Squarings' poems in *Seeing Things*, she cites the word 'corroborative' from Heaney himself.[33] Formal indebtedness of the kind I have been considering here is something substantively, and ethically, distinct from intertextuality. In Julia Kristeva, in fact, the theorist who first, in her readings of Bakhtin, gave the term currency, intertextuality has nothing whatever to do with human agency, with intersubjectivity, but with the 'transposition of one (or several) sign-system(s) into another': the use of the term 'intertextuality' to denote the 'study of sources' is, she says, 'banal'.[34] It is far too late now in literary history and criticism to avoid that banality, and in any case I hope that what I have offered here has been something more complex in its poetics, ethics and politics than the *de haut en bas* Kristevan phrase 'study of sources', which seems intended as a slur, might suggest. In my view, to attempt an engagement with form, to show how and why particular forms both derive from, and meet, specific contingencies, necessarily involves criticism in the processes of agency, and not only the agency of the individual poet, but the agency also of historical and political circumstance.

In any such consideration, questions of value also matter. Heaney is braced but not bound by the Yeatsian heritage, difficult as that is to approach and assimilate, and in this he differs from many lesser poets. 'Casualty' is not so much a 'map of misreading' as the graph of a brave engagement with the best that is itself one of the signatures of the newly excellent. This engagement is figured explicitly in one of the 'Squarings' poems of *Seeing Things*, poem xxii of the sub-sequence 'Settings'. This ends with a reference to Yeats as, now, himself the revenant, here become the object of the poet's questions. These have their gnomic or riddling element, but they are clearly to do with the cohabitation between what the poem calls 'spirit', which is a substantial word in Yeats, and what it calls 'perfected form'. 'Spirit' I take to be what it is traditionally, the animating principle, cognate with the more explicitly religious term 'soul', which is a word the poem also risks. And 'perfected form' is, I think, the initially daunting architecture of the Yeatsian poem, or poetic sequence (that very Yeatsian genre). The imagery of this 'Squarings' poem, with its birds, its dawn cold, its stone tower, its Big House statuary and horticulture, is all Yeatsian. The questions it ends with are those of a Seamus Heaney who, even if now undaunted, turns aside, in the parenthesis of the final line, with what I take to be a wry, even embarrassed, but saving, *moue* at this act of his own presumption – the poet suddenly become examiner of the schoolboy Yeats, asking impossibly large questions which, if they can be answered at all, can be answered only by the next, and then the next, and then, again, the next poem:

> How habitable is perfected form?
> And how inhabited the windy light?
>
> What's the use of a held note or held line
> That cannot be assailed for reassurance?
> (Set questions for the ghost of W.B.)

CHAPTER 6

The Same Again? Louis MacNeice's Repetitions

I

The enlarged edition of the excellent *Princeton Encyclopedia of Poetry and Poetics* published in 1974 makes Louis MacNeice prominent in its entry for 'repetition'. One of the many kinds of repetition it catalogues is when the verses of a poem are linked by the repetition in the opening line of each new one of the final word of the previous one, and the example given is 'Leaving Barra'. That exquisite poem, written in 1937, was published in MacNeice's unclassifiable potboiler, would-be travel book *I Crossed the Minch* in 1938, where he tells us that he did in fact write it on board the boat *Lochearn* as he left the Hebrides. The poem does what the *Encyclopedia* says it does, as the word 'island' is picked up from the first quatrain by the second, 'garbage' from the second by the third, and so on through the poem's thirteen verses, in a way musically mimetic, it seems, of the mind in progress – self-scrutinizing, self-corrective, advancing hesitantly but keeping moving – while also sustaining an ear-delighting system of aural patterning.

In fact, MacNeice's systems of repetition in this poem are more varied than the encyclopedia tells us, since the poem features other kinds of repetition too: when the phrase 'phantom hunger', for instance, at the end of the fifth verse, is separated out into its parts, so that both 'hunger' and 'phantom' form end-words of lines in the next; when words are echoed within lines – 'The belief that is disbelieving' in the seventh verse, and 'Loving the rain and the rainbow' in the eighth; and when the mode of repetition that is alliteration operates in 'Wake with the knack of knowledge' in the tenth, with its sudden knock of Anglo-Saxon metre. All of the end-words of the poem's lines – 'darling', 'channel', 'taking' and 'island' in the opening verse, for instance – constitute a form of repetition too, since all fifty-two of them have trochaic feminine endings – stressed followed by unstressed syllables – a cadence presumably picked up from both words of the poem's title, 'Leaving Barra': so, you might say, a cadence inhering in the action being evoked – 'leaving' – and in the very name of the place being left, 'Barra'. And – one final repetition – the last line of all, the final ending, includes the first line of all, as the poem ends by closing its circle or eating its tail:

> The dazzle on the sea, my darling,
> Leads from the western channel,
> A carpet of brilliance taking
> My leave forever of the island.
> …
>
> For few are able to keep moving,
> They drag and flag in the traffic;
> While you are alive beyond question
> Like the dazzle on the sea, my darling.

The effect of the repeated feminine endings may be usefully glossed by what Christopher Ricks in his book *Dylan's Visions of Sin* says about comparable endings, also picked up from the proper name in the title, in Bob Dylan's great song 'The Lonesome Death of Hattie Carroll'. 'The feminine ending,' Ricks says, 'naturally evokes a dying fall or courage in the face either of death or of loss, something falling poignantly away'.[1] In 'Leaving Barra' the island is falling poignantly away, as MacNeice realizes he will never revisit it and compares its imagined ideal of existence to the reality he returns to. Not, in fact, that he had much wish to revisit it, since the two visits to the Hebrides which are the subject of *I Crossed the Minch* were not, according to the book's account, particularly happy ones. This was despite the fact that MacNeice was accompanied there by the painter Nancy Sharp (Coldstream), who contributed some drawings to the book. She must be the addressee of 'Leaving the Island', even though she is never included in the book's prose narrative, presumably because this was an adulterous relationship – albeit, Jon Stallworthy tells us in his biography, one conducted with her husband's agreement.

Something else, however, is also falling poignantly away, as it does in many of MacNeice's poems: that thing imagined in this poem as a 'hankering after Atlantis'. This may be a general metaphysical longing in this son of the episcopal palace; and the persistent desirability of such a mythical place is figured in the poem as a quasi-Petrine betrayal of a secular humanism committed, in a now collusively ironic alliterative repetition, to 'Loving the beast and the bubble'. But this fictional, unobtainable Atlantis may also be that idea or ideal of the West that ghosts much of the sense of longing in MacNeice. *I Crossed the Minch* makes it plain that he comes to understand in the Hebrides the depth of his alienation from the inhabitants of the Western Isles because of his inability to speak Gaelic.[2] By implication, MacNeice must have also been realizing on Barra, therefore, how such incapacity cut him off too from the lives of those who continued to speak Irish in the West of Ireland.

'Leaving Barra' resolves the urgency of its longings finally into a set of 'inklings' of what might offer and sustain a scale of value distinct from the materialist one dominant in the culture of metropolitan London to which the poet is returning (and where he is just about to write probably the most notably inclusive and analytical poem of his time and its values, *Autumn Journal*). These inklings are: 'The beauty of the moon and music, / The routine courage of the worker, / The gay endurance of women.' The aestheticism of the first is unexceptionable if a little sentimental; the implicitly socialist politics – or at least leftish obeisance – of the second seems, in context, a bit *voulu* and itself 'routine' in this poem of the 1930s; but the third line's celebration of women is heartfelt, genuine and strongly declarative, possibly in large part because the poem's formal play with enduring feminine endings has prepared our ears for precisely such a declaration. In addition, the word 'gay' is striking, partly since the phrase 'gay endurance' is almost an oxymoron. The word now has specific connotations which it would almost certainly not have had for MacNeice; but it has never in fact been an easy word, as Yeats knows when he activates various connotations of it in 'Lapis Lazuli', moving from the women of his opening lines who are 'sick of ... / poets that are always gay' to the famously ringing, if problematic, assertion that 'Hamlet and Lear are gay'. MacNeice's appreciative near-oxymoron in 'Leaving Barra' surely picks the word up from Yeats who in 'Lapis Lazuli' transfuses its initial connotations of airiness and self-indulgence – this being what the women object to in poets – with the immense stiffening of its association with the endurance of tragedy in his paradoxical line. Not long after writing 'Leaving Barra' MacNeice was to write the first full-length critical book on Yeats, *The Poetry of W. B. Yeats* (1941), which remains an excellent introductory study.

If the feminine endings of 'Leaving Barra' evoke courage in the face of loss, something falling poignantly away, they also provoke here an image of delighted appreciation, something set determinedly against loss, 'alive beyond question'. And both inhere in that remarkable trope which is sudden, surprising, unforgettable and pretty impatient of explication, as MacNeice sometimes is, when the woman is celebrated in the poem's penultimate quatrain for 'the example / Of living like a fugue'. What does MacNeice have in mind here? Assuming that he means the musical form of fugue, we might conceive of someone living like counter-pointed music, I suppose, if she lived with a kind of regulated, always charming variety of interest and affect; and this might be exactly the kind of thing the celebrant in 'Snow' of 'the drunkenness of things being various' would find desirable in a woman – or in anyone. And the verse repetitions of 'Leaving Barra' may themselves be thought to form an appropriate fugal counterpoint to this theme, or even to constitute a linguistic fugue of their own, as words are repeated with a difference: the difference made by their new contexts, in which they sometimes match, sometimes modify, their preceding connotations.

There is also at least the possibility, though, in this instance of what 'Donegal Triptych' calls 'the glad sad poetry of departure', in this poem entitled with a 'leaving', that the word 'fugue' is ghosted here by its use in Freudian psychoanalytic theory: the fugue as a flight from identity which may involve travel to some unconsciously desired locality. The poet Louis MacNeice may well find such a thing, together with its associated repetition compulsion, almost perversely exemplary, given that one thing you can certainly sense being repeated in various forms in his work is that melancholy-depressive thing conjured in the poem 'Autobiography' (written in 1940) – 'When I was five the black dreams came; / Nothing after was quite the same' – with its dejected, even abject, refrain which itself contains a repetition, circling on itself, *'Come back early or never come'*. The MacNeicean autobiography, of which this is, as it were, the poetically distilled essence, prominently includes the death of the mother and the ensuing catastrophe of the child's permanently inconsolable distress. Nothing after was quite the same; but repetition is always quite the same again, with a difference.

In fact, 'Autobiography' can be read in terrible tandem with that essay in which Freud analyses repetition compulsion, 'Beyond the Pleasure Principle', where the (temporary) disappearance of the mother is assuaged by the control or revenge of the *fort / da* game in which the child's compelled passivity in the face of loss is combated by the game's repetitions. All poetry may be read as compensatory repetition of this kind, of course, retrieving with the toy of verse what has inexorably disappeared from experience, and all poetry involves repetition, since rhythm and rhyme are themselves repetitions, and even free verse is disciplined and recognizable by the necessity that one line stop and another begin, again and again and again. Nevertheless, the chilly, minatory repetitions of the eight rhyming tetrameter couplets and the eight repeats of the tetrameter refrain in 'Autobiography' make the poem readable almost as an allegory of Freudian repetition. The couplets and refrain turn into the game of poetry the suffering before which the child was of necessity passive in life. And who is commanded by the refrain's imperative, who is being ordered to come back early or never come? Is it the mother who, by never coming, is ordered vengefully away forever? Or is it the son himself who, by endlessly repeating the traumatic event in the repetitive game of poetry, is ordering himself never to re-enter the primal scene of his distress?

II

Both 'Leaving Barra' and 'Autobiography', then, illustrate some of the ways in which repetition at the formal or technical levels is thematically, emotionally or psychologically functional in MacNeice. Many other poems underwrite the point. Some examples. There is the cascade of 'I give you's that forms a long toast in the last five stanzas of 'Train to Dublin', where the repetition is a generously cumulative expansiveness, 'turning a sentence', but is also, in negative form, an explicit political refusal:

> But I will not give you any idol or idea, creed or king,
> I give you the incidental things which pass
> Outward through space exactly as each was.

There is the woven intricacy of 'The Sunlight on the Garden', where the rhymes repeated at line-beginnings as well as line-endings, and then repeated across opening and closing verses, create a gorgeously memorable verbal music. Irony becomes virtually a principle of form here, since the attractively harmonious musicality is so threateningly apocalyptic too in the period immediately preceding the Second World War; and the poem actually envisages the time about to come as the time when music must end: 'And soon, my friend, / We shall have no time for dances.' There is the phrase 'On those islands' in 'The Hebrides', also first published in *I Crossed the Minch* (where it is actually entitled 'On those islands'), which has an almost Homerically insistent reiterativeness as it opens each syntactically sinuous section of this lengthy poem, situating a topography and a culture both analytically and tenderly. There is 'It is no go' in 'Bagpipe Music' whose almost demented repetitiveness propels the poem's hurdy-gurdy rhythmic relentlessness, as if the repeated phrase has taken over the poem, the lunatic has taken over the asylum. There is the repeated opening and closing line of each stanza of 'Meeting Point', that almost archetypal MacNeicean love poem of enraptured mutuality, beginning 'Time was away and somewhere else', and closing 'Time was away and she was here'. The device, working almost like a series of variant refrains, poignantly but also proudly establishes the separate togetherness of lovers, isolated in a crowd, and the distinction between the time they spend together and ordinary, quotidian time. In verse after verse of 'Meeting Point' the repeated lines meet pointedly, enclosing an ecstasy.

'What will you have, my dear? The same again?' asks the drinker, repeatedly, in 'Homage to Clichés', that very artful poem in which MacNeice writes virtually a knowing meta-poem on this aspect of his work. The poem celebrates 'the automatic, the reflex, the cliché of velvet' as the source of erotic allure but also of panic at what it calls 'finality'. It rings the changes through its eighty-two lines on a tiny cluster of images associated with fish, cat and bell until finality encroaches inexorably on temporality, reminding us how the inexorable is also, always, necessarily, an aspect of refrain:

> Somewhere behind us stands a man, a counter
> A timekeeper with a watch and a pistol
> Ready to shoot and with his shot destroy
> This whole delightful world of cliché and refrain –
> What will you have, my dear? The same again?

In the delightful world of cliché and refrain, having the same again seems both an avoidance of the knowledge of death, and an inevitable confrontation with it: both at once, the same again. Woven into the very fabric of cliché and refrain is the knowledge of termination; and poems employing metre, 'numbers' and rhyme are always 'counters' too, as they count their stresses or construct their rhyme schemes. In this sense, all poems are about time and its passing. It seems wholly characteristic of MacNeice that his figure for this should be the invitation to have another drink; you have to get one in of course before time is called. The often only artificially intimate bonhomie of drinking companions may hide an abyss; and it is a figure inspired, probably, by the seasoned drinker's (alcoholic's?) knowledge that, where drinking is concerned, repetition may lead all too literally to death.

III

That repetition is the same again, but the same again with a difference, is the ambiguous knowledge plotted into MacNeice's extensive use of the 'delightful' device of refrain. A few examples. In his obituary for MacNeice Philip Larkin says, approvingly, that his lyricism and musicality as a poet were sometimes akin to those of popular songwriters.[3] He could, Larkin thinks, have written 'These Foolish Things'; and in fact games with assonance and internal rhyme, often very witty ones indeed, are probably more characteristic of writers of the classic American songbook such as Cole Porter and Ira Gershwin than they are of conventional poets. MacNeice does write a kind of would-be popular song in 'Swing-song', a poem written in the character of what it calls 'a wartime working girl' in a deafening machine shop. The poem's refrain is her figuring to herself of the way her bomber pilot 'young man' talks on his intercom:

> So there's no one in the world, I sometimes think,
> Such a wallflower as I
> For I must talk to myself on the ground

> While he is talking to his friends in the sky:
>   K for Kitty calling P for Prue ...
>   Bomb Doors Open ...
>   Over to You.

The three-line refrain here takes the sharpness of its edge from the fact that her bereft loneliness must cope with the way the code-names of his 'friends' – his fellow bomber pilots, or their aircraft – are gendered as female and, of course, from the way the innocently girlish diminutives Kitty and Prue disguise and contrast with the murderous nature of the bombing raids being undertaken in which, no doubt, other working girls talking to themselves on the ground will be horribly killed and mutilated. In an introduction to his radio plays in 1947 MacNeice says of the writer lucky enough to be involved in a radio production of his own work that he cannot get 'more closely in touch with his work-in-performance than he can be anywhere else unless he is Mr Noel Coward'.[4] This seems both admiring and a little envious of a popular singer–songwriter. If MacNeice could have written 'These Foolish Things', however, maybe Coward could have written 'Swing-song', and it would have been excellent to have had a musical setting and accompaniment for MacNeice's words.

Then there is 'Babel' in *Springboard* (1944), which could be said to have, in a way appropriate to its title, three refrains; or – an alternative way of regarding it – it is most unusually a poem which has more refrain than verse. The three repeated lines – 'There was a tower that went before a fall', 'Can't we ever, my love, speak in the same language?' and 'Have we no aims in common?' – are all bent around the remaining seven lines in four rhyming quatrains. The poem therefore seems a lot like a villanelle, in a structure, however, which is not at all that of a villanelle. The result is a kind of stuck-in-the-groove monotony, an inability either to communicate or to advance an argument. This is the point of a poem that, as far as the relationship between its lovers is concerned, might be regarded as an out-of-love poem, the repetitive refrains as functional as a gagging in the throat. Yet the ramifying repetitions also insist that the personal babel the lovers manage to create by their linguistic confusions, evasions and misunderstandings becomes quickly a public and political linguistic hell too, as 'Patriots, dreamers, die-hards, theoreticians, all, / ... go, still quarrelling over words, to the wall', where the cliché is disturbingly electrified, so that going to the wall while still quarrelling is not just to register a willingness to go to the ultimate point of an argument but to face a firing squad for one's contrarian beliefs. Repetition is itself hell here, and the poem hideously performs a kind of satanic reversal of Christ's consolatory insistence that where two or three are gathered together there he will be also. In MacNeice's Babel, on the contrary, 'The more there are together, Togetherness recedes'. Formal repetition in 'Babel' is therefore an instruction in the alienatingly recessive ability of human beings to be together at all, ever, in any state of harmony; and the MacNeice of such poems is no distance at all from the Larkin for whom, in 'Wants', 'Beneath it all, desire of oblivion runs'.

Then there is the just-posthumous book *The Burning Perch* (1963), a volume much given to thematic repetitions and returns of various kinds: to MacNeice's own childhood, certainly, but also, as Peter McDonald demonstrates in *Louis MacNeice: The Poet in his Contexts*, to the ghosts of 'the poet MacNeice once was'. Amongst so much returning and repeating, refrain in this volume becomes destabilized, self-deconstructing and altogether anxiety-inducing; and 'The Taxis', written in 1961, is paradigmatic.

Strictly, 'tra-la' in that poem, occurring once or twice in each of four quatrains which all figure a taxi ride of vertiginous, even uncanny eeriness, is not really a refrain. It is a 'repetend', a term defined by the *Princeton Encyclopedia* as 'a recurring word, phrase or line. As distinguished from refrain, repetend usually refers to a repetition occurring irregularly rather than regularly in a poem, or to a partial rather than a complete repetition'. But 'tra-la' is not really a word or a phrase or a line: it is a sort of interrupted or fragmentary musical phrase. The phrase is usually taken to be 'tra-la-la'; 'tra-la' does in fact feature famously in Nanki Poo's solo 'The flowers that bloom in the spring tra-la' in *The Gondoliers*, and MacNeice, the admirer of popular song, may even have had Gilbert's lyric and Sullivan's music in mind when he wrote the poem. The fact that it seems interrupted, however, or fragmentary, and is spoken, not sung, makes for a dead weight, a dead hand and a dead echo in the poem, as the repetend moves from the end of the opening lines of the first three stanzas, where we might at least expect to find it (and do find it of course in Gilbert and Sullivan), to the disconcerting mid-final line of the second stanza and the opening of the second line of the final stanza ('As for the fourth taxi, he was alone / Tra-la when he hailed it ...'). These repetitions include its final appearance in the taxi driver's quoted speech – '"I can't tra-la well take / So many people, not to speak of the dog."' – where it may be intended as a print euphemism for the now outraged 'I can't fucking well take ...'.

That the repeated 'tra-la' – spondaic, unsung and in print – is actually hard to voice is apparent when we remember the opening of *A Portrait of the Artist as a Young Man*. The linguistic hornpipe danced there has its rhythm completed:

> Tralalala lala
> Tralala tralaladdy
> Tralala lala
> Tralala lala

But 'tra-la'? Its musical inertia is a function of the wryly skewed black comedy being enacted in the poem. It is also more black, probably, than comic, even though a large part of the poem's memorability has to do with its spooky unresolvedness of tone, and the concluding dog is a joke, certainly, self-reflexively suggesting that the poem is something of a shaggy dog story bathetically lacking a punchline.

'The Taxis' may, however, owe something to the taxi rides that conclude Elizabeth Bowen's novel *The Death of the Heart* and short story 'The Demon Lover'. At the end of *The Death of the Heart* the much-put-upon servant Matchett is put into a taxi without knowing its destination and has to endure the vaguely threatening hostility of its driver; and at the end of the truly terrifying wartime story 'The Demon Lover', which is much taken up with repetitions of a sadistic and masochistic kind, the terrified Mrs Drover is driven off by a taxi driver who appears to be the ghost of her lover long since killed in the First World War: he may be driving her to a loathsome shared eternity. Certainly, the more they are compelled to be together, as this taxi recedes, the more Togetherness will recede too. Not only the uncanny element of 'The Taxis' but also its hallucinatory cinematic quality is shared with Bowen's story, one of her greatest.[5]

The deconstructed refrain 'tra-la' in 'The Taxis' seems to do the opposite of what the OED tells us the musical phrase 'tra-la-la' should do: be expressive of gaiety or joy. It trivializes the taxi occupant's predicament while also sinisterly emphasizing it. He is of no consequence, tra-la, but being of no consequence is his predicament, he who seems to have several selves but is still looked through as if, transparently, he has none. This crisis of identity and high pitch of anxiety can be read under the rubric of various kinds of existential predicament; and the taxi driver's presumptuous authoritativeness is forbiddingly judgemental and discountenancing. MacNeice certainly picks up here, as Bowen does too, on what can sometimes be the all too real anxiety of taking a taxi alone, especially in a strange place. It is after all one of the very few situations in which you voluntarily place yourself alone under the total control of someone completely unknown.[6]

Given the parabolic nature of some of MacNeice's late poems, however, it is also feasible, I think, to read 'The Taxis' as a representation of what a poet might become in his or her poems: dissolved – sometimes, it must seem, unnervingly and discountenancingly, even uncannily – into language, and then into the opinions and interpretations of reviewers and critics. 'The Taxis' may even be glossed by what MacNeice wittily but almost tauntingly says about himself as poet in *The Poetry of W. B. Yeats*, discussing the Crazy Jane poems, those poems that also prominently employ refrain and seem in some oblique ways related to these parable poems of MacNeice's. MacNeice evinces there what might seem almost a postmodern conception of identity, were it not that so much that has been classified as 'postmodern' is actually a feature of the 'modern' too: 'If you know what my whole self and my only self is, you know a lot more than I do. As far as I can make out, I not only have many different selves but I am often, as they say, not myself at all.'[7] Not myself at all; or, the same again?

With appropriate finality, MacNeice's last published poem, 'Coda', written in 1962 and published as the final poem in *The Burning Perch*, is a perfectly pitched exercise in the repetitive:

> Maybe we knew each other better
> When the night was young and unrepeated
> And the moon stood still over Jericho.
>
> So much for the past; in the present
> There are moments caught between heart-beats
> When maybe we know each other better.
>
> But what is that clinking in the darkness?
> Maybe we shall know each other better
> When the tunnels meet beneath the mountain.

The repeat here is very much a repetition with variation – 'Maybe we knew each other better', 'When maybe we know each other better', 'Maybe we shall know each other better'. Past, present and future are all rendered uncertain and unstable by that slippery, repeated, Janus-faced adverb of contingency, expressive of both possibility and regret, 'maybe'. And there is variation too in the positioning of the repeat across the poem's three tercets – opening line in the first, closing line in the second, middle line in the third. This is a wavering of positioning – maybe – to reflect the wavering uncertainty of the thought. And the poem's title is also waveringly uncertain. Is this poem a coda to the volume *The Burning Perch*, or is it a coda to the relationship being represented in its ruminative address? (It can certainly be read as a coda to 'Babel'.) The relationship is not exactly over, clearly, despite the title, but it has never been engaged wholly successfully either, it appears, since mutual knowledge is speculative even at the point of apparent origin when, significantly, things were 'unrepeated'. The mysterious suggestiveness of the poem's final lines – 'Maybe we shall know each other better / When the tunnels meet beneath the mountain.' – is apparently inspired by the building of the Mont Blanc tunnel which was still uncompleted at the time of the poem's writing. The image conjures therefore an indefinitely postponed insecurity about another 'meeting point'. This poem of repetitions, by including in the second line of its first tercet the word 'unrepeated', seems held in tension by the consideration that repetition itself may be the coda to relationship, that repetition may be a living death.

IV

And indeed the quick poetic liveliness of repetition, refrain and repetend in MacNeice – even when, as in 'The Taxis', the repetend is being more emotionally (but not poetically) deadly than lively – may be one way in which this poet defies what his work frequently finds wearyingly repetitive: that is, the actual, unavoidable routines of ordinary living. Louis MacNeice's poetry sometimes conveys a strong sense of staving off boredom. One of his major figures for this is that of the parrot; who, of course, can only copy and repeat what he hears. *Autumn Sequel* opens with such a bird, in a perhaps mimetically garrulous hypermetric line: 'August. Render to Caesar. Speak parrot: a gimmick for Poll'; and several lines further on, the bird appears again, dignified, or mock-dignified, with an initial capital: 'the Parrot is loose on the world / Clapping his trap with gay but meaningless wings'. Clapping his trap, the Parrot must be beating with his wings a device once known as a 'claptrap' and now usually known simply as a clapper, in order to applaud himself narcissistically: but he is also speaking claptrap, whose meaning has varied from 'cheap, showy sentiment' to its current almost exclusive use for nonsense or rubbish. This claptrapping Parrot appears also to trick out the parrot of John Skelton's scathing fifteenth-century satirical poem 'Speke Parrot' – a poem much admired by poets of the 1930s – with the modern plumage of Yeats's 'The Second Coming'. The Parrot 'loose on the world' evokes but also renders bathetic the 'rough beast' apocalyptically 'loosed upon the world' in that poem, offering a preposterous bird in a state of purposeless unrestraint ('loose') in place of a terrifyingly indeterminate animal all too determined in its malevolence ('loosed').

It has always seemed to me that at the beginning of *Autumn Sequel*, a very long poem with a Dantean shape, this figure of MacNeice's which aligns fifteenth-century Skeltonic satirical invective with quasi-Yeatsian apocalyptic modernity had at least the potential to become one of the great modern poetic figurations, one of the great modernist intertexts. So it is a distressing irony that the poetic repetitions of *Autumn Sequel* are so jejune compared with some of those I have been discussing, seeming as they do so often mechanical or flaccid rather than thematically, emotionally or symbolically functional or telling. Notably, the brilliant repetitiveness of the rhetoric of *Autumn Journal* with its hammering polysyndeton – the word 'And' repeated propulsively again and again and again – is replaced by the inert, inexpertly managed derivativeness of the repetitions of terza rima in *Autumn Sequel*; and the poem is, as a consequence, no true sequel at all but hypertrophic succession. MacNeice in fact appears to make his own damningly accurate self-assessment of this in Canto V: that 'the Muse has defaulted // And left me an apparatus, rivet and link, / With nothing to link or rivet'. After such self-knowledge, the reader might well ask, what forgiveness for allowing the poetic enterprise to extend for a further twenty-one cantos? MacNeice had undoubtedly mistaken himself and is, at least over this distance, neither a satirical nor a mythological poet.

But there is no point in labouring the failures of much of *Autumn Sequel* once again; except that raising the issue gives me the chance to make what is not, I hope, just a smart-aleck point: that this poem unwittingly throws into the sharpest possible relief how, in *Autumn Journal*, history makes poetry happen. In that poem the time itself is link and rivet as MacNeice's journal, and journalistic, dailiness in a London both claustrophobic and exhilarating is darkly shadowed by looming European catastrophe. History makes poetry happen in *Autumn Journal*, however, only by means of MacNeice's hypersensitive poetic attunement to his moment, by the extremely well-judged sharpness, intensity and clarity of his imagistic selectivity and rhythmic evocativeness. The poet and his moment seem in *Autumn Journal* in fact not so much linked or riveted as soldered inseparably together.

Still, the richly accoutred parrot of *Autumn Sequel* returns, maybe, even if a little the worse for wear, in 'Budgie', the poem from which the title of *The Burning Perch* derives. Given that the Yeats of 'The Second Coming' is part of the Parrot's generation, this new bird figures in the appropriately apocalyptic context of what appears to be an intimation of nuclear catastrophe. The caged budgie once again narcissistically stares into its mirror, repeating, *'Let me attitudinize, / Let me attitudinize, let me attitudinize'*, 'Its voice a small I Am', 'peep[ing] like a television / Actor admiring himself in the monitor' while his perch burns as 'the human / Race recedes and dwindles, the giant / Reptiles cackle in their graves, the mountain / Gorillas exchange their final messages'. The repetitions in MacNeice's poems may be regarded as engaged in a tacit battle with this kind of parroting narcissism – with psittacism, indeed, from the Greek for parrot, *psittakos*: 'the mechanical repetition of previously received ideas or images that reflects neither true reasoning nor feeling', as the OED puts it, with almost Leavisian disdain.[8] MacNeice also realizes that poetry itself may be psittacism, an inertly parroting kind of repetition of various masters' voices; and Derek Mahon has provocatively suggested that we read 'Budgie' as 'perhaps … a satire on the poetic vocation'.[9] A satire on the poetic vocation, maybe; but possibly also a self-lacerating satire on one potential of MacNeice's own work: its tendency to prolixity, the tendency which, as we have seen, he himself castigates *Autumn Sequel* for indulging, even while in the very act of continuing to write it, and its propensity to indulge a merely journalistic image or impulse, or to purvey what Tom Paulin once memorably called a 'throwaway lyricism'.[10] Although these are temptations from which MacNeice's most memorable and enduring work seems to cast itself clear with disciplined resourcefulness, both parrot and budgie include their poet too in the inclusivity of their figurations.

V

Louis MacNeice is manifestly aware, then, of what is at issue, and also of what he risks, in repetition; but he spells it out in *The Poetry of W. B. Yeats* when he discusses refrain in the Crazy Jane poems.[11] In the twentieth century, he says, refrain has been in many circles for a long time under taboo, considered merely decorative or sentimental, regarded as nothing but 'a rhetorical seductiveness'. The epithet 'rhetorical' here picks up what Yeats famously opposes to the argument with oneself that constitutes poetry: the argument with others that constitutes rhetoric. This prejudiced taboo, MacNeice insists, with a tacit allusion now to Eliot, 'is based on the assumption that a complex, unmusical world demands – in all cases – a complex, unmusical poetry – an assumption which Yeats never makes'. It is an assumption that MacNeice never makes either; and, although Derek Mahon may be right to insist that MacNeice was never 'influenced' by Yeats, this critical prose strongly suggests that some of his own poetic practices were at least sanctioned by Yeats. Even so, it is worth saying that MacNeice's refrains never sound at all like Yeats's. Those of other poets of the 1930s sometimes do. This, for instance, from a poem of 1935: 'Cried the cripples to the silent statue, / The six beggared cripples'. Not the later W. B. Yeats, not even the W. B. Yeats of the Crazy Jane poems published in 1932, but the earlier W. H. Auden, in 'Song of the Beggars' from the 'Twelve Songs' of 1936.

When MacNeice says that Yeats had 'a quite child-like liking for the simple poetry of the folk type', particularly Irish folk song and street ballad (and, we might add, nursery rhyme), he is also talking about himself, I think, and in his critical writing elsewhere he makes it plain that for him sentimentality is a danger the poet ought to risk. He also defends his use of the word 'vulgarity' as a term of approbation: poetry should be of the *vulgus*, of the crowd. MacNeice believes this despite his very firm objections to the view of Irish poetry expounded by F. R. Higgins in the 1939 BBC radio dialogue published as 'Tendencies in Modern Poetry' and made prominent by Paul Muldoon as the 'prologue' to his controversial *Faber Book of Contemporary Irish Poetry* in 1986.

Lurking in Higgins's conception of the 'magic' of Irish poetry MacNeice finds a reprehensible, dangerously sentimental form of nationalistic 'race-consciousness'.[12] There is a principled, democratizing, anti-authoritarian impulse in this discrimination of MacNeice's in favour of a form of vulgarity that never courts opportunistic or instrumental populism. His modernism, for all that it opposes a preening psittacism of modernity, is equally untempted by modernist hauteur of the Eliotic or Poundian varieties, however indebted MacNeice's practice is, in some of its forms, to an Eliotic model. This is a further reason why his satirical, mythological Parrot never gets very far off the ground in *Autumn Sequel*. Successful modernist myth in poetry (as opposed to prose, where *Ulysses* is always the counter-example) seems to demand hauteur of the patrician and varyingly reactionary variety. Scandalously, perhaps, such hauteur is rich with poetic possibility: but there is very little in MacNeice that can rise, or stoop, to such occasions. In *Autumn Sequel*, to his credit but unfortunately not greatly to the credit of the poetry, he is all too easily distracted from detraction.

In his critical essays MacNeice sometimes admires the ways in which repetition and refrain can bring to what would otherwise be mere flux the structure of an architectonic; and we should read MacNeice's own practice in the light of this. Indeed, if we substitute for the notion of flux something of what inheres in MacNeice's conception of psittacism – the parrot's mechanical, repetitive, vain, narcissistic preenings as a function and outstanding feature of modernity – then the repetitions of his own poems, which acknowledge old cultural continuities, affiliations and attachments, become a mode of critique. In his prose MacNeice also understands poetry as developing from the desire to combine accessible communication and some kind of ritual. Poetry as communication, not solipsism, is a form of hostility to some of the kinds of modernism which developed from symbolism: but the concept of ritual returns the element of symbolist or modernist magic or metaphysic to the communicative act, slyly retrieving with the left hand what the right has just appeared to give away.

Coda

Communication made very strange to itself by surface ritual is one way of regarding two late poems of MacNeice's that actually take repetition as preoccupation and theme: 'Reflections' in his penultimate volume *Solstices* (1961) and 'Soap Suds' in *The Burning Perch*.

In the former, in a kind of apotheosis of the imagery of mirror and window which figures so significantly elsewhere too in MacNeice and, as we have seen, in 'Budgie', the mirror repeats the image of the self already mirrored in the window of the room. In this dizzyingly multiple reflectivity the self becomes uncannily self-estranged: to the point, indeed, of being able to recognize itself only in its self-estrangement. It becomes even surrealistically self-estranged, since the poem's image of 'standing back to my back' recalls and may remember Magritte's painting *La Reproduction interdite* (1937) and its representation of the terrifying depersonalization involved in looking into a mirror and seeing there the back of your own head and shoulders: turning away from yourself, giving yourself the cold shoulder.[13] The repeated reflections of this extraordinarily, even syntactically, reflexive and self-reflexive poem bring the idea of the self to a point of comparably radical destabilization. They also bring the writer at his desk to an impossible and unsustainable position; since, in the poem's final lines, his reflection reverses his writing right hand to make him left-handed, so that he is unable to write at all. He becomes therefore a writer unable to 'reflect' any further, at least in writing; and the poem's reflections culminate in a form of writerly self-deconstruction.

'Soap Suds' repeats through the agency of smell the child's experience in the adult's, a 'return' in memory effected by a very delicately managed quasi-cinematic dissolve and then by a brilliantly speedy linguistic fast-forward. Self-reflexively too, the poem actually uses the word 'dissolves' as it evokes a long-since completed game of croquet. The far-off moment of childhood returns to the adult by way of the recollected smell of soap while he is washing his hands.

Washing his hands of what, though? The poem catalogues the 'joys' of the big house he visited when he was 8, where he played the recalled croquet game: but it fixes on, or is fixated on, an adult voice crying 'Play!' The first time the voice does so, in the third verse, it does so neutrally, with no qualifying adjective: but when it does so again in the next verse and once again in the final one the voice is 'angry' and it cries from the grass of a croquet lawn now grown impossibly 'head-high'. It is anger that survives in the ageing memory, then, not joy, anger all the more disconcerting for the lack of specification of its origin or motive. 'But the ball is lost and the mallet slipped long since from the hands / Under the running tap that are not the hands of the child': the loss, the slippage, the repetition and the return recall once more the game or 'play' of 'Beyond the Pleasure Principle'. The poem retrieves the moment but still says to the moment, '*Come back early or never come*'; and some of Louis MacNeice's most powerful poems are those in which the past returns to shadow or even dominate the present, without mercy and without release.

CHAPTER 7

The Celebration of Waiting: Moments in the History of Modern Irish Poetry and the Visual Arts

I

Despite the best efforts of Kingsley Amis, who notoriously said in 1955 that 'nobody wants any more poems about paintings', poetry's engagement with the visual arts has been constant since the Imagism of the early twentieth century in which modernism first conceived itself, and conceived of itself, as painterly in its very self-definition.[1] Ekphrasis – poetry about visual representations – has been endemic to modern poetry and has attracted a large body of critical and theoretical activity. Modern Irish poetry, which has W. B. Yeats at its origins, and is still in many ways shadowed by him, has the relationship consequently almost programmed into its DNA. The son of a painter and the brother of a great painter, Yeats himself trained briefly in an art school. Both his poetry and prose frequently refer to painting and sculpture, and the first item in his *Oxford Book of Modern Verse* in 1936 is a 'free verse' lineation of Walter Pater's famous passage on 'La Gioconda' in *The Renaissance*. 'Only by putting it in free verse,' says Yeats, 'can one show its revolutionary importance'; but the extremely undistinguished free verse that results, which Yeats is ill-advised to advertise so recklessly, may be allowed, rather, to indicate his sense of the inextricability of poetry and painting in the foundational aesthetics of modernity.[2]

Yeats is fascinated early in his life by the Pre-Raphaelites, notably by Dante Gabriel Rossetti, a painter who sometimes illustrated poems such as his sister Christina Rossetti's *Goblin Market* and who was also an outstanding ekphrastic sonneteer. He is permanently fascinated by Blake, whose poetry and painting are deeply intertwined, and in 1893 he edited, with Edwin Ellis, a three-volume collection of Blake's works. The painters of the Italian Quattrocento figure in major poems of Yeats's, including 'Leda and the Swan' and 'Among School Children'. His conversion by Hugh Lane to the French Impressionists led to one of the major controversies of Yeats's life and is one of the circumstances behind the bitterness of his poem 'September 1913' with its castigating refrain, 'Romantic Ireland's dead and gone, / It's with O'Leary in the grave'. At the end of the 'B' edition of his extraordinary work of symbolic and esoteric synthesis, *A Vision*, in 1937, he compares his own systematizing to Wyndham Lewis's cubes and Brancusi's ovoids; and in its 'Dove or Swan' chapter, which is by far the most interesting one for any unconvinced reader, he attempts an understanding of historical process by means of a history of sculpture.

Nevertheless, Yeats rarely writes purely ekphrastic poems. 'On a Picture of a Black Centaur by Edmund Dulac' only appears to be an exception because of its title, since the image it evokes is in fact composite, and the poem is therefore an example of what John Hollander usefully distinguishes as 'notional' rather than real ekphrasis.[3] Poignantly, however, 'A Bronze Head' in Yeats's *Last Poems*, which was indeed his last poem about Maud Gonne, originates in Lawrence Campbell's painted bronze plaster cast in Dublin's Municipal Gallery, which represents Gonne in age. 'A Bronze Head' is a genuine ekphrastic poem which reads out of the sculpture the terrible image of 'a bird's round eye / Everything else withered and mummy-dead'. This poetic image justly describes the sculptured one and outstares many of the more sparing images of Gonne in Yeats's work, acting as a terrible counterpart to those representing her as a Pre-Raphaelite beauty. It therefore powerfully complements 'In Memory of Eva Gore-Booth and Con Markiewicz' and 'Among School Children' as an implicit exercise in the tragic incommensurability of youthful beauty and the ravages of age in women.

Certain of Yeats's poems, however, among them some of his greatest, are so intimately involved with the visual arts as to evoke from critics a language of the painterly and sculptural. Such poems as 'Leda and the Swan' (which introduces 'Dove or Swan' as well as taking its place in *The Tower* in 1928), 'Lapis Lazuli', 'Sailing to Byzantium', 'Among School Children', 'Under Ben Bulben' and 'Long-legged Fly' are deeply pondered responses to the visual, and testaments to its pre-existing plastic power, in ways variously admiring and competitive. Such poems invite readings of that agonistic kind characteristic of many contemporary theorists of ekphrasis, who tend to perceive the relationship between *poesis* and *pictura* as a combination of iconophilia and iconophobia.

The relationship between 'Leda and the Swan', for instance, and the image of Michelangelo's which is probably its most significant source would appear a prime case, even an allegory, of what James

A. W. Heffernan in his excellent book *Museum of Words* reads as the 'paragonal' – from Leonardo's *paragone* – and gendered nature of ekphrasis, its posing of a competitive, even antagonistic, relationship between language gendered as male and visual representation gendered as female. Furthermore, when Heffernan characterizes the dynamic and obstetric nature of ekphrasis, in which the poem narrativizes the 'pregnant moment' of the visual representation, he is using terms almost demanded by Yeats's magnificently perturbing, volcanically dynamic sonnet of divine violation and its eventual outcome – since the daughter of Zeus and Leda was Helen – in the catastrophe of Troy, 'the burning roof and tower / And Agamemnon dead'.[4]

The poem therefore realizes, as ekphrasis often does, but not often with such power, the potent narrative and linguistic energy inherent in the stasis of the pictorial image. It electrifies the stillness of that image into a linguistic object no longer still but, like the swan's 'great wings' of its opening line, 'beating still'. Yeats's essay of 1910, 'The Tragic Theatre', shows that he understands all of this theoretically as well as creatively when he says, with reference to Titian and medieval Chinese painting, and with a superb confidence of discrimination, that 'it seems at times as if the graphic art, unlike poetry which sings the crisis itself, were the celebration of waiting'.[5] At such moments, when the magnificence of Yeats's prose virtually matches that of his greatest poetry, exactly defining superb insight and recognition, he himself sings the crisis of representation to which any act of ekphrasis may give rise.

Not only does Yeats write poems prominently preoccupied with the visual arts and poems enacting both the stresses and the opportunities of the ekphrastic in some of the most excruciated ways, but he also writes, in 'The Municipal Gallery Revisited', published in *New Poems* in 1938, one of the great poems of the institution in which the visual arts are given validity and made universally available by modernity. Published in the same year as the other great foundational poem of the modern museum, W. H. Auden's 'Musée des Beaux Arts', 'The Municipal Gallery Revisited' offers the concept of the public gallery as the church of a secular modernity. The gallery is the domain of commemoration; the preserver of the values of a community, a nation or a state; the site of reverence; and even the opportunity for transcendence.

The Dublin gallery's paintings as Yeats evokes them transform the revolutionary Ireland of his immediate past into permanent testamentary image and do so by painting 'an Ireland / The poets have imagined, terrible and gay'. Here Yeats is fantasizing a kind of reverse ekphrasis in which the paintings reconfigure already existing poetry; but of course many paintings do originate in poetry: some of Rossetti's, as I have said, and J. M. W. Turner's 'The Golden Bough', which deeply impressed Yeats in his youth. Since the concept of tragic gaiety figures so largely in Yeats's work and is crucial to 'Lapis Lazuli', and since the word 'terrible' resounds so memorably in the refrain of 'Easter, 1916', Yeats must, himself, be one of the poets who have imaginatively enabled the Ireland of these painters. The relationship between poetry and painting appears as a competitive agon here, then, in which the poet makes himself pre-eminent and victorious; but it is also reciprocal. The reciprocity enables a form of self-transcendence for this poet, who has of course been acquainted with the sitters for many of the gallery's portraits. So that the poem's resounding final lines – 'Think where man's glory most begins and ends / And say my glory was I had such friends' – themselves transform the desire for fame, which might seem arrogance or vainglory, into a splendour and effulgence retaining something of the aura of the word 'glory' in Christian theology.

This is an exhilarating reversal of both the feeling and the gesture that the paintings initially provoke in the ageing poet ('Heart smitten with emotion I sink down'); and at its close 'The Municipal Gallery Revisited' assumes the language of theological transformation to enact what is virtually a secular theophany. The gallery of modern art, 'this hallowed place', becomes the scene of worldly redemption, which is what painting and sculpture are, at their most intense and exalted, for W. B. Yeats; and the poem, like the gallery itself, takes on the aspect of the monumental. Doing so, it becomes in Irish literature, to steal a phrase from Seamus Heaney's 'The Settle Bed', an 'un-get-roundable weight'.

Yeats's poems involving the visual arts might indeed seem formidably un-get-roundable to his successors, particularly if we agree with James Heffernan that ekphrasis is doubly paragonal in that it stages a contest not only between word and image but also between one poet and another.[6] Derek Mahon in fact has a poem in his volume *Harbour Lights* (2005) entitled 'Lapis Lazuli' and dedicated, as Yeats's poem of the same title is, to Harry Clifton. We must assume that Mahon's dedicatee is a different man and poet: but title and dedication appear to parade the inevitability of the relationship with Yeats while at the same time deflecting it with a characteristically elegant and wry literary joke. In fact, however, engagements with the visual arts in Irish poetry after Yeats seem to me to reveal no deep anxiety about his influence or achievement, and neither are they inevitably agonistic, despite much ekphrastic theory. The spirit of poetry bloweth where it listeth, and relations between poetry and painting may signal many things other than the competitive: the genuinely tributary, the cooperative, the self-reflexive, the self-identifying, the tutelary.[7] The other is not always rival. Even so, the competitive is clearly sometimes involved too. I want now to consider several poems significantly engaged with this relationship by some of the best Irish poets writing after Yeats.

II

John Montague's early quartet poem sequence 'Cultural Centre: *Musée Imaginaire'*, first published in his volume *Poisoned Lands* in 1961, where it lacked its subtitle, is subscribed 'New Haven, 1954': so the cultural centre of its title is an Eastern-seaboard American one. The subtitle it later acquired quotes the phrase made current by André Malraux in *Les Voix du Silence* (1951), a study offering what was at the time a revolutionary, controversial theory of artistic representation. For Malraux, the phrase 'imaginary museum' acts as an index of modernity's relationship with art in a 'museum without walls', where images from many cultures and chronological periods are endlessly reproduced and circulated; and his book proposes ways in which this inevitably modifies aesthetic categories or, indeed, the category of the aesthetic itself. The 'cultural centre' of Montague's title is also knowingly alert to the way the idea and institution of the 'gallery' has been democratized in the post-war world. Yeats's 'municipal gallery' was so named in co-ordination with administrative and governmental principle, designed to celebrate the status of an urban capital; Montague's 'cultural centre' nominates, alternatively, a demotic space.

Hence the four poems of his sequence are entitled 'Room I', 'Room II', 'Room III' and 'Entrance Hall', and each commemorates the shared space of hitherto quite distinct, and distinctive, cultures: a Catalan crucifix and a many-handed Indian god; a Botticelli-derived Virgin and a Japanese mountain; a canvas figuring 'slaughtered forms' and one which is a 'complete abstraction'. The image of the 'minatory' crucifix hangs over the whole, however, and meets, in the final lines of the final poem the 'minute harmless god of silver plate' hanging at the waist of a 'tiny nun' taking her class on a cultural visit; and the poem ends with her standing 'possessively beneath / The lean, accusing, Catalan crucifix'.

'Cultural Centre: *Musée Imaginaire'* is the poem of an Irish Catholic, or Irish-American Catholic, or lapsed Catholic, in the early 1950s taking countenance of the facts of both cultural relativism and religious desuetude. The nun's assumption of cultural, religious and, as it were, professional possession is radically undercut by the diminution of the force of the traditional Catholic image at her waist, now ineffectual and made out of base metal; by her diminutive size; and by the threateningly accusatory Catalan image, which is the product of a culture of deep belief and awe produced by, and responsive to, great human suffering and grief. That image too, though, by being transposed to this 'cultural centre' from, presumably, its initial home in a Christian church, has become cultural object rather than religious icon and so, inevitably, debased too, or at least suffering the loss of aura of its primary meaning and associations. The poem knows that this fiercely numinous power, still readable in the image by an Irish Catholic poet of John Montague's generation, will become less and less available to an increasingly secular society whose only church is a cultural centre. 'Cultural Centre: *Musée Imaginaire*' is a young poet's poem, and its own terms and images are perhaps a little over-manipulated in the interests of the palpable design it has upon us: but this is still an impressively haunted and haunting poem, a balance of gains and losses and the index of a transitional moment in Irish modernity. Poem and poet are uncertain of their own emotions and allegiances and of what might constitute their own equable cultural centre, of what might any longer suffice in the imaginary museum of the Irish Catholic imagination. As such, the uncertainty is poetically fruitful and also initiates a fruitful line of cultural examination and self-examination too in this poet's now lengthy career.

Appropriately, then, John Montague has also written an outstanding ekphrastic poem, on an image in Bruges by the early Renaissance Netherlandish painter Gerard David (*c*.1460–1523). A prose poem in his volume *Tides* (1971) with the ominous title 'Coming Events', it seems deeply to have internalized Auden's 'Musée des Beaux Arts'. It is the only ekphrastic poem Montague has written and one of his very few prose poems. Genre and form are appropriately matched, as the unemphatic register of Montague's distinguished prose inspects David's hideously oxymoronic image of a man being flayed almost decorously: the torturers, the onlookers and even the victim himself display very little emotion. The poem's final sentence, playing on the cliché of being 'led to admire', is responsive to the painting's image in its own understated insouciance, with the result that this poem's real work is done by the silence – by the voice of a silence, indeed – in which the poem's title, 'Coming Events', communes in an ironically discrepant way with this sentence: 'The whole scene may be intended as an allegory of human suffering but what the line of perspective leads us to admire is the brown calfskin of the principal executioner's boots.' 'Coming events', then, in this poem from Ireland in the early 1970s: but also a complement to Auden's 'how everything turns away / Quite leisurely from the disaster'. Including, of course, the implicated viewer of the image too: this poet, first, and us, now, as we read, turning violence and suffering into aesthetics.

III

Michael Longley, Derek Mahon and Seamus Heaney all have early poems dedicated to the Northern Irish painter Colin Middleton. In his volume *An Exploded View* (1973) Longley also has a poem entitled 'In Memory of Gerard Dillon'. In the poem's memorial trope Dillon, the Belfast painter who died in 1971, has become 'a room full of self-portraits, / A face that follows us everywhere', which seems a variant of Auden's famous figuration in 'In Memory of W. B. Yeats' that the poet on his death 'became his admirers'. Longley's poem also commemorates Dillon by recollecting in its final numbered section attributes of the Catholic Belfast of the painter's origins: 'Christening robes, communion dresses, / The shawls of factory workers, / A blind drawn on the Lower Falls'. This is despite the fact that Dillon is almost certainly best known for his paintings of the landscapes and people of Roundstone in Connemara in the West of Ireland. Longley's poem therefore celebrates not just the dead painter but the decencies and probities of the place and community that nurtured him. In 1973, when it appeared in *An Exploded View*, whose punning title is drawn from the visual arts, this must have seemed a decent gesture of its own, a tactfully understated signal of rapprochement in a city divided by sectarianism and all too literally exploding.[8] The signal would probably have been the more easily deciphered by the poem's first readers because Dillon and Longley had in fact engaged in an exchange of letters in the *Irish Times* in 1969 about Dillon's controversial decision to pull his paintings from an exhibition of Irish art in Belfast in protest against 'the arrogance of the Unionist mob'. Longley's commemorative poem stills these controversies into elegiac lament by making a graceful acknowledgement of the inescapability of origins as well as ends in the shaping of an artistic life.

Longley's persistent interest in the visual arts throughout his career is apparent. He has collaborated with painters on limited editions, including *Patchwork* with Jim Allen in 1981 and *Out of the Cold* with his daughter Sarah Longley in 1999 – about whose own work he has a poem in *Snow Water* (2004), 'Primary Colours' – and he has written entries for exhibition catalogues. In one of these, *Playthings for the Soul: The Art of Felim Egan*, in 1996, he evokes the Northern Irish painter's canvases and methods by quoting both John Ashbery and Emily Dickinson; by reading paintings through poems, therefore. When he says that Egan's 'rich tonalities depend on a frugality of means', he appears to supply a definition wholly appropriate to his own often minimalist work too, and in fact his note concludes by quoting a phrase from his poem 'Stilts', the phrase which supplies his piece with its title, 'playthings for the soul', as also appropriate to Egan, and then going on to quote a stanza from the poem. We could hardly have a clearer indication of the way in which a poet reading a painter is also reading himself. And what about this, also written of Egan? 'Purged of rhetoric, Beckettian almost, earthy and yet etherial, his is a pianissimo world where whimsy swells into vision.'[9]

Not Beckettian, maybe: but the other terms apply, and apply to the poem which gives its title to Longley's 1976 volume, *Man Lying on a Wall*. This is an ekphrastic poem subtitled *Homage to L. S. Lowry*, and it takes Lowry's well-known painting of that title as its subject. The poem has its whimsical element, as it speculates on the painting's geometry and imagines that the man lying without the support of the wall would be a kind of miracle or conjuring trick. This seems psychologically acute about what we actually do, sometimes, in front of paintings, as we separate out formal from material properties by tracing shapes, proportions, the squares and triangles of geometrical observation behind the work's design. The Lowry painting is perhaps more likely than most to promote such speculation since its spare, precise means emphasize the geometry of the repeated brick rectangles of the wall itself and of chimney, clock tower and cigarette pointing upwards into what Longley accurately calls 'the enormous weight of the sky'. But the poem then turns, still in its opening verse, from formal speculation to the image itself, drawing an analogy which also very much makes the image over into Longley's own in its apparently far-fetched fantasticality: the man lying on the wall wears the 'serious expression / Of popes and kings in their final slumber' and his 'deportment' is 'not dissimilar / To their stiff, reluctant exits from this world / Above the shoulders of the multitude'. But the poem then turns, in the way a sonnet might turn from octet into sestet, to draw a moral or to point a tale:

> It is difficult to judge whether or not
> He is sleeping or merely disinclined
> To arrive punctually at the office
> Or to return home in time for his tea.
> He is wearing a pinstripe suit, black shoes
> And a bowler hat: on the pavement
> Below him, like a relic or something
> He is trying to forget, his briefcase
> With everybody's initials on it.

Fran Brearton reads this poem as congruent with this volume's preoccupations with alternative and divided selves and with 'moments of self-conscious fictionality', and she elegantly says that it is a poem 'inspired by [a work] of art and self-consciously about the workings of art'.[10] This is true, and the poem takes its place in the history of ekphrastic self-reflexivity: but it is more peculiar than this too. Inspired by the Lowry image, which is one of his most famous and widely available in reproduction, the poem nevertheless misreads it or mistakes it. The man in Lowry is not wearing a pinstripe suit, but a black jacket and brown trousers, and he is not wearing a hat, although what may be a bowler is resting on his stomach. In addition, it is not at all difficult to judge whether he is sleeping or not since his left eye, which we can clearly see, is wide open (and he is smoking a cigarette). Longley has either misremembered the painting or deliberately varied it for the purposes of his poem. He has, in other words, made it his own. But this is what all ekphrastic poets do with paintings, even if usually not by so manifestly altering the original image.

Longley also makes it his own when the poem's originating whimsy culminates if not in 'vision' exactly then in that thing into which this poet's work often wanders or turns, a form of ramifyingly peculiar rumination which raises more questions than it is ever likely to answer. In those lines which have a faintly Larkinesque cadence, why is the briefcase like a relic, exactly, or something he is trying to forget? We assume that it has everybody's initials on it because everybody has their relics and their things they wish to forget. But that detail too is one final appropriation of the painting's actuality since, very strikingly, the initials on the briefcase in the painting are LSL – Lowry's own, of course. By obliterating them and replacing them with everybody's, Longley is also replacing them with his own, assuming possession of the painting in the way he assumes possession of Lowry's title for his book.

Taking possession of the image in this way, he is surely also offering it as a very Longleyesque *memento mori*. The briefcase become relic recalls the serious expression of final slumber and reluctant exit in the opening verse, and everybody's initials are on the relic because relics of what everyone has once been are what everybody will eventually leave; and what we lie on, or in, when the wall, the 'supporting structure', is taken away will not be the product of miracle or conjuring trick but the grave. In its appropriative insouciance, this poem may therefore be read almost as an emblem of one possibility of ekphrasis. In fact, Longley turns Lowry's real image into what is virtually an instance of 'notional' ekphrasis (and one of the painting's most notable appurtenances, a large umbrella leaning against the wall, goes entirely unremarked). Narrativizing, or fictionalizing, Lowry in this way, Longley also, however, penetrates to the chilly solitude at the heart of this very peculiar painter. It is as if within the dimensions of Lowry's 'Man Lying On A Wall', at the very heart of his whimsy, Michael Longley has discovered something of the desolating, quasi-abstract visionary emptiness of his seascapes.

When Longley writes about the making of his own portrait in 1983 by the Irish painter Edward McGuire in the poem 'Sitting for Eddie' in *The Ghost Orchid* (1995), which is also a poem written in memory of McGuire, who died in 1986, he makes its signal element the fact that McGuire gets the colour of his eyes wrong. This must have been galling, and the poem refers to 'crazed arguments / About the colour of my eyes'. McGuire could also be regarded, though, as trumping the strange mistake, if it is that, which Longley makes about Lowry's painting. Poems and paintings, and perhaps paintings and people too when people are their subject, need not correspond and be equivalent.

IV

Derek Mahon is probably the most thoroughgoing ekphrastic Irish poet of his generation. His poem for Colin Middleton, 'A Portrait of the Artist' (first published as 'Van Gogh among the Miners' in Mahon's first book, *Night-Crossing*, in 1968), is spoken for Van Gogh and finds a brilliant image for the way the aesthetics of his art displace into a humanistic vision the evangelical Christianity he had once espoused, when van Gogh projects his future work as 'Setting fierce fire to the eyes / Of sunflowers and fishing boats, / Each one a miner in disguise'. There is an intensity of empathy in this that is Mahon's for Van Gogh as well as Van Gogh's for the miners, and the displacement of Protestant evangelicalism by the alternative luminosity of art must carry implications close to home for this poet born in Protestant Belfast. Subsequently, his work offers many further readings of painters and paintings including, outstandingly, the work of Edvard Munch, Paolo Uccello, Pieter de Hooch and William Scott. Mahon's 1982 volume, taking its title from one of its poems, is called *The Hunt By Night*, after the great painting by Uccello in the Ashmolean in Oxford; and 'Art Notes' in *Life on Earth* (2008) is a sequence of nine ekphrastic poems on work by such painters as Edward Hopper, René Magritte and Howard Hodgkin.

Mahon's finest achievement as an ekphrastic poet, however, is 'Courtyards in Delft' which opens *The Hunt by Night*. Affixed to the poem's title are the painting's artist and date: Pieter de Hooch, 1659; and the poem constitutes a reading of the Dutch painting 'The Courtyard of a House in Delft' in the National Gallery in London.[11]

The poem's first three stanzas describe the painting in terms emphasizing what the image excludes ('No breeze ... / No spinet-playing ... / No lewd fish, no fruit, no wide-eyed bird ...') and suggest even that it makes its exclusivity explicit, since it prominently features water-tap, broom and wooden pail, the mechanics of a physical cleanliness that may be designed to propose or reflect a moral purity or, at least, exclusivity. In Mahon's reading of the painting even the trees have their 'trim composure'; and the poem's stanza is, up to a point, a formal mimesis of composure too. In fact, though, these eight-line stanzas of loose iambics irregularly rhyming may be designed to suggest something of the weight of Yeats's *ottava rima* stanza even as, discomposing it a bit, they reject its hieratic monumentality.

Not only are the literal dust and dirt swept out of the image, however, so is the complicating mess of love and sex which in other seventeenth-century Dutch genre paintings might be emblematized by spinet-playing, 'lewd fish' and a bird about to fly its cage: paintings by de Hooch himself, and by Vermeer, for instance, whose images are sometimes tense with secret or potential narratives. However, Mahon's poem says of the painting's image that 'this is life too'. Housewifely care is a reality in seventeenth-century Delft, and de Hooch has unforgettably memorialized it, made it 'vividly mnemonic' in that artistic afterlife towards which the poem 'Courtyards in Delft' is admiring and scrupulously, minutely attentive.

And then the poem's penultimate stanza suddenly turns, even lurches, from an evocation of the painting to the poet's personal pronoun:

I lived there as a boy and know the coal
Glittering in its shed, late-afternoon
Lambency informing the deal table,
The ceiling cradled in a radiant spoon.
I must be lying low in a room there,
A strange child with a taste for verse,
While my hard-nosed companions dream of fire
And sword upon parched veldt and fields of rain-wept gorse.

This is a recognition scene that comes as a genuine shock, as Mahon literalizes, as it were, the metaphor of reading oneself into a painting, crossing the working-class Belfast of his childhood with the courtyards of seventeenth-century Delft in an unpredictable piece of deft analogizing. One obvious element of the analogy is reticently withheld: that both cultures are Protestant and, indeed, that they are directly linked through the presence of 'King Billy', William of Orange, in Northern Irish Protestant iconology. Clearly enough, however, what Mahon is recognizing in the de Hooch is the cleanliness which is next to godliness in Protestant virtue. In fact, although Mahon does not say so, the National Gallery painting prominently includes, in the form of a written tablet above its arch, a piece of homiletic advice recommending patience and meekness.[12]

Also implicit in the analogy, however, is the fact that both cultures are engaged in, or products of, imperial adventure. This is insinuated by the word 'veldt', which summons the open spaces of South Africa in which the men of seventeenth-century Holland busily built their empire while women such as those depicted in the painting kept the homeland clean. What de Hooch's painting ultimately excludes is the 'fire' of imperial plunder, of imperialism as Protestant moral obligation, that thing magnificently fictionalized, for instance, in J. M. Coetzee's *Dusklands*; and what lies just behind Mahon's poem is the conflagration of Northern Ireland at the time of its writing, the violence of which the 'hard-nosed companions' of his childhood dream in a Belfast of barely contained sectarian suppressions and repressions.

In printings of this poem other than that in *The Hunt by Night*, including the Gallery Press *Collected Poems* of 1999, this restlessly self-revising poet strips 'Courtyards in Delft' of its final stanza; most unfortunately, and greatly to the poem's detriment, in my view. In the version published in *The Hunt By Night*, repressed violence returns with, as it were, a vengeance. Dutch imperialism goes on the march when 'the pale light of that provincial town / Will spread itself like ink or oil / Over the not yet accurate linen / Map of the world', and the exclusionary stasis of de Hooch's image is galvanized into narrative consequence when the poem's final lines voice a desire that is the clamorous voice of repression itself: 'If only now the Maenads, as of right, / Came smashing crockery, with fire and sword, / We could sleep easier in our beds at night.' The Maenads who follow Dionysus in Greek mythology and who tear Pentheus apart at the end of Euripedes's *Bacchae* are of course women: so that Mahon's poem ends by converting, in an act of radical discomposure, the house-proud wives of its opening stanza into the furiously released forces of Dionysiac destructiveness. What Mahon calls in the title of a poem from *Lives* (1972), drawing on Wallace Stevens, the 'rage for order' collapses now into a terrifying vision of raging disorder, as the domestic space of crockery is ravaged by plunder and pillage. So that the poem's own apparently demented paradox, that easier sleep would be achieved by such rage asserting its rights, suggests that only by the articulation of excluded violence can the nightmares of Protestant repression be calmed.

This probably remembers the history of South Africa after Dutch colonization but it is also, manifestly, tuned to the frequencies of Northern Irish atrocity and outrage. It may be that his anxious recognition of the scandal of such paradox is what impelled Mahon's own eventual exclusion of this final stanza; and it is a compositional irony that a poem about exclusion should itself become the victim of authorial exclusion. It is one of the scandals of true poetry, however, that it does not always stem from the finer feelings of its writers. The history of poets' anxious ethical self-revisions – from Wordsworth, say, to W. H. Auden – is not a history of aesthetic improvement. In its original form 'Courtyards in Delft' is almost as perturbed in its sense of consequence as Yeats's 'Leda and the Swan', that poem which knows enough to leave ill alone; and Mahon's relationship to de Hooch is manifestly agonistic as well as admiring.[13]

Delft's pale light, the excluded stanza says, will spread itself 'like ink or oil': like, therefore, the medium of poetry or the medium of painting. Reading himself into de Hooch's painting as a 'strange child with a taste for verse', Derek Mahon is also self-reflexively crossing his own nascent poetry with de Hooch's work. The child lying low – hiding out, biding his time, in an act of almost guerrilla-like stealth – will eventually emerge as the poet of such work as this very poem who, in the act of reading a painting with such powerful and intimate originality, will get his place and time and self into perspective; into, in fact, the long perspectives of artistic representation. With brilliantly understated implication, Derek Mahon writes ekphrasis in 'Courtyards in Delft' as a form of historical analogy, discernment and critique.

V

Seamus Heaney's relations with the visual arts are explicit from the beginning. 'In Small Townlands', his poem for Colin Middleton in his first book *Death of a Naturalist* (1966), evokes Middleton's creative processes as a strenuous confrontation between the painter's 'hogshair wedge' and the unremitting antagonism of the natural world, in what is one of Heaney's most Hughesian early exercises. And 'Bogland' in his second book, *Door into the Dark* (1969), is dedicated to the Northern Irish landscape painter T. P. Flanagan. The poem's title corresponds with that of Flanagan's 1967 painting 'Boglands – for Seamus Heaney', one of a series of paintings under the general title 'Gortahork'. 'Bogland', the final poem in *Door into the Dark*, placed as if it knows what it is leading to, is an extremely significant poem because the bog becomes at least as rich a poetic resource for Heaney as it is a painterly one for Flanagan, notably in the 'bog poems' of the books immediately succeeding *Door into the Dark*, *Wintering Out* (1972) and *North* (1975). The bog becomes indeed a crucial image, motif, symbol and myth in Heaney; and although its origins are undoubtedly autobiographical it is of real interest that Heaney should so early in his writing life have discovered it already made over into artwork. The dedication of 'Bogland' to Flanagan may well, therefore, have been no more than a necessary acknowledgement, the payment of a genuine debt, or, at the very least, the generous acknowledgement of a mutually enabling fascination or obsession between poet and painter. Heaney writes very engagingly about his friendship with Flanagan as well as his relationship with his art in the foreword he wrote for a retrospective exhibition at the Ulster Museum in 1995, where he refers to the 'mutual inspiration' of shared visits to Gortahork in County Donegal in the late 1960s.[14]

Years later, the 'Squarings' sequence published in *Seeing Things* (1991) had its origins in a collaborative exhibition with Felim Egan, and was separately published as a limited edition with Egan's lithographs. In an author's note to the 'special copy' of this edition Heaney says that certain images of Egan's and some of his own poems are jointly about 'natural landmarks that had become marked absences', and in a catalogue note for an Egan exhibition in 1992 he defines 'the exquisite ache which the physical world induces'.[15] Both phrases are markedly apposite to 'Squarings' too; and the intense, burnished visuality of some of the poems in the very accurately named *Seeing Things* have a markedly painterly quality. (The Heaney-Egan collaboration was published by Graphic Studio Dublin, which has a long, if intermittent, history of collaborative relationship with Irish poets.)[16]

Heaney also dedicates other poems to artists, and artists figure in poems: the sculptor Oisin Kelly in the 'Glanmore Sonnets' sequence in *Field Work* (1979), for instance; the potter Sonja Landweer in 'To a Dutch Potter in Ireland' in *The Spirit Level* (1996); and Barrie Cooke painting 'godbeams' in 'Saw Music' in the sequence 'Out of This World' in *District and Circle* (2006). In the conversations with Dennis O'Driscoll collected as *Stepping Stones* in 2008, Heaney's friendships with painters from the 1960s on is commented on, as is his deeply informed knowledge and appreciation of the visual arts generally.[17] The Heaney bibliography compiled by Rand Brandes and Michael J. Durkan is instructive about his interactions with painters: in the form of limited-edition collaborations, occasional writings about painters, catalogue introductions for, mainly, contemporary Irish artists (but also for Howard Hodgkin), and, notably, his curatorship of the Ulster Museum exhibition of 1982, *A Personal Selection*. In the catalogue for that exhibition Heaney writes notes on his choices, and a reiterated term of approbation is 'lyric', as in the phrase 'lyric precision'. This is impressionistic as art-descriptive terminology, but nevertheless interestingly reveals Heaney's tendency to conflate the visual and the poetic, or to reconfigure pictorial or plastic artwork in poetic terms.[18]

Heaney writes ekphrastic poems too, including 'Grotus and Coventina' in *The Haw Lantern* (1987), on a Roman altar bas-relief; the second section of 'Seeing Things', on an unspecified cathedral facade; '"Poet's Chair"' in *The Spirit Level*, on a street sculpture in Dublin by Carolyn Mulholland, which includes a comic allusion to Yeats's great ekphrastic poem 'Sailing to Byzantium'; and 'The Mud Vision' in *The Haw Lantern*, which is a kind of disguised ekphrastic poem deriving partly from Richard Long's 'Mud Hand Circle'. In that poem, as elsewhere too, Heaney is inventively exploratory in his inherited genre, reading a history of Irish national opportunity and disappointment out of Long's striking image, in which a 'mud vision' is perceived 'as if a rose window of mud / Had invented itself out of the glittery damp, / A gossamer wheel, concentric with its own hub / Of nebulous dirt, sullied yet lucent'. Although Heaney's poem does not tell us that it is ekphrastic, this is brilliant ekphrastic evocation.[19]

Such invention is matched by that of 'To a Dutch Potter in Ireland', a remarkable instance of the dialogism potentially inherent in all ekphrasis. Heaney's meditation on glazes by this artist, who grew up in occupied wartime Holland, embraces both moments from his own childhood in Northern Ireland and his translation of a poem called 'After Liberation' by the Dutch poet J. C. Bloem. 'To a Dutch Potter in Ireland' opens with an italicized epigraphic section in which words themselves are imagined as having 'come through the fire': so an implicit relation is established between poetry and pottery before the potter summoned by title and dedication is addressed. Her life and the poet's are then crossed as he moves towards an ekphrastic evocation of her glazes which, in a phrase quoted from her, 'bring down the sun'; and finally the poem includes her history and culture and, in translation, her language too. It also includes a reference to the burning Kuwaiti oilfields of the Gulf War in 1991, one of its most memorable and terrible images. The dialogism of ekphrasis, then, promotes here a very rich socializing of the lyric voice, in which poet is joined to potter, poet to poet, Heaney's poem to Bloem's – to which it gives new life in English – and the Second World War to the Gulf War, in a celebration of what art may offer as survival or consolation in the face of human and historical depredation.

So the subject of Heaney's relationship with the visual arts is a large one. Here, I want to think about its impact on *North* (1975) and about a later ekphrastic poem on his portrait by Edward McGuire, a reproduction of which appeared on the back cover of the original Faber edition.

North opens with 'Mossbawn: Two Poems in Dedication', which set the much fiercer poems of the rest of the volume under the affectionate aegis of recollections of Heaney's own childhood Northern home. The first, 'Sunlight', with its evocation of the sun 'against the wall / of each long afternoon' and its portrait of a woman at work in a domestic interior using as a duster an archaic 'goose's wing', seems to have Dutch seventeenth-century domestic interiors, such as those by Vermeer and de Hooch, in mind. The second, a sonnet called 'The Seed Cutters', summons Breughel to authenticate the truth of its own representation of this Northern Irish community's rural 'calendar customs' ('Breughel, you'll know them if I can get them true'). The sonnet skilfully defines an allegiance to an original place and community in the same gesture in which it acknowledges an artistic mentor or confirmatory presence who was also rooted in a Northern artistic landscape. The poet, as a sophisticated, gallery-going contemporary, is therefore allied, without strain, to the inhabitant of rural County Derry. Although this poet appeals to a validating authority, the appeal itself cannot but carry an authenticating self-validation too. Such dual recognition of the self in both original attachments and secondary, educated mobility is entirely characteristic of Heaney; and it is the tonal strength of this sonnet that justifies its own gesture, since in any poem less assured the apostrophe to Breughel would almost certainly seem presumption.

Set under these northern painterly stars, the subsequent poems in *North* frequently include elements of ekphrasis, as they scrutinize various objects into the precisions of an appropriately spare language: quernstones; Viking archaeological finds and 'trial pieces'; the anatomical plates of Baudelaire's 'Le Squelette Laboureur', which Heaney translates as 'The Digging Skeleton' (no doubt recalling that Baudelaire was intensely preoccupied with the visual arts and an outstanding ekphrastic poet); and Goya's paintings, in an extended ekphrasis at the end of 'Summer 1969'.

In that poem Heaney situates himself in Madrid as Belfast explodes. He pictures himself listening to advice to return home and assume some form of responsibility, in public stance and in writing, towards his place and its catastrophic political moment, but instead choosing to 'retreat' to the Prado, where he takes instruction from Goya, the devastating painter of the extreme violence and brutality of war. Heaney names the painting 'The Shootings of the Third of May' and evokes 'Saturn Devouring his Son': but it is his description of the 'Duel with Clubs' as 'that holmgang / Where two berserks club each other to death / For honour's sake, greaved in a bog, and sinking' that seems to correspond most directly to the situation in the North. One of the works known as

121

Goya's Black Paintings, it is an image not only of appalling ferocity but of total futility, since the bog will claim both men anyway, even if one manages to club the other to death first. The relatively peculiar words 'holmgang' and 'berserk' used as a noun call attention to themselves. The former is the Old Norse for a duel to the death and the latter, from the Icelandic – more usually 'berserker' – means a wild Norse warrior. Heaney's prominently Northern vocabulary, in an act of commanding ekphrastic appropriation, tears Goya's image from its Spanish location and gives it, as it were, a newly relevant topography in the same act in which it gives it a newly contemporary political dimension.

These ekphrastic moments in *North* also bring into relief the act of ekphrasis involved in the 'bog poems' themselves; and indeed this holmgang in a bog makes 'Summer 1969' a bog poem too. This is a sequence of poems that originated, in 'The Tollund Man' in *Wintering Out* (1972), not with the viewing of an actual body retrieved from the bog but with the photograph of such a body as it appears in P. V. Glob's book *The Bog People*. The promissory dedication of the opening line of 'The Tollund Man' – 'Some day I will go to Aarhus' – has, it seems, been kept by the time of 'The Grauballe Man' in *North*, where the poet says, 'I first saw his twisted face // in a photograph ... // but now he lies / perfected in my memory'. The ekphrastic moments of *North* all put their weight on Heaney's figuration of himself as an 'artful voyeur' in 'Punishment'; and, beyond its immediate context in that poem, the phrase may do duty for the ethical awkwardness inevitable in some forms of ekphrasis too. The varied critical reception of the bog poems strongly suggests that these poems give rise, of their very nature, to awkward ethical issues. These are continuous, in fact, with those raised by the agonistic relationship between writing and image in ekphrasis more generally; and it could be that this poet's telling us, in a poem, that he kept a promise made in a previous poem, is to be read as attempted ethical reparation or self-validation.

Edward McGuire's celebrated portrait of Heaney seems almost calculated to emphasize the relationship between the poems of *North* and the visual arts.[20] Having the portrait of a poet on the jacket of what was only a fourth collection was unusual; but it was all the more so because, as Heaney says in *Stepping Stones*, 'it was the first time Faber broke with the old house style, which had never featured author photographs or jacket art'.[21] This now well-known image seems exceptionally well attuned to the poetic persona implicit in the volume's many uses of the first person singular, although it was presumably completed before these poems were actually written. Heaney, wearing a dark polo neck sweater, sits at a small table in front of a window with a book open in his hands but looking straight ahead at his portraitist in a way that seems clenched, even cornered. There is perhaps something Hamlet-like about him; and one of the *North* poems figures the poet as 'Hamlet the Dane, / skull-handler, parablist'. A tree with very large leaves, and two large-headed birds in its branches, turned towards each other, fills the window. The table is covered in a white cloth with a geometrical design. This portrait makes its subject an icon: the solitary, dark-clothed figure at a kind of altar seems almost monastically dedicated, both to his book and to the natural – or is it a mythological or fabulous? – world beyond the window. McGuire's portrait is, superbly, a representation of Seamus Heaney as one of his own *North* poems.

In 'A Basket of Chestnuts' in *Seeing Things* Heaney revisits the portrait. The poem's opening stanzas describe swinging a loaded basket in that way Heaney has of almost preternaturally getting into language something we have often experienced but hardly ever even acknowledged. Reading him in this mode is always to experience the shock of recognition. Then, again entirely characteristically, the delicacy of physical evocation ramifies into a whole system of value – in this case, into the knowledge of both dismay and ratification. Heaney quotes Wallace Stevens at the opening of 'Fosterage' in the 'Singing School' sequence in *North*: 'Description is revelation!'; and the strength of his work always lies, before it lies anywhere else, in the exactness of its visual record. Which is one reason why painting means so much to him; and why 'A Basket of Chestnuts' envies that other art, saying of its eponymous chestnuts:

> And I wish they could be painted, known for what
> Pigment might see beyond them, what the reach
> Of sense despairs of as it fails to reach it,
> Especially the thwarted sense of touch.

'Known for what / Pigment might see beyond them': a visionary epistemology is made to depend on the activity of painting here, when it becomes impersonally active, its very medium credited with sight, with 'seeing things'.

But the poem then remembers that chestnuts were available to Edward McGuire for the Heaney portrait, which he had considered using as 'a decoy or a coffer for the light' but which he in fact chose not to use, reflecting the light instead – and strikingly so – off Heaney's shoes. The basket of chestnuts therefore 'wasn't in the picture and is not':

> What's there is comeback, especially for him.
> In oils and brushwork we are ratified.
> And the basket shines and foxfire chestnuts gleam
> Where he passed through, unburdened and dismayed.

In these lines the language of dismay and ratification with which the poem opens is transferred to McGuire himself, in tributary elegy (he died in 1986). Heaney's descriptive accuracy – 'foxfire' could not be bettered – matches the painter's; and it is this accuracy which makes for the outlasting capacity of art. 'Especially for him', since he is the maker of this enduring object: but, by implication, for his sitter too, who will go on sitting there for as long as the portrait stays.

So these lines join painter and poet in memorial evocation, and in the ambivalent triumph and terror of making. They do so too in a very peculiar form of ekphrasis. 'A Basket of Chestnuts' is both an ekphrastic poem by a poet on his own portrait and a poem about a painting that does not exist. Summoning the idea of an alternative composition, the poem holds the relationship between writing and painting in an admiring but almost awkward tension. It has, in a way endemic to ekphrasis, both a genuine complementarity and a competitive edge. The poem is tribute and displacement; and since it is a self-representation that is being displaced, the competition is not only with the painter but with an earlier self and poet too. 'A Basket of Chestnuts' is therefore a paradigm of a certain kind of Heaney poem as his oeuvre advances: the poem in which former selves and former poems are revisited in ways that complicate, extend or even subvert original significance.

CHAPTER 8

The Pools of Shiloh:
On Paul Muldoon's
'Our Lady of Ardboe'

I was an undergraduate in Oxford when I first read a Paul Muldoon poem. Someone came around the rooms in college in, it must have been, 1972, selling a little magazine called *Caret*.[1] This pedlar was clearly a very enterprising enthusiast because this is one of the very few times I remember any such thing happening, although I do remember the neatly coiffured Jon Silkin hawking copies of *Stand* around the pubs – ever ready, it seemed, for a rigorous intellectual debate, even in pretty raucous surroundings and with those not blessed with his preternatural sobriety. I bought *Caret* and read a poem by Muldoon about what I would in those days, I suppose, have called Red Indians. I am pretty sure that he did not publish this poem subsequently, and I cannot remember its title: but of course aspects of this subject matter became hugely important to him and reached a kind of apotheosis in *Madoc - A Mystery* in 1990.

I do not think I understood the *Caret* poem very well, but it did register. I probably spent some time trying to figure it out, and I remember passing the magazine on to a pal and discussing the poem with him. So of course I bought *New Weather* when it came out in 1973. I liked 'Wind and Tree' very much, and still do – especially since its author restored the absolutely necessary second 'together' to its tenth line in *Poems 1968-1998* – but I was a bit put off the book by the fact that it was printed entirely in italics. These seemed pretentious, or whimsical, or both to me; and I remain unclear about whether they were the consequence of design or bizarre accident. Perhaps I should chastise my younger self for being so puritanically po-faced about this, but actually I still think the italics look ridiculous.

I first really took to Muldoon with the next book, *Mules*, in 1977. 'Our Lady of Ardboe' was the poem that did it for me. I do not think that it has been written about very much by his commentators, but

Muldoon himself clearly thinks very well of it, since he has published it subsequently in his *Selected Poems* of 1986, his *New Selected Poems* in 1996, and, as I have said, the *Poems 1968-1998* in 2001. I shall try to say first of all what mattered to me about the poem then (in so far as I can accurately recall this about a poem I must have read a thousand times since), and then I shall try to say why it still matters to me; which involves, in addition to what I liked about it first, both what I have discovered about it since, and also my sense of its place in Muldoon's now substantial (in several senses) oeuvre, reading it backwards through the thicket of what he has published in the over thirty years since.

The poem's subject seemed important to me. I took it to be the registering of an attitude to an inherited Catholicism that was sceptical but not hostile. I surmised – knew with gut instinct, I suppose – that Muldoon's education had been very similar to my own: that is, that it had been at the hands of Irish Catholic priests, members of a religious order. In my case, these priests were stationed at a remote outpost of the Irish Catholic Empire virtually on top of Hadrian's Wall, in Carlisle, in the county of England then called Cumberland. Why they were there, educating droves of Cumbrian farmers' sons, sad waifs and strays from the loins of the British (and occasionally American) armed forces overseas, and Catholic city boys like me who had passed the Eleven Plus, is still, like *Madoc*, a bit of a mystery to me. However, possibly because they were priests who had chosen to work outside the Ireland of the 1960s, and occasionally articulated, in public, a delight that they were no longer there, they seemed, in the main, a remarkably liberal, well-educated and open-minded lot. One of them, my history teacher, Gabriel Daly, went on to become a celebrated liberal theologian and broadcaster in Ireland who spoke out, sometimes bravely, on ethical issues, and another, my headmaster, Dominic Daly, edited the diaries of Douglas Hyde. I had no reason, that is to say, to feel hostile towards, or aggrieved about, the Catholic Church as a consequence of the education I received, and even 'tried my vocation', as the saying was, for a year or so after school. However, I met people in Oxford who did feel such hostility and grievances, and I knew, therefore, how ungainsayable such responses can be. During my first year there, in any case, I stopped practising the faith, and this was a matter of real anxiety or even distress to me, I think, in so far as I can now recall it, and was certainly something a first-year undergraduate under many other pressures could have done without. By 1977 this had evaporated, although it left what I even now retain, a kind of residual nostalgia that is like a little knot at the back of the mind, which it gets more and more unlikely that I shall ever untie. Still, in 1977, 'Our Lady of Ardboe' seemed the poem for me.

Its three sections present three almost independent attitudes to the figure or icon named in the title. I had never heard of this Virgin, nor of Ardboe, although I assumed (correctly) that she was a figure of veneration in local Irish Catholic piety. The first section of the poem, a quatrain and a couplet interconnected by rhyme, describes the appearance of this figure, referred to simply as 'She', to a girl 'in a corner of the whin-field /... One night in nineteen fifty-three or four'. It is presented quite neutrally, as though attesting to the reality of the vision, which also includes cattle kneeling in reverence in a way that encourages the girl to kneel. I knew cattle kneeling in worship in poems by Thomas Hardy and David Jones, so I assumed this to be an old folk belief in Ireland as well as England. The first section of 'Our Lady of Ardboe' credits the mystery of such belief, we might say, in a way that acts as a kind of poetic equivalent of free indirect speech in narrative prose.

The second section is a sonnet, of unorthodox rhyme scheme, and this book was beginning to establish the sonnet as a staple, if almost plastically variable, form in this poet's work. This one offers a rumination on the vision by the poem's 'I' which is, clearly enough, a representation of the poet's own subjectivity. Here, the neutrality of section I, readable even as awe-struck belief, is complemented by something more complex and ambiguous. Statement in the opening section succeeds to supposition and inquiry: 'Who's to know what's knowable?' The longing to which a vision of the Virgin might be a response, and which it might fulfil, is rendered metaphorically as sacred watery oppositions to 'the fixity of running water' which is the routine life of domesticity and acquisition:

> For I like to think, as I step these acres,
> That a holy well is no more shallow
> Nor plummetless than the pools of Shiloh,
> The fairy thorn no less true than the Cross.

The miracles of rural Irish Catholicism and of ancient folk tradition appear to be held in a relatively sympathetic form of apposition; but this sonnet is nevertheless linguistically slippery in the way *Mules* is, provocatively, throughout. Although it appears concessive, the poem plays with notions that, even though they possess a zany surreal poetry, can only make miracle or vision appear ridiculous. The idea of a winding road to Christ's navel, the concepts of milk from the Virgin's breast and a feather from the Holy Ghost, the stuff of demented scholasticism and outrageous superstition, together with the lack of specificity in the date of the vision itself – 'in nineteen fifty-three or four' – all seem to place the religion as equivalent to folk belief only in a shared preposterousness. And the final quatrain plays very ambivalently with the phrases 'like to think', 'no more shallow' and 'no less true'. What kinds of equivalence are these proposing? If a holy well is no more shallow than the pools of Shiloh, then both are possibly equally shallow rather than equally deep; and if the fairy thorn is 'no less true' than the Cross, then how true is the Cross? Is the fairy thorn in fact 'no more true' than the Cross? Are such equivalences merely forms of equivocation? The OED defines equivocation as 'the use of words or expressions that are susceptible of a double signification, with a view to mislead; *esp.* the expression of a virtual falsehood in the form of a proposition which (in order to satisfy the speaker's conscience) is verbally true'. 'In order to satisfy the speaker's conscience': a great deal of Catholicism in my generation required us to manage that, and to do so we might well have 'like[d] to think' several impossible things at the same time, where 'like' means less 'to find agreeable' than 'to entertain the fancy'. And equivocation is the Jesuitical concept that attracts Shakespeare's interest in *Macbeth*.

The poem's final section, which is formally once again what the opening section is, a quatrain and a couplet interlinked by what we might now call almost-rhyme, changes tack once more, and in a way so surprising that I can still remember the shock, and the shock of recognition, I felt when I first read it. The quatrain is a direct quotation of eight invocations from the 'Litany of the Blessed Virgin Mary', a lengthy celebration of Our Lady through various titles given to her by the medieval church ('Tower of ivory, House of gold' are others, famously quoted by James Joyce in *A Portrait of the Artist as a Young Man*). Recited during my childhood (and presumably Muldoon's), but probably no longer, at the end of various liturgical or quasi-liturgical events, and chanted by the entire congregation, the Litany always seemed a kind of poem in public recitation and is indeed very beautiful. Now, in 'Our Lady of Ardboe', Muldoon is making it over into an actual poem of his own. The sacred poem, however, becomes the cue for exit:

> And I walk waist-deep among purples and golds
> With one arm as long as the other.

These lines represent, I assumed, a way of walking away from the subject without too much drama or anguish, giving it its due without being any longer in hock to it. The purples and golds are the liturgical colours of priestly vestments; but walking among them with equivalent arm lengths is to walk in a state of equanimity. Equivalence, equivocation, equanimity: the three emotional or ethical qualities of 'Our Lady of Ardboe' are expressed many times elsewhere too in Paul Muldoon. 'I give them all, I give them all their due', as another uncollected poem, which turns the poets of Northern Ireland into a cheeseboard, says; 'And for myself a little *Caprice des Dieux*'.[2] Turning the at least potential trauma of separating oneself from childhood Catholicism to the caprice of 'Our Lady of Ardboe' seems not a bad thing to do with it and not a bad thing to have managed, even a way of getting it off your conscience. And in 1977 I liked that very much.

I thought one other thing about the poem then. Its penultimate line seemed to echo the opening of Seamus Heaney's 'The Other Side', published in *Wintering Out* in 1972. There, a Protestant 'neighbour' visits a Catholic house and waits courteously outside until the recitation of the rosary is over. The rosary is a domestic act of Marian piety to which the Litany of the Blessed Virgin Mary was occasionally, I think, also attached. Heaney's neighbour approaches the house 'thigh-deep in sedge and marigolds'; Muldoon's 'I' exits 'waist-deep in purples and golds'. I do not know that I thought about this for long – I just noticed it – and in 1977 I knew nothing about Paul Muldoon's relationship with Seamus Heaney, and would not have cared to know. I have cared to know since, and have written about connections between the two poets in an article that has itself been subject to some suspicious 'interrogation'.[3]

Nevertheless, I was a bit taken aback when I interviewed Muldoon during a conference on his work in 2000. The remit of the interview was that he would read aloud poems chosen by me, on which I would then comment and ask him questions, inviting the audience (some of whom had given or were about to give conference papers) to comment further or ask questions of their own. My intentions in asking about 'Our Lady of Ardboe' were first to hear Muldoon reading a favourite poem of mine and secondly to use the opportunity to try to get him to talk about Catholicism, which I continue to find more interesting and problematic in his work than some of his critics seem to. And in fact largely through the intervention of the critic Tim Kendall, who has published a book on Muldoon, he did talk extremely interestingly about what might be regarded as a displacement of the forms of Catholicism into the almost occult later forms of his own poems.

But he also talked – with rather more initial enthusiasm, I felt – about the way 'Our Lady of Ardboe' relates to Seamus Heaney. When I asked whether the poem betrays an 'envy of unsophistication', he said that it 'owes a great deal to Seamus Heaney, it is a kind of Heaney poem'. Ardboe has strong Heaney associations, he said, without specifying: but as it is the place where Heaney's wife, Marie, comes from, it is a place in which Heaney himself has spent a lot of time. Muldoon goes so far as to say, jocularly but not only so, that 'this poem was written by Seamus Heaney'; and when I pursue the matter perhaps beyond all reason by asking what in his own work 'is saved from irony', he says, 'Only the occasional Seamus Heaney poem'. Medbh McGuckian, present in the audience, picks all of this up by asking, 'So that's what Shiloh is there for?'; and Muldoon says, 'That's right, "S H". Well spotted.'[4] McGuckian has picked up here on the kind of alphabetical effect that some of Muldoon's later poems almost cry out for critics to pick up on; but this is an early instance which no one before McGuckian on this occasion had, as far as I am aware, 'spotted'. We might regard it, then, I suppose, as 'that first *sh* the strangers found / difficult to manage', that brilliantly loaded echo offered by Muldoon's 'The More a Man Has the More a Man Wants' in *Quoof* (1983) to the famous call made by Heaney's 'Broagh' in *Wintering Out* (1972), 'that last *gh* / the strangers found / difficult to manage'.

There is manifestly, therefore, a kind of code in operation, even in

Muldoon's early poems. It is a code that, no doubt, helps him to write them and, in this one, may help him, almost privately, to overcome certain anxieties of a (Harold) Bloomian, 'anxiety of influence' kind. 'Overcome' would be the word, for the fact is that while 'Our Lady of Ardboe' may include a property or two patented by Seamus Heaney and may both inscribe and occlude a reference to the initial letters of his name, it is most certainly not 'a Seamus Heaney poem' or anything remotely like one. It is most manifestly not so in its abjuration of single voice or, given the context, we might say, single 'vision'. The multivalence of its ironic perspectivizing might even lead us to think of its title as a scent-distracting misnomer. Whereas a genuine Heaney poem might well be called 'Our Lady of Ardboe' – but, interestingly, given the opportunities of the local miracle with which he must have been extremely familiar, one is not – Muldoon's might more appropriately be called, for instance, 'Three Ways of Looking at a Miracle of the Virgin' or, in inverted commas, '"Our Lady of Ardboe"'.[5]

Does the intertextual relationship of this poem to Seamus Heaney matter? It seemed to matter sufficiently to its author long after its first publication to bring it to the attention of a roomful of his critics and admirers. And I can hardly claim to find it of no interest myself, since I have, as I have said, written about these interconnections. But I persist in finding this less important than the things I first found interesting in the poem, which I have tried to define here. I continue to find these things interesting; and they seem to me, I suppose, of larger cultural moment than any relationship between writers. I regard the presence of Heaney's work in 'Our Lady of Ardboe', then, as a kind of enablement for the young poet Paul Muldoon who presumably needed to take on – to brave – this encounter in order to become himself, or his self in poetry. Having done so, however, maintaining a primary responsibility to the art itself and its own potential future, he writes a poem whose truest value and whose most lasting effects lie altogether elsewhere, fixing in form a crucial moment in Irish religious and cultural life.

In retrospect, this poem seems to me to have been in at the beginning of things other than the alphabetical in Muldoon too. The poem's form is not just that of a sonnet but of a sonnet topped and tailed by two sort-of sestets that modify or even contradict it. As I have said, the sonnet becomes a staple in Muldoon; but so too does the inventive and exploratory playing with, and opening up of, traditional forms as a means to the invention of long poems, notably the deployment of sestina in a mode of expansion or even gigantism. The tripartite structure of 'Our Lady of Ardboe' may be the origin of that. It is a structure that enables irony, scepticism and multivalence but that still finds a space for the approval of unsophistication. It is also a mode of simultaneity, of having several responses at once and holding them, if not in a single thought, then still in a single movement of mind; and Muldoon is variously interested in that.

Notably, there is the way 'Madoc – A Mystery' (1990) tells the story of an alternative Coleridgean Pantisocracy, one that actually makes it to America, as if it is also the story of contemporary Northern Ireland, or contemporary Northern Irish poetry and its critics; and the way 'The Bangle (Slight Return)' in *Hay* (1998), taking its subtitle from Jimi Hendrix, appears to tell three stories at the same time, privileging none, in a poem partly about privilege. There are risks as well as pleasures and satisfactions in such ways of proceeding in poems. The playfulness can become exhausting the more it tends to the exhaustive; and about Muldoon you can feel that less is more, sometimes much more, and that poems can be thinner for being fatter.

One particular long poem by Muldoon, however, casts a shadow over 'Our Lady of Ardboe' for me nowadays whenever I turn back to it. 'Yarrow' in *The Annals of Chile* (1994) is a kind of poetic *Bildungsroman*, a portrait of the artist as a young man, in which the mother figures in her function as almost the incarnation of the now certainly repressive Catholicism of this poet's childhood, the mother as 'Fidei Defensor', Defender of the Faith. It is always difficult with Muldoon to know what relationship obtains between autobiography and poetry, but the poems do extend the invitation to think about this; and the figure of the repressive mother is an enduring one. It appears in such poems as 'Profumo' in *Meeting the British* (1987), in which the mother 'shifts from ham to snobbish ham'; in what seems almost an epigraph poem for 'Yarrow', 'Milkweed and Monarch', also in *The Annals of Chile*, where 'He'd mistaken his mother's name, "Regan", for "Anger"'; in 'Errata' in *Hay*, where one erratum is 'For "mother" read "other"', which has seemed to at least one critic a modish appeal to the contemporary (or recent) academy, but which surely draws more nourishment from the genuinely extensive and threatening alterity of the 'mother' in Muldoon.[6]

This would be, in particular, the mother of her two most terrible realizations: that of 'Homesickness' in *Moy Sand and Gravel* (2002) where, like the 'black-winged angel' of the Magritte painting which this poem is named after and tacitly evokes, she 'turns away', making no concession whatever to the diagnosis of the father's terminal cancer; and that of 'They That Wash on Thursday' in *Hay*, where the word 'hand' hammers itself into itself in an extended performance of the possibilities of identical rhyme:

> She was a dab hand, my mother. Such a dab hand
> at raising her hand
> to a child. At bringing a cane down across my hand
> in such a seemingly off-hand
> manner I almost have to hand
> it to her.

Beyond these thematic preoccupations, the extraordinarily elaborate rhyme schemes of certain interconnected long poems in Muldoon's work have been read by one of his most astute critics, Clair Wills, as formally employing 'a kind of ghostly maternal template'; which is a genuinely disturbing notion, both morbid and uncanny.[7]

Such apparent recriminations from the abused poet-son can hardly now fail to trail their unforgotten and unappeasable memories, miseries and accusations across the final part of 'Our Lady of Ardboe' and the figure of the young poet who wrote there, quoting the Litany, 'Mother most amiable, Mother most admirable / ... Mother inviolate, mother undefiled'. In such a context, the references to Heaney in his work must remind us how incapable Muldoon is of drawing on his childhood as the source of benignity and beneficence in the way Heaney does again and again; even if one of the things the sonnet sequence 'Clearances' in *The Haw Lantern* makes plain is that the relationship with the mother was not an entirely straightforward one in Heaney's case either. Even so, it is entirely appropriate that Wordsworth should stand so prominently over Heaney's work, and it is testimony to Muldoon's self-knowledge that he should make Coleridge, who was positioned so problematically in relation to both first and second families, the hapless hero of 'Madoc – A Mystery'. The relationship with the mother seems the location of trauma, or at least of damage, that fuels Muldoon's work from very deeply down. 'On Not Being Seamus Heaney' might well be the name for this strain in Paul Muldoon; and it could be that his frequent references to that poet include an element of longing or even of a kind of envy which has nothing to do with literary 'anxiety'.

In some more recent poems, however, the trope of the repressive or abusive mother is newly focused under the most compelling of biographical or genetic necessities. Now, the deeply loved daughter reminds the poet of the mother. This happens, in a way continuous with the examples I have been discussing, in 'The Throwback' in *Hay*. In this poem, the recognition of similarity prompts a further memory of the mother as embattled and aggressive, when the poet imagines his daughter's patch of psoriasis 'suddenly flar[ing] up into the helmet / she [the mother] wore when she stood firm against Xerxes', where 'Xerxes', the Persian king who invaded Greece, is presumably coded for the unruly son himself. It also happens in 'The Windshield' in *Maggot* (2010). Here, the poet waiting in his car for his daughter receives 'a rear view mirror's jolt' in which he recalls his mother waiting to collect him from a school debate; and the poem moves towards conclusion when the recalled debate turns into a piece of contemporary self-admonishment: 'This house proposes that we not sully / the memory of a parent, least of all one who sends a judder / through a child'.

In 'It Is What It Is' in *Horse Latitudes* (2006) Muldoon figures himself, in relation to yet another episode in his childhood involving his mother, spending 'fifty years ... trying to put it together'. (Seamus Heaney, alternatively, had to 'wait until [he] was nearly fifty / to credit marvels', he tells us in the second of his poems to be called 'Fosterling', in *Seeing*

Things.) Is the poet Paul Muldoon finally enabled to put it together through the redemptive agency of the daughter? Can he put it together at last when he can put the daughter together with the mother and figure them together in the same poem? If so, this can hardly be expected to produce from Muldoon's oeuvre the image of a mother inviolate, a mother undefiled, and least of all a mother forgiven; but it might produce the figure of a dangerous, damaging mother finally allayed. The debate is proposed but not won in 'The Windshield'; but who's to know what's knowable? Who's to know what poetry, or paternity, or the poetry of paternity, might make knowable or possible to the poet who has so frequently figured an extremely difficult filiality? 'Go figure', as the poet says.

PART III

CHAPTER 9

Everyone and I: Frank O'Hara, Billie Holiday and Modern Elegy

A poem must be a holiday of Mind. It can be nothing else.

Paul Valéry

I

An impulse towards elegy, towards the melancholy attendant on a profound consciousness of mutability and transience, is often present in Frank O'Hara's poetry, which is characteristically buoyantly celebratory and delighted, even ecstatic, too. Such an impulse is one of the things he notices and admires in Jackson Pollock, on whom he wrote a short illustrated monograph in 1959. Of Pollock's 'heroic' painting *Blue Poles* O'Hara says that it is 'a painfully beautiful celebration of what will disappear, or has disappeared already, from his world, of what may be destroyed at any moment'.[1] Within this we can certainly hear the accents of a sensibility necessarily constrained by the Cold War moment, with its relentlessly threatening maintenance of 'peace' as the 'balance of terror'; and we also remember that O'Hara was partly formed and conditioned by serving in the US Navy during the Second World War while still only in his teens. Reading American Abstract Expressionism more generally, O'Hara is defining himself and his own work too when he says that burgeoning within it is 'the traumatic consciousness of emergency and crisis expressed as personal event, the artist assuming responsibility for being, however accidentally, alive here and now'. The art of Gorky, de Kooning and Newman is, he says, both 'somber and joyful': 'somber because it does not merely reflect but sees what is about it, and joyful because it is able to exist'.[2] This is a salutary reminder that the work O'Hara most admired in his own time, and his own work too, is art made by those who perceived themselves as survivors and were forced to recognize the fragility of human life in the face of potential nuclear disaster.

In O'Hara the elegiac impulse is notably an element of what he famously calls in 'Getting Up Ahead of Someone (Sun)' his 'I do this I do that' poems. In 'A Step Away from Them', for instance, O'Hara jauntily does this and does that during his lunch hour in New York City – the poem was collected in his book *Lunch Poems* in 1964 – and, with an eroticized focus, describes such things as the glistening torsos of labourers, women's skirts blown up over grates, Puerto Ricans on the avenue ('which / makes it beautiful and warm') and the Manhattan Storage Warehouse ('which they'll soon tear down'). The riot of metropolitan particulars is meticulously recorded, as it is in other such poems of O'Hara's, the meticulousness stretching to the use of upper-case typography to represent or reproduce what the poet sees as he drifts by. As in other such poems too, meticulousness is a matter of chronological specificity: 'Everything / suddenly honks: it is 12.40 of / a Thursday'. The particulars are striking and the evocation of a moment in the life of a great city has considerable documentary interest and attractiveness in itself. It is as though O'Hara is doing in verse for the American city something of what the Italian post-war neo-realists were doing in cinema for Italian cities. 'A Step Away from Them', written on 16 August 1956, actually mentions Federico Fellini, whose *I Vitteloni*, a prominent example of the genre, had won the Venice Film Festival Silver Lion in 1953 (O'Hara is reminded of Fellini by free-associating 'JULIET'S CORNER' with Fellini's wife, the *'bell' attrice* Giulietta Masina); and O'Hara was a huge fan of the movies, referring to them and to their stars frequently in his poems, notably in one of the best-known, 'Ave Maria'.

In these poems, O'Hara's is an aesthetic of the spontaneous, the improvisatory, the arrested momentary. The poems are what he says such paintings of Pollock's as *Full Fathom Five* (which embed in the paint of their surfaces actual objects – a cigarette, keys, tacks, 'paint-tube tops making little blind eyes here and there') are: 'souvenirs of accident'.[3] These poems might also be regarded, however, in relation to longer-sanctioned literary histories, of which O'Hara was a sophisticated, if subversive, inheritor. They are poems in which the reiterated 'I' of the poet is a variant on Baudelaire's nineteenth-century Parisian *flâneur*, for instance, and therefore inevitably intricated in the consumerist society whose appurtenances he so relentlessly catalogues; and they are poems in which the poet, maintaining a responsibility of praise, becomes the mid-twentieth-century metropolitan inheritor of the late romanticism of the Rilke of the *Duino Elegies* ('such saying / as never the things themselves hoped so intensely to be'). This poet is markedly also the conveyor of a certain kind of camp sensibility, itself a transformation of the pose of the nineteenth-century Wildean dandy, in which, as Susan Sontag says in her influential essay 'Notes on Camp', the world is seen as 'an aesthetic phenomenon'.[4] As attractive as all of this is, however, collections of particulars, however finely and meticulously evoked and recorded, may come to seem merely whimsical if they are the sole raison d'être of poems, and debilitatingly so; and there are poems – inevitably, given the vast scale of O'Hara's output – which make themselves subject to such censure.

'A Step Away from Them', however, gathers its particulars in the face of, or against, a particular of another kind altogether, which explains the poem's title. After the poet notices the Puerto Ricans, in a way that is eroticized, certainly, but also politically sensitive (since this kind of approval inevitably opposed itself in 1959 to a then prevalent American prejudice: witness the great Bernstein–Sondheim musical *West Side Story*, of 1957), this happens:

> First
> Bunny died, then John Latouche,
> then Jackson Pollock. But is the
> earth as full as life was full, of them?

And the poem's final lines combine the annotation of the poet's lunch with something much stranger:

> A glass of papaya juice
> and back to work. My heart is in my
> pocket, it is Poems by Pierre Reverdy.

In these lines the declarative register of 'A Step Away from Them' warps into the elliptical, as the intrusion of mortality forces a variation in the poem's syntactical register. Death provokes a mournful rhetorical question which insinuates a sense of absolute loss, since the question's answer must be in the negative – no, earth is not as full as life was full, of them, since their absence inevitably robs O'Hara's earth of a previous plenitude – and that negativity casts its darkness over the poem's catalogue of life's fullness. It also provokes a joltingly odd statement of identity and the surprise of a heart-breaking line-break. Not 'My heart is in my / mouth', as it might well be, but 'My heart is in my / pocket, it is Poems by Pierre Reverdy'. The poet's lunch hour has been fatally interrupted, and his heart bruised, by thoughts of the friends who have died, and he can be steadied only by art itself, by life-enhancing poems; and by this poet especially, it may be, whose importance for O'Hara is glossed by the last line of another of the *Lunch Poems*, 'Adieu to Norman, Bon Jour to Joan and Jean-Paul': 'I love Reverdy for saying yes, though I don't believe it'.[5] In 'A Step Away from Them' the fact that the recent deaths of friends and artists are recounted almost in parenthesis means that nothing is being insisted; nevertheless, everything is altered. In what the jacket blurb of *Lunch Poems*, which O'Hara wrote himself, calls 'the noisy splintered glare of a Manhattan noon', the poet is always only a step away from his ghosts, and his ghosts keep in permanent step with the poet.

II

O'Hara's is a poetry often depending on, and feeding off, a sustaining coterie: and the coterie functions primarily in the work itself by means of proper names like these, usually those of friends and acquaintances. Because O'Hara's friends were primarily writers, artists and musicians, they often had public fame. Even so, some were more famous than others; and O'Hara names them in 'A Step Away from Them' as though differentiating them by the degrees of their intimacy with him: 'Bunny' was his close friend, the poet Bunny Lang; John Latouche was the writer and musician whose rented house O'Hara lived in for a while; Jackson Pollock was of course the famous 'action' painter. 'A Step Away from Them' is characteristic of O'Hara's 'I do this I do that' poems in the density of its naming: but naming the dead is testamentary and memorial, where naming the other objects of the poet's attention is vividly to itemize the actual. Naming the dead makes the poem the scene of an absence, the site of a haunting, as it does in Yeats's great elegiac poems, including 'Easter, 1916', where the recitation of names occasions a disturbance of gender in the male speaker of the poem: 'As a mother names her child / When sleep at last has come / On limbs that had run wild'. Given the interest in Yeats intermittently apparent in O'Hara's work – itself one manifest of the importance of his Irish-American background, which in various ways he rejected but never denied in his maturity – it is not inconceivable that the naming of friends in his work is an American vernacular equivalent of Yeats's proudly hieratic naming in his poems, where the names are sometimes those of well-known painters too. It is Dublin's Municipal Gallery after all that prompts his ringing self-advertisement, 'And say my glory was I had such friends'.

The melancholy tenderness attendant on naming in O'Hara is, I think, also a function of his chronological specificity. Mark Ford says of the lines culminating in 'it is 12.40 of / a Thursday' in 'A Step Away from Them' that 'they make us feel that poetry is not in opposition to time but somehow parallel to it'.[6] There is truth in this, and it is one of the essential ways in which the poem is for O'Hara, as John Ashbery has said, 'the chronicle of the creative act that produces it'.[7] Even so, the insistently reiterative keeping of time cannot but emphasize its passing too, particularly since we must be aware that however quickly and soon after experience O'Hara wrote his poems the act of writing 'it is 12.40' has to be already a memorial since, at the moment of writing, it is, of necessity, no longer the 12.40 of the actual lunch hour described.[8] The poem's present tense is a fiction, in which the past is written as if it were the present: but it is not. In that fictional *as if* the poem becomes memorial inscription. Chronology in O'Hara is therefore anxious or uneasy as well as exhilarated; there is the potential for panic in the poems' clocking of temporality, which is always a reminder of 'what may be destroyed at any moment'.

Such a recognition prompts the thought that 'Back to work' at the end of 'A Step Away from Them' may even be read as the poet deliberately pulling himself together, an acknowledgement of the way work can act as the displacement of melancholy. In this way, the O'Hara of 'A Step Away from Them' suddenly and quite unpredictably joins hands with the Philip Larkin of 'Toads Revisited' addressing what an earlier poem of his calls 'the toad work': 'Give me your arm, old toad; / Help me down Cemetery Road'. In this respect too, another moment in O'Hara's art criticism appears revealingly self-referential, as he distinguishes between Jackson Pollock and Franz Kline. The latter, he says, 'did not wish to be "in" his painting, as Pollock did, but to create the event of his passage, at whatever intersection of space and time, through the world'.[9] It could be that the word 'event' here has something of its seventeenth-century sense restored to it – O'Hara is always etymologically alert – and so means not just 'happening' but 'consequence' or 'outcome'. The 'event' in Kline would, then, be the painting itself, just as in O'Hara it would be the poem.

The elegiac is, in these ways, frequently an accompanying motion in O'Hara's emotional chronicles; but he rarely writes actual elegy, and when he does he does not always do so very successfully. 'The Tomb of Arnold Schoenberg', written in 1951, is laboured and mannered in a way one can hardly credit of this poet. A relatively orthodox, although unconventionally rhyming, sonnet, it is ridiculously stiff in its carriage, conventional in its imagery and as syntactically contorted as early John Berryman. The attempt to discover a formal means of addressing the greatly admired, recently dead composer betrays O'Hara into absurdly baroque posturing: 'I weep upon your bier, this glacial shore'. The poems commemorating James Dean – 'For James Dean', 'Thinking of James Dean' and 'Four Little Elegies' – are neither stiff nor formal in this way but they too strive to absorb and refract elegiac tropes in stylistically inept ways. Adapting the classical trope of chastising the gods or the fates, O'Hara manages to sound only petulant: 'you / have cut him from your table / which is built, how unfairly / for us! not on trees, but on clouds', where the over-insistence of the unnecessary exclamation point betrays an underlying insecurity about the viability of the imitation. In these poems elegiac obligation is corrupted by both self-identification and a capitulation to the popular mythologizing of the actor. The poet seems both self-pitying and self-aggrandizing when he writes, 'now I am this dead man's voice'. O'Hara's sexuality is obviously profoundly involved in this, but the male poet's identification with the (male) subject of elegy is by no means confined in literary history to gay poets. Even so, a strain of modern elegy involves guilt about, precisely, making the dead the subject of possibly opportunistic poetry: Thomas Hardy's *Poems of 1912-13* is a classic case. In this context, O'Hara's sentimental self-identification seems artlessly presumptuous and peculiarly graceless. The end of 'Thinking of James Dean' does, nevertheless, more mutedly and reflectively offer an image, in piercing appositional phrasing, of what true elegy may manage in the way of memorial witness: 'A leaving word in the sand, odor of tides: his name'. The word, which is James Dean's name, the name commemorated in this poem's title, is as potentially impermanent as a word written in the sand, which will be erased by the incoming tide; which is hardly more permanent than the epitaph John Keats conceived for his memorial stone shortly before his death: 'Here lies one whose name was writ in water'. Self-identification thereby takes a harsher, more self-lacerating edge, since the poem may be the 'leaving word' too, placed, like the actor's name, at the risk of tide and time.

By ending his elegy on the word 'name' itself, though, O'Hara is drawing attention to the responsible act which the recitation of names, such as that offered in 'A Step Away from Them', involves. Honouring the names is a form of ethical scruple quite distinct from, or even antithetical to, the camp 'theatricalization of experience' (Sontag) which can also be found in O'Hara; and his literary-critical prose, notably but not uniquely when he writes on Boris Pasternak in 'About Zhivago and His Poems', can be strikingly ethical in tendency and character; and Pasternak recurs several times as, in effect, a form of ethical touchstone in O'Hara's poems too. In the essay, O'Hara even writes wholly approvingly about the moral strength of Pasternak's Christianity, of its stern but loving opposition to what O'Hara calls 'the cheap tempestuousness of our time'; which is an empathetic acknowledgement truly remarkable from this flagrantly renegade ex-Catholic who writes, in 'Now That I am in Madrid and Can Think', that 'it's well known that God and I don't get along together'.[10]

'The Day Lady Died', O'Hara's quasi-elegy for Billie Holiday – a poem, that is, that registers powerful elegiac feeling without deploying any of the motifs characteristically associated with traditional elegy – appears almost camp in its political disengagement from the figure it commemorates, since it names neither her nor any of the circumstances of her life: the camp sensibility, Susan Sontag says, 'is disengaged, depoliticized – or at least apolitical', although this fails to appreciate what is often genuinely politically subversive or oppositional in it too.[11] In fact, however, 'The Day Lady Died' appears to reintroduce a politics of self-alignment by means of referential stealth. Doing so, it becomes a poem in which a strong but occluded or covert element of social or political responsibility protects O'Hara from the deleterious forms of self-interest to which he succumbs in his altogether too self-interested James Dean poems. The fact that the name of the celebrated figure is occluded in this poem also makes it impossible for O'Hara to indulge the popular mythology of Holiday's fame and persona, as he undoubtedly does when he prominently uses the too seductive name 'James Dean'.

As a consequence, 'The Day Lady Died' amply exemplifies the statement of poetic credo which O'Hara uncharacteristically made when he opposed what he regarded as a wrong-headed critique of the work of his fellow New York poet Kenneth Koch: 'I do not believe', he said then, that '"poetry is still a matter of private taste" but rather one of public responsibility'.[12] 'The Day Lady Died' is an 'I do this I do that' poem in which, despite the fact that it contains fifteen instances of the word 'I' in its twenty-eight lines, the 'I' is not egotistical, as O'Hara witheringly thought it was in the confessional poetics of Robert Lowell. The refusal to name the subject of the elegy is, paradoxically, a liberating act of disciplined continence, a self-denying ordinance. If this is spontaneously intuitive on O'Hara's part, as the poem's style and tone emphatically (but delicately) suggest it to be, it is also an aspect of his deep absorption of literary history, of his knowledge for instance of another great English elegy, Milton's 'Lycidas', of which he says that 'the subject ... has freed the poet's sensibility from the rather arch stylistic considerations of many other poems of that period. Stylistic preoccupation often makes for sameness, the trap of the look, of performance'.[13] This poem wonderfully liberates itself from the trap of the look:

The Day Lady Died

It is 12:20 in New York a Friday
three days after Bastille Day, yes
it is 1959, and I go get a shoeshine
because I will get off the 4:19 in East Hampton
at 7:15 and then go straight to dinner
and I don't know the people who will feed me

I walk up the muggy street beginning to sun
and have a hamburger and a malted and buy
an ugly NEW WORLD WRITING to see what the poets
in Ghana are doing these days
                              I go on to the bank
and Miss Stillwagon (first name Linda I once heard)
doesn't even look up my balance for once in her life
and in the GOLDEN GRIFFIN I get a little Verlaine
for Patsy with drawings by Bonnard although I do
think of Hesiod, trans. Richmond Lattimore or
Brendan Behan's new play or *Le Balcon* or *Les Nègres*
of Genet, but I don't, I stick with Verlaine
after practically going to sleep with quandariness

and for Mike I just stroll into the PARK LANE
Liquor Store and ask for a bottle of Strega, and
then I go back where I came from to 6th Avenue
and the tobacconist in the Ziegfeld Theater and
casually ask for a carton of Gauloises and a carton
of Picayunes, and a NEW YORK POST with her face on it

and I am sweating a lot by now and thinking of
leaning on the john door in the 5 SPOT
while she whispered a song along the keyboard
to Mal Waldron and everyone and I stopped breathing

III

Billie Holiday was nicknamed 'Lady Day' by the great jazz saxophonist Lester Young; O'Hara's title therefore plays with the nickname by reversing it to form a statement of elegiac chronology. Holiday died on 17 July 1959 at the age of 44. In an extremely difficult, damaged life, she had been addicted to alcohol and heroin; she had also been openly bisexual at a time when that was a flagrant breach of conventional American sexual mores. Constantly subject to police attention, she was jailed for eight months in 1947 and subsequently forbidden to sing where liquor was served. She was therefore possibly singing illegally in the 5 SPOT when O'Hara heard her, as he recalls at the end of his poem, although Joe LeSueur, who says he was there too, tells us in *Digressions on Some Poems by Frank O'Hara* that she had been there – at 'that shabby, unimposing jazz club' – privately that evening before agreeing to sing; he also thinks that it was probably the last time she ever did sing in public.[14]

Possibly Holiday's most famous song and certainly her most controversial, 'Strange Fruit', written and recorded in 1939, was virtually a Civil Rights song long *avant la lettre*, a precursor of such songs of the American 1960s as Bob Dylan's 'Only a Pawn in Their Game' and 'The Lonesome Death of Hattie Carroll'.[15] A song about the lynching of black people in the American South, it had begun as a poem by Abel Meeropol, a white Jewish schoolteacher from the Bronx, written under the pseudonym Lewis Allan; and, as such, it took its place, horribly, in a genre of 'lynch poetry' whose primary exponents were Langston Hughes, Gwendolyn Brooks and Robert Hayden. Meeropol's musical setting for his poem may have been developed by Holiday with her piano accompanist, Sonny White.[16] The lyrics alone are extraordinarily striking, with their traumatized and scathingly ironic metaphor of a 'pastoral scene of the gallant South' composed of trees bearing the 'strange fruit' of burning black flesh. Holiday's performances of the song left audiences in stunned silence, and her recorded rendering, both stoical and fraught, is devastating.[17] In 1933 Holiday had been signed to Columbia Records by the maverick producer John Hammond (who signed Dylan nearly thirty years later), but despite Holiday's subsequent popularity Columbia refused to record the song in 1939, and she was obliged to bring it out with another label, the leftish-inclined Commodore. She died of cirrhosis of the liver, a customary death for chronic alcoholics, and was once again under arrest at the time of her death.

O'Hara's strong emotional investment in Holiday is obvious in the poem. Her music was clearly of immense importance to him, even though he was himself classically trained and had at one time considered a career as a classical composer. Beyond this, the poem makes it clear too, without at all insisting on it, that both Holiday's blackness and her sexuality are of significance to him. David Lehman, in *The Last Avant-Garde: The Making of the New York School of Poets*, says that O'Hara was 'one of the first American poets to include [black people] matter-of-factly in his vision of America'; and in three poems, 'Personal Poem', 'Ode: Salute to the French Negro Poets' and 'Answer to Voznesensky & Evtushenko', the condition of American blacks in pre-Civil Rights days is alluded to or addressed. In 'Personal Poem', at the poet's lunchtime meeting with the black poet LeRoi Jones (who later changed his name to Amira Baraka), he learns that 'Miles Davis was clubbed 12 / times last night outside BIRDLAND by a cop': the poem, by so casually recording this shocking information and immediately moving on, makes it plain that in New York in 1959 such things are simply to be expected. Both of the other poems include – more problematically – O'Hara's registering of his own attitude. The former names Aimé Césaire, observing that 'if there is fortuity it's in the love we bear each other's differences / in race which is the poetic ground on which we rear our smiles'. The latter, an uncharacteristically vituperative poem, chastises the Russian poets of its title who during their visit to America in 1963 appear to have expressed opinions to which O'Hara took profound objection: 'we are tired', he says, 'of your dreary tourist ideas of our Negro selves'. Opposing such ideas, O'Hara celebrates 'the strange black cock which has become ours despite your envy' and offers a kind of taunting challenge: 'I consider myself to be black and you not even part'. This self-identification resembles that of the James Dean poems, although it is, obviously, more explicit and also more explicitly, boastfully sexual; which makes it unsurprising that Yusef Komunyakaa should have criticized the 'conspicuous exoticism' which O'Hara sometimes ascribes to blacks: 'When the human body becomes mere object,' he says, 'this kind of voyeurism dehumanises us'.[18] In 'Answer to Voznesensky & Evtushenko' O'Hara does come much too close for comfort both to indulging the stereotype of black people and to the phenomenon famously defined by Norman Mailer in an essay published in 1957: that of 'the white negro', the American hipster who enviously, or self-hatefully, apes black and jazz styles and lifestyles.[19]

'The Day Lady Died', however, is delicately tactful, oblique and reticent where that poem is almost shrilly insistent. Self-identification is now skilfully dispersed into the recorded particulars themselves, and these include a register of sexuality as well as ethnicity and, ultimately, of a shared mortality. This results in a poem of infinitely superior ethical scruple, responsibility and authority, and one in which the apparent spontaneity of O'Hara's casually improvisatory bebop poetics has astonishingly loaded every rift with ore. That the poem was in fact written fairly speedily, on the hoof, is attested by Joe LeSueur's account in *Digressions*. He was with O'Hara on the train trip to East Hampton – which, he tells us, is how it should be written, and not, as in the poem, 'Easthampton' – and over hors d'oeuvres, while a Billie Holiday record was playing, O'Hara read the poem he had written that afternoon. If this was indeed the case, then 'The Day Lady Died' is eloquent testimony to the way that, when O'Hara was writing at his most intensely concentrated, the riot of his particulars gathers itself – almost, it seems, by a centripetal aesthetics of the automatic – around a radiant nucleus of implication.

Although the poem opens with the registering of clock time characteristic of the 'I do this I do that' poems, it then – uniquely among them, I think – places clock time in the context of calendar time and of the more extensive calendar of historical time itself: 'three days after Bastille Day'. In France, Bastille Day is called 'Quatorze Juillet', and in fact there is a Bastille Day parade in Manhattan: so O'Hara's line tells us that the day Lady died is 17 July 1959. Bastille Day commemorates, of course, the storming of the Bastille on 14 July 1789 and the liberation of its prisoners at the beginning of the French Revolution. O'Hara's reference to it is, clearly, not simply an extension or ramification of chronological exactitude but carries emblematic weight. It proposes, I think, an idea, or an ideal, of liberation, of freedom from entrenched servitude, that inheres in his tribute to Billie Holiday, and initiates what becomes the poem's marked political edge. In the USA of 1959, just prior to the Civil Rights movement, in a country that, nearly two centuries since, had had its own revolution on the French model, the black singer Billie Holiday was frequently subject to the humiliations of segregation. She tells us in her autobiography *Lady Sings the Blues*, for instance, that she left Artie Shaw's band when she was obliged to use the back door of the hotel they were all staying in in New York. She could take it, or at least force herself to stand it, in the South, but not there. 'You can be up to your boobies in white satin,' she says, inimitably, 'with gardenias in your hair and no sugar cane for miles, but you can still be working on a plantation'.[20]

The concept of historical liberation inheres also in the only apparently casual reference to the magazine O'Hara buys, NEW WORLD WRITING, and his motive for buying it. The magazine, which in fact folded after eight years and fifteen issues in June 1959 – so that the poem must refer to its final issue – was, as its title makes clear, internationalist in aim and scope; and O'Hara's desire to find out from this issue 'what the poets in Ghana are doing these days' would have been motivated partly by the very recent history of the country: Ghana had gained its independence from Britain, its liberation from colonial status, only two years previously, in March 1957. O'Hara wants to find out, in a great American city in the middle of the twentieth century, how black poets in Africa are responding to liberation, whereas a great black American artist, Billie Holiday, descendant of African slaves, had been subjected to ancient servitudes in what had once also been a politically optimistic 'New World'. In this context, 'Lady Day', Holiday's nickname and the name coded into this poem's title, becomes a tenderly quasi-aristocratic honorific, of a kind few black women of Holiday's generation were ever likely to have been awarded by white men. (For O'Hara, what Holiday tells us in *Lady Sings the Blues* about her mixed ethnic origin as the inheritor of white Irish plantation-owning genes too, would undoubtedly have had poignant resonance if he knew it. Her birth-name was Eleanora Fagan.)

When the O'Hara of the poem enters the GOLDEN GRIFFIN bookshop the books he considers as possible gifts for a friend – she is Patsy Southgate, the writer and translator from the French – include a work congruent with the poem's concern with black ethnicity: Jean Genet's *Les Nègres* is a shockingly confrontational ritualistic play in which black actors re-enact the murder of a white woman for the entertainment of an audience of white establishment figures played by black actors in whiteface make-up. The play, a radical rehearsal of racial stereotypes, was written to commemorate Ghana's independence. Published in 1958, it was subsequently staged in a long off-Broadway production beginning in 1961. Genet seems equally significant in this context, though, because of his homosexuality, since the other books O'Hara considers buying are written by bisexuals. Paul Verlaine had a sexual relationship with the young Arthur Rimbaud, one richly commemorated in their jointly composed poem 'Le sonnet du trou du cul', which was published only posthumously, and clandestinely, in 1904 as the final poem in Verlaine's *Hombres*, a short sequence about gay sex. The Irish writer Brendan Behan's new play in 1959 was *The Hostage*, staged on Broadway, which concerns a young member of the IRA accused of killing a policeman. Behan had himself belonged to the organization, which of course considered itself a national liberation movement; and Behan was also bisexual. Although this was not publicly known during Behan's lifetime, O'Hara may well have been in the know.

The books O'Hara ponders in the GOLDEN GRIFFIN are, then, covertly aligned with Billie Holiday's sexuality and with O'Hara's own; and, in the USA in 1959 homosexual acts were subject to criminal prosecution. O'Hara is therefore coding into his elegy for Holiday an aspect of human identity in addition to ethnicity which, in his contemporary historical moment and geographical location, also requires liberation. Codings of his sexuality are everywhere in O'Hara's work; most usually, as we have seen, as a mode of camp sensibility (although camp is of course not exclusively gay). In this poem, for instance, the line 'after practically going to sleep with quandariness' is richly camp in its theatrical archness and also in the way it resists real understanding, since the state of being in a quandary might normally be expected to provoke anxious alertness rather than sleep: but this line is not 'normal', and 'quandariness' is not even in the OED. Possibly, sexuality rises a little out of the implicit just prior to this in the poem with the information that 'Miss Stillwagon (first name Linda I once heard) / doesn't even look up my balance for once in her life': is she being judgemental about a rather raffish (or 'gay-'looking) character, someone apparently well outside the norm of banking conventions? If so, O'Hara's Dickensian or Eliotic naming allows him to get his own back, making her appear chilly and prissy, joylessly still on the wagon. But in fact O'Hara's very interest in Billie Holiday in 1959 may well have been read as itself implicitly gay: John Hammond, tolerantly liberal and ahead of his time in so many ways, nevertheless apparently regarded it as a problem in her later career that 'homosexuals just *fell* for Billie' because, he thought, it made her 'mannered'.[21]

However, even if his sexuality is usually an implicit element, although a prominent one, of style, sensibility and address, there is at least one moment in O'Hara's work when he becomes resentfully explicit. The lengthy, capacious 'Biotherm (For Bill Berkson)', written in late 1961 and early 1962, includes this vignette:

> then too, the other day I was walking through a train
> with my suitcase and I overheard someone say 'speaking of faggots'
> now isn't life difficult enough without that
> and why am I always carrying something
> well it was a shitty looking person anyway
> better a faggot than a farthead
> or as fathers have often said to friends of mine
> 'better dead than a dope' 'if I thought you were queer I'd kill you'
> you'd be right to, DAD, daddio, addled annie pad-lark (Brit. 19th C.)
> > well everything can't be perfect
> > you said it

The puerile name-calling of O'Hara's response to the puerile name-calling he has endured – his almost shocking abandonment of customary ironic pose – suggests the bruising damage done by such abusive encounters; and we must assume that, although he included such a thing in a poem only once, he must have experienced it far more than once. Indeed, we should probably read the line 'And why am I always carrying something' as metaphorical as well as literal, referring not just to the encumbrance of suitcases and suchlike but to the encumbrance of a sexuality constantly prey to prejudice and to the violence implicit in prejudice. 'Now isn't life difficult enough without that', indeed; and O'Hara's more reflective response is not on the same level as that of his abuser, but a deconstruction of the authoritative paternal or patriarchal figure of the upper-case 'DAD' who would kill a queer son, by diminishing him derisively into the 1950s and 1960s hip patois 'daddio' and then, it appears, by discovering in an act of self-protective, hostile etymological scholarship an obscure or obsolete nineteenth-century rebuke (whose cryptic nature, however, has foiled my researches and inquiries).

'Well everything can't be perfect / you said it': but, actually, opposing all this 'shitty looking' stuff, some things can, and these are things that feature sometimes in O'Hara's poetry. One of them occurs in 'The Day Lady Died' after the poet buys 'a NEW YORK POST with her face on it' – so that her face, a sad, mechanically reproduced relic and metonym, appears in the poem, even if her name does not – and the concluding lines change everything, as they move from present to past tense, making 'The Day Lady Died' a poem you cannot really read, only reread. The fact that these lines are separated off from what precedes them also reveals with what deliberate care this poem is lineated. Its three longer verse divisions describe the lunchtime walking, and its fourth, final verse section – a quatrain – moves into the past and into reflection. It is almost as though the ghost of Shakespearean sonnet structure, with its four-part division – into three quatrains and concluding couplet – is somewhere in the poem's literary-historical memory too, turning free verse rapidity and lower-case linear initials into beautifully poised and shapely elegance of form. The poem ends like this:

> and I am sweating a lot by now and thinking of
> leaning on the john door in the 5 SPOT
> while she whispered a song along the keyboard
> to Mal Waldron and everyone and I stopped breathing

Not only does the poem never name Billie Holiday, it never actually specifies her death: only its title does that. But O'Hara's final lines conjure, and concentrate, an overwhelming presence in the space of elision or absence, even if this is a presence now only in the poet's own memory.

But who is 'The Day Lady Died' an elegy for, exactly? '[A]nd everyone and I stopped breathing' is ambivalent, even as it brings the wonderment of Holiday's artistry almost to our ears by literalizing the cliché of a 'breath-taking' performance. The absence of punctuation is itself a form of punctuation, as we have seen in Zbigniew Herbert's 'Elegy of Fortinbras'; and O'Hara's characteristic lack of punctuation means that phrases look syntactically backwards as well as forwards, so that poems catch us out, or overtake us, and we must try to catch up with them. Did she whisper the song to Mal Waldron and everyone, and then 'I [Frank O'Hara] stopped breathing'? Did she whisper the song along the keyboard to Mal Waldron and then 'everyone and I' stopped breathing? ('Whisper' is accurate about Holiday's later voice, while also tenderly making the song seem an open secret.) The stopping breathing is the response, the intake of breath, in spontaneous reaction to the astonishment of what Holiday is, or was, doing; to, that is, her genius. But 'stopping breathing' is also literally what Billie Holiday did on 17 July 1959. And stopping breathing is what 'everyone and I' will all eventually do. The poem also itself stops – we pause for breath if we are reading it aloud – at the moment that the phrase 'stopped breathing' stops.

In this way 'The Day Lady Died', which is in many ways one of the most unconventional elegies ever written, sophisticatedly rewrites one of the crucially complicating motifs of elegy: that is, that it always includes the elegist as well as the elegized and is inevitably therefore a form of narcissism, that motif given memorable parenthetical and ambiguous expression in Geoffrey Hill's 'September Song': '(I have made / an elegy for myself it / is true)'. Milton commemorating Edward King in 'Lycidas', Shelley commemorating Keats in 'Adonais', Auden commemorating Yeats in 'In Memory of W. B. Yeats', Berryman commemorating Stevens in 'So Long? Stevens': all are self-referential too, reflecting on their own mortality, and on matters of poetic heritage. In addition, such poems, in which one artist commemorates another, often have a competitively oedipal edge: Berryman's poem, for instance, acts as a vehicle for the judgement that Stevens is 'better than us; less wide', which is an acidly ambiguous, decidedly non-deferential compliment. 'The Day Lady Died' stands at an oblique angle to this tradition. Narcissistic of necessity, since thinking of anyone's death is inevitably to ponder one's own mortality, O'Hara is entirely free of artistic envy, lost in wonder at the art made possible by a woman whose life was so egregiously difficult. As a consequence, the poem manages the strangest of tones. For most of its length it is insouciant in its register of a sophisticated, urbane, middle-class metropolitan life – even if this evoked or performed ego can seem vulnerably self-conscious too – while at the same time insinuating in gesture and reference an altogether alternative world to which this wandering 'I' is also profoundly attached. But then, finally, while still saying nothing that would assert the value or quality of the life that has just ceased, the poem is truly devastated in the face of this death; and the silence into which it lapses at its close is that of genuine elegiac lament.

CHAPTER 10

Poison and Cure: Ted Hughes's Prose

I

'I have but an indifferent opinion of the prose-style of poets: not that it is not sometimes good, nay, excellent; but it is never the better, and generally the worse from the habit of writing verse', says Hazlitt, with characteristic pugnacity, at the opening of 'On the Prose-Style of Poets'.[1] Composer exclusively of prose, Hazlitt has his own axe to grind here: but his strictures about the prose of the Romantics that follow in this essay, and his opposing recommendation of the virtues of another exclusive writer of prose, Edmund Burke, are still worthy of attention in the way they suggest that poets can easily forget the strengths prose needs. Even if we have long since learned to admire the varied virtues of, say, *Biographia Literaria* and the *Preface* to *Lyrical Ballads*, which is itself extensively taken up with the similarities and dissimilarities of verse and prose, it is salutary to attend to Hazlitt on the magnificence of a prose style which differs from poetry 'like the chamois from the eagle'; whereas a poet's style, craving 'continual excitement' and therefore always aspiring to the condition of the eagle, may have scant respect for the necessary agility, persistence and level-headedness of the chamois, in for the long haul.

Necessarily, however, such strictures are less appropriate to a post-Romantic period initiated by Ezra Pound's recommendation that poetry be at least as well-written as prose; one in which by far the dominant form of poetry has been free verse, not metre; in which successive 'ages of criticism' have flourished; and in which poets have varyingly accommodated themselves to or even, in the cases at least of Eliot and Empson, moulded the forms and styles of the literary-critical academy. As a consequence, we are likely to be sceptical about what may well now seem Hazlitt's prescriptivism, and to admire rather than derogate a prose developed from, or dependent on, the habit of writing verse. We may even admire a prose congruent with a poet's verse, in which a poem may be discovered in gestation, or the motive or movement of mind or sensibility necessary to a poem may be found compellingly acknowledged. Such diverse instances as Wallace Stevens's *The Necessary Angel*, by turns pellucid and resisting the intelligence almost successfully; passages of meditative near-entrancement in Seamus Heaney; and the spiritedly acerbic camp, both comically spontaneous and genuinely self-explanatory, of Frank O'Hara's 'Personism: A Manifesto' are all ungainsayable adjuncts to the muse's diadem.

In such a context it becomes possible to say at least neutrally but even admiringly that Ted Hughes's prose is often poetry by other means. Here are four examples from what are normally considered quite different types of prose writing.

In one of the *Tales of the Early World*, a children's book, Woman wants a playmate and God tries to fathom what she has in mind. She wants it to be 'beautiful and exciting', she says, 'like the sea'. God gets the idea and plunges into the ocean, creating 'a white commotion':

> And as he rode up into the breakers a huge shaggy head reared out of the water ahead of him. She saw its deep-sea staring eyes. It reared a long neck, draped with seaweed … Then its shoulders heaved up, and as the great comber burst around it, it turned. She saw its long side, like a giant white-silver shark. For a moment it seemed to writhe and melt, as if it were itself exploding into foam, and the next thing God was rolling up the beach, battered by foam.[2]

God, by the process of accident and approximation that characterizes his creative endeavours in these tales, has generously attuned himself to Woman's desire and has fashioned her a horse. This is an event in nature and, simultaneously, in language. The horse is created by the similitude of shape which the rising and arching wave, the excited behaviour of the sea, shares with a horse's head, that similitude which, in a mode of back-formation, brings the expression 'white horses' into the language. It is also created out of what Woman perceives elsewhere in this passage as 'the sea's hoarse, constant roar'. God creates, that is, by means of a visual and aural pun. Woman's own similitude, in which the sea's metamorphosis is first perceived as a 'white-silver shark', has to be re-educated as God's new animal simultaneously enters the world, language and her cognition, all of which are themselves writhing and melting in this virtuoso passage of enthusiastic imagining.

In 'Sylvia Plath and Her Journals', one of the many places in which Hughes's prose accompanies his poetry's enduring engagement with the writer and her work, he evokes what he regards as distinctively essential to her by adducing Shakespeare's Ariel and Plath's own – Ariel was the name of her horse and *Ariel* the title of her most famous volume – as a combinatory metaphor to distinguish her from 'the normal flowering and fruiting kind of writer'. Plath, says Hughes, is a writer whose work is 'roots only':

> Almost as if her entire oeuvre were enclosed within those processes and transformations that happen in other poets before they can even begin, before the muse can hold out a leaf. Or as if all poetry were made up of the feats and shows performed by the poetic spirit Ariel. Whereas her poetry is the biology of Ariel, the ontology of Ariel – the story of Ariel's imprisonment in the pine, before Prospero opened it.[3]

The Ariel metaphor acts almost as an electrification of what might otherwise seem a slightly precious, derivatively Coleridgean organicism here, conveying with justness the sheer scale of Plath's difference from other writers. That difference is characterized too by a strong hint of dark magic in Plath's 'roots', the magic which is Sycorax's before it is Prospero's; and Hughes's *Birthday Letters* reveals how strongly he figured not only Plath's poetry but his own too, and his relationship with Plath, in terms offered by Shakespeare's play. The passage therefore richly conveys Hughes's sense of Plath's exceptionalism, which is implicitly made to echo or even rival Shakespeare's, and which Hughes registers in everything he writes about her. His prose here seems virtually a form of cohabitation with the deep structures of her verse and is almost biomorphically definitive. Present in its few sentences too is a view of Plath intimated throughout the course of Hughes's writing about her. She is a poet of a heroic but ultimately unwinnable struggle against overwhelming psychological odds; but she is attuned always to a plot of mythical articulation and transformation, in the single long poem of which her individual poems are component, sometimes warring, parts, and she is not at all an exponent of confessional discourse, as she has frequently been (disastrously) misread.

When Hughes discusses his own poems in his prose it can be interpretatively transformative. On 'The Thought-Fox' in *Poetry in the Making* and on 'In the Likeness of a Grasshopper' in the 'Myths, Metres, Rhythms' essay collected in *Winter Pollen* he is mesmerizing. The latter is given an aura of melancholy by Hughes's knowledge that, in writing a poem about a grasshopper at all, he is writing ecological elegy about 'any grassy place in England before Agrochemicals imposed their final solution'; and his genuinely helpful prose gloss on the poem enters into serious poetic competition with it: 'Soon, a Song (silent, still uncaught) comes along, searching for the sexual life – on which it lives (Song being nourished by love)'.[4] It is almost as though Hughes is back in the creative place itself, setting an illuminating lamp of prose beside the poem's original manuscript, inserting a second co-creative self between poem and reader in a uniquely sympathetic form of close reading; reading, as it were, from the inside out.

Despite such performances polished for publication – although in this case Hughes is quoting his own responses in a letter to a 'courteous and yet baffled' inquirer – what he says briefly of the poem 'Thistles' in a little note to his sister Olwyn shortly after he had first published it is almost as valuable in the way it turns one of his greatest poems in an altogether unpredictable light. This prose is not so much mirror or lamp as, in a metaphor he himself deploys elsewhere, the laser light of a radically experimental modernism:

> Thistles was a sort of Picasso thistles – the plant, you see, from an academic point of view, being the nucleus of associations on the whole more important than the plant. Also a sort of Walt Disney thistles, and Klee thistles. Not really thistles. Their plume isn't red, each has several plumes, etc. It's a scherzo, not very serious. The idea of the decayed Viking was really the main one – the one I'd had before & been amused by.[5]

A scherzo and not really serious, maybe, but only as Picasso, Disney and Klee are not really serious in their playful (or popular) forms of attention; and a scherzo serious enough to open this poet's greatest single volume, *Wodwo*, in 1967. *Wodwo* stays unmanageable, disconcerting and plain weird in all sorts of ways, and always excitingly so; but it is, since the publication of this letter, at least the kind of thing we might almost expect from a poet who finds the idea of a decayed Viking amusing, and tells his sister so. The few sentences also reveal, though, how Hughes, while he is most definitely a 'nature poet', one of the strongest English poetry has had, has a sophisticated conception, early in his creative life, of the way the natural image is always, in writing, emblem too, as he defines these thistles which are 'not really thistles' and indicates that in a poem a plant may be itself but is also, and more importantly, a 'nucleus of associations'. These words to his sister may seem casually thrown off in a letter but they are dense with implication for the recovery of a Hughesian aesthetic.

We may be well used to reading the letters of writers, many of which, we must assume, were not written for publication, although this is always hard to tell: but private letters not written for publication always to some extent put us in the position of voyeurs, hardly knowing how to position ourselves in relation to the prurient interest they permit or provoke. This is intensely so with some of Ted Hughes's letters since his biography has, in some of its detail, been the subject of such extensive, often melodramatic speculation. In fact, in Christopher Reid's selection the profile of Hughes that emerges is at least as much that of a father as it is of a lover and husband, and we must think hard about a man left alone with the daunting prospect of bringing up young children. The letters to his son Nick in this volume are admirable: in the patient dedication of their paternal concern and counsel; in their delighted apprehension of shared interests; and notably in the strength of their readiness to discuss the thing father and son share of absolute necessity, Sylvia Plath and her memory. Even very deep affection between fathers and sons is sometimes, I think, expressed only through irony. Ted Hughes's letters to Nick are not like that. This brief passage, written towards the very end of Hughes's life, in a letter in which he eventually accounts for *Birthday Letters*, his volume of poems addressed to Plath, makes vibrantly articulate between father and son both vulnerable human necessity and the fundamental necessity for a writer of the act of writing out of – in both senses – that vulnerability:

> What I was needing to do, all those years, was deal with what had happened to your mother and me. That was the big unmanageable event in my life, that had somehow to be managed – internally – by me. Somehow through my writing – because that's the method I've developed to deal with myself. In Ireland, I did find a way of dealing with it – not by writing about it directly, but dealing with the deep emotional tangle of it <u>indirectly</u>, through other symbols, which is the best and most natural way.[6]

This needs little comment, other than to note that the 'method' defended here, which gave us, we must assume, such volumes as *Crow*, *Gaudete* and *Cave Birds*, is also the one Hughes identifies and defines in Plath herself; and that something else, externally now, between father and son, rather than internally, is also being managed here, very well.

II

These passages focus aspects of Hughes's prose which I want to consider in this chapter: his work for children; his observations on poetry; and the new thing added to our conception and understanding of this poet by the publication of his letters. But first Hughes's deep ambivalence about writing prose at all needs to be considered. This is peculiar, since the prose is remarkably extensive, including five books of children's stories; a collection of radio talks for children; a large volume of literary and other essays which omits a considerable amount of published material but includes the outstanding essay on English versification, 'Myths, Metres, Rhythms', and a vast, controversial study of Shakespeare, both of which I have discussed extensively elsewhere;[7] the stories originally published together with poems in *Wodwo*, reprinted along with others as *Difficulties of a Bridegroom* (1995); and Christopher Reid's selection from, it appears, a huge archive of letters. In addition, prose of a highly charged, sometimes lineated, kind – 'rough verse', Hughes calls it – constitutes the form of *Gaudete* (1977).[8]

Two other works, in which poetry and prose are interdependent, are also relevant to a consideration of Hughes's ambivalence: the ur-*Crow*, in which the poems eventually published in 1970 as *Crow: From the Life and Songs of the Crow* were to have been plotted into a prose narrative;[9] and his laureate poems, some of which are freighted with mythological and arcane reference and extensively annotated in lengthy, essayistic and opinionated footnotes, in a way possibly owing something to David Jones, whom Hughes admired. *Rain-Charm for the Duchy and Other Laureate Poems* (1992) is not often considered very seriously by people who write about Hughes, but it could be argued that the relationship between poem and prose which obtains in it emblematizes an essential in Hughes's work, since some of the Laureate Poems are virtually incomprehensible without their notes. The prose is therefore essential to the poems' semantic survival, in a form of responsive and responsible authorial-critical behaviour; although whether the notes justify the opacity of the poems is another matter. Hughes's letters suggest that prose was similarly vital, if not exactly in this way, to the survival of his poetry, even that he regarded his poetry and prose as in some sense sharing a symbiotic relationship. The letters also offer an arresting chronology, making it plain that Hughes was in fact at work on children's stories prior to the publication of his first volume of poetry, *The Hawk in the Rain*, in 1957.

Writing to Olwyn as early as 1956, he says he has discovered his 'secret': that he can write poems only when he is busy with prose at the same time.[10] This early perception of prose as poetic enablement is maintained in a letter to his brother in 1957 in which, while admitting the desirability of the financial benefits of children's stories to a freelance writer, he still insists that they 'come to me absolutely naturally so I'm not prostituting my imagination', and he hyperbolically envisages writing about 5,000 of them.[11] In 1961 he tells the Irish poet John Montague, also a writer of short stories as well as verse, that prose stories 'help me write verse – get the machine going unself-consciously, very necessary in my case'.[12] And in 1969 he tells Richard Murphy that the *Crow* poems 'make more sense with the prose story', clearly then regarding the work as an integration of prose and poetry. As such, it would probably have further developed the dual form initiated by *Wodwo*, itself possibly prompted by Robert Lowell's revolutionary 1959 volume, *Life Studies*. Our knowledge of its original conception means that *Crow* must have, even for its admirers, what Hughes's subtitle may imply and what he says Coleridge's 'Ballad of the Dark Ladie' actually does have, 'an amputated kind of completeness'.[13] This is an oxymoronic notion; but, transferred to the way the poems of *Crow* seem provokingly both fragmentary and at the service of an occulted teleology, it has persuasive hermeneutic power.

Nevertheless, prose is also for Hughes, and from the beginning too, a kind of catastrophe. At issue here is prominently but not exclusively the prose of speculative or argumentative discourse rather than fictional narrative. Hughes makes a point of preserving, in the brief essay 'The Burnt Fox' in *Winter Pollen*, his often reiterated undergraduate dream of a smouldering, bloody-handed, anthropoid fox which convinces him to change his degree from English to Archaeology and Anthropology because, the fox says, the writing of critical prose is 'destroying us'.[14] Even if this seems too perfect a Hughesian-mythical fit, another kind of 'story', to be entirely credible as an actual dream, or at least as an accurate transcription of a dream, the letters are, corroboratively, frequently negative about prose. In 1983, disparaging in humorously crude terms his long essay on Leonard Baskin, Hughes registers extreme exasperation, saying he will write no more prose and claiming that he cannot recognize himself in it.[15] A decade later he explains that he abandoned writing stories for adults because those in *Wodwo* turned out to be 'prophecies about my own life'.[16] This is eerie and also tantalizing: but the apparent ability of these stories to tap into an obviously terrifying authorial uncanny could hardly have been more powerfully expressed than by Hughes's decision to stop writing them; which must have been to risk a form of permanent blockage for a writer who has regarded prose as necessary to verse composition.

This self-protective self-denial consorts with Hughes's feelings about the vast prose effort represented by *Shakespeare and the Goddess of Complete Being* (1992). In a letter to Seamus Heaney in 1998, the last year of Hughes's life, he raises the symbiotic inter-relationship between his poetry and prose in a form especially piercing because self-doubting when he says, 'I sometimes wondered if that Shakes [*sic*] tome wasn't the poem I should have written – decoded, hugely deflected and dumped on shoulders that could carry it'.[17] Some readers of the *Goddess* have wondered not this exactly, but almost the obverse: whether the book was not, by other (prose) means, the poem which he did in fact write as virtually his life's work, in extended sequences which discover alternative ways of both approaching and deflecting a single, inescapable node of distress and finding new encodings for it, a distress whose simplest name is 'Sylvia Plath'. That these sequences acted in part therapeutically is what he admits in the letter to Nick quoted above. It is the distress of writing the cognate Shakespeare prose, though, which prompts the harrowing negativity of letters in which Hughes blames it for destroying his 'immune system'.[18]

By preventing Hughes from writing English essays, the fox of his undergraduate dream had presumably prevented a community of dream-foxes from being killed: but, by backsliding so catastrophically into prose, Hughes had, he appears to have thought towards the end of his life, virtually killed himself. It may seem heartless to say so but there must be fantastication, even of a melodramatic kind, in this. Nevertheless, it is clear that for Ted Hughes prose is simultaneously obligation and exacerbation, essential to his life as a poet and at the same time dangerous to his life as a man. It may even be said that prose is for this writer a kind of *pharmakon*, the Greek word meaning both poison and cure which Jacques Derrida famously discussed as an almost vertiginously endless play of irresolvable signification.

III

As cure, Hughes's prose is prominently associated with children. Although children's stories were there from the beginning for him, as I have shown, their importance has not always been recognized by those who write primarily about his poetry, although it is always recognized by poets who write for children and by other children's writers. Some of Hughes's stories engage riches of anthropological material of the kind which also fuel a great deal of his poetry; and his 'creation tales', eventually collected in *The Dreamfighter* (2003), may be contemporary 'just so' stories on the Kipling model but they are also continuous with the mythical and metaphysical effort and effects of some of his poetic sequences. In particular, the figure they identify as 'God' almost scandalously diverges from the figure so named in the Bible; to the extent, I assume, of making some of these stories extremely problematical for Christian or quasi-Christian classrooms. They appear to subvert the narrative of Genesis or, at the very least, to relativize its truth-value. Even in a largely post-Christian or post-religious culture the word 'God' continues to carry high valency. José Saramago wonders in *The Gospel According to Jesus Christ* whether one of the things wrong with God is that, unlike everyone else, he does not share his name with anyone; in Ted Hughes he does.

Hughes's is an anthropomorphic God subject to nightmare, for instance, and to a hectoring mother who, like Hamm's parents in their dustbins in *Endgame*, lives submerged under rubbish. Far more significantly, this is a God for whom Creation is not the serene authoritativeness of a seven-day plan but a matter of frustrated accident and happenstance. He therefore bears a strong family resemblance to the figure named 'God' in *Crow*; and in this context the original prose-and-verse conception of that sequence takes on added significance. Neil Roberts tells us that 'Earth-Moon', which was published as a children's poem in *Moon-Whales and Other Poems* (1976), was originally written for *Crow* and that Hughes once, 'perhaps provocatively', described *Crow* as a children's story.[19] Anyone who remembers Hughes's readings from that book in the 1970s, with their combinations of verse and apparently partly improvised prose, will find this tantalizing. His beguiling, sometimes almost hypnotic, voice, with its slow Yorkshire inflections, had the paradoxically almost assuaging power necessary to a bedtime story; and

Crow does in fact include a poem called 'A Bedtime Story'. For all its bleakness, *Crow* is not entirely unlike Hughes's children's stories, which are unsparing of children's emotional aptitudes as they are conventionally, perhaps sentimentally, conceived. The stories frequently engage forms of sadness and distress without anxiety or condescension: in this story of creation such things just are. Exhaustion with life may lead to thoughts of suicide, for instance; and one haunting moment figures the bee's labour of pollination as the carrying of a demon's tears in his veins. He needs the sweetness of flowers to make him happy, but 'When he is angry and stings, the smart of his sting is the tear of the demon'.[20] The tears of things smart and sting in these stories too.

Hughes appears to have possessed and nourished a rapport with children probably unusual in a man of his generation. His prose for children is profoundly at one with the elements of wonder, mystery and amazement that may also be read out of some of the poetry. This is in part a romantic indebtedness, a keeping of the imaginative lines of communication open by keeping them attuned to the virtue of original impulse and the poignancy of its falling-off; and Hughes is, in this sense, after Yeats and Lawrence, another of the last romantics, given that 'romanticism' seems, as literary history advances, a diagnostic term less relevant to chronology than to individual temper.

IV

Hughes's prose for children is earthed, though, in anthropology at least as much as in aesthetics, and specifically in the belief expressed epigrammatically in the essay 'Myth and Education' that 'Every new child is nature's chance to correct culture's error'.[21]

One of Hughes's most compelling, if eccentric, prose pieces is a contribution to a 60th birthday *festschrift* for William Golding in 1986. Entitled 'Baboons and Neanderthalers', and nominally taking *The Inheritors* for theme, the essay displays knowledge of the anthropological theories of Eugene Marais, which Hughes finds credible, even compelling. People, says Beckett's Estragon in *Waiting for Godot*, 'are bloody ignorant apes'. Quite the contrary, thinks Marais, according to Hughes: people are over-intelligent apes; premature baboons, in fact, miscarried at a developmental stage when intelligence far outran affective and instinctual capacities. Hughes's unforgettable figure for Marais man is thus 'a jittery Ariel among the Calibans'; and this is appropriately Shakespearean, since what *Shakespeare and the Goddess of Complete Being* calls 'the Shakespearean moment' is, in one of its aspects, 'the inevitable crime of Civilization, or even the inevitable crime of consciousness'.[22] Art and culture are to be understood as compensation for the repression in the unconscious of the consequences of baboon miscarriage, which produced humans suffering a tragic misfit between intelligence and instinct.

As far as I know, Marais' theory is held in no repute by contemporary science, and its undoubted poetry is at least as comic as it is tragic. But its view of human nature as animal perversion and of art's compensatory necessity account for a great deal in Ted Hughes: notably, for his valorizing of the identity between animal intelligence and instinct as the very ground of his poetic endeavour and its occasions, and his interest in anthropological accounts of the way the curative powers of shamanic figures work in so-called 'primitive' societies. The effort of some of Hughes's prose has itself a quasi-shamanic function: its diagnostic attention is engaged as thoroughly as it is because it attempts to draw the poison of civilization and consciousness; and any potentially curative capacity it might have involves its author in the risk of being, himself, poisoned. However far-fetched this may seem, some such view of the urgency of his prose occasions does appear to underwrite the engagements of his later career.

In *Shakespeare and the Goddess of Complete Being* the crime of consciousness finds a local habitation in the mapping of Shakespeare's agonized sexuality onto the religio-political crisis of his time. The long essays on poetry and poets written in the latter part of Hughes's life – written, we might say, against time – are wracked by comparable efforts of identification. They make comparable demands of attention on their readers too when Hughes almost naively trusts that reiteration, microscopic attentiveness, variations of perspective and, occasionally, a Lawrentian resort to exclamatory enthusiasm and hyperbole will supply for conventional discursive argument. Secure architectonic control is not a Hughesian virtue in these long pieces; and we might well find ourselves returning in exhaustion to Hazlitt's relevant praising of the chamois.

'Sylvia Plath: The Evolution of "Sheep in Fog"', 'The Poetic Self: A Centenary Tribute to T. S. Eliot' and 'The Snake in the Oak', on Coleridge, all derive ultimately, as *Shakespeare and the Goddess of Complete Being* does, from Yeats, who is in all sorts of ways the originary poet for Hughes. The Shakespeare book makes its Yeatsian inception epigraphic:

> The Greeks, a certain scholar has told me, considered that myths are the activities of the Daimons, and that the Daimons shape our characters and our lives. I have often had the fancy that there is some one myth for every man, which, if we but knew it, would make us understand all he did and thought.[23]

Hughes's essential effort in these essays is, consequently, to identify the single myth in these poets – which might in fact be syncretic, as when Plath is discovered combining Phaeton and Icarus – and to unravel, with a species of agonistic patience, the way this is a 'daemonic' given which the poet must first identify and locate and then work through in the accumulating individual poems of an entire life. These poems therefore become, for Hughes, phases of self-knowledge and self-development, 'chapters in a mythology', as he calls them in relation to Plath. Poems have what Hughes calls, also apropos Plath, 'inexorable inner laws' which must be obeyed under penalty of emotional and artistic disintegration. They are the symbolic representation or projection of the very struggle to constitute psychological and emotional equilibrium, or the humbled or desperate confession of an ultimate inability to do so.[24]

The human risk of poetry is therefore almost appallingly high: the cost is potentially not less than everything. In these essays, then, Hughes is not so much a literary critic as both the intuitive diviner and the practised investigator of the occult secret of the individual oeuvre. For all that his archetypal mythologizing has an avatar in Jung, his procedures sometimes resemble Freud's in his case studies, the Freud who loved Conan Doyle and sometimes reads like him, in transposed register; and Hughes can evince, too, a comparably almost unnerving assurance in both his procedures and their results. Sometimes, as in the Plath essay, this assurance dazzles with illumination, and Hughes's insights cannot be ignored, although they can, of course, be challenged. At other times, however, it seems to dazzle Hughes himself. Despite the immensely high regard for, and estimate of, Eliot displayed by 'The Poetic Self', that essay illuminates no poet of that name recognizable to me. Unjustified assurance comes to seem therefore, as it always does, presumptive, and leads only to our questioning the grounds on which judgement and discrimination are being made. Hughes's method is manifestly intended as its own justification, as much a form of medical as of literary diagnosis; and one cannot help but think that an invitation is implicitly being extended to the reader to explicate the single myth of Hughes's own oeuvre.

Hughes's valuation of poems is, then, something other than aesthetics. In attempting to trace the contours of the activities of the daimons, 'the powers in control of our life, the ultimate suffering and decision in us', these late, nominally literary essays share some of the occult interests which disconcerted otherwise appreciative reviewers of the letters. This is an unignorable aspect of Hughes's prose, in which such matters as astrology, witchcraft, superstition, shamanism and occult Neoplatonism often arrest and sometimes consume his attention, impeding progress. Disconcertion is probably inevitable unless the reader shares at least some of Hughes's idiosyncratic beliefs; and the letters in particular manifest the obsessive-compulsive in this regard, notably when their recipients appear to be uncritical admirers. The idiosyncrasy, however, is at root a suspicion of the reflex assumptions of rationality, a hostility to scientism, and an underwriting of the ecology apparent throughout Hughes's life and writing and rendered parabolic in *The Iron Woman* (1993).

It is one of the paradoxes of Hughes's prose therefore that it relishes contemporary scientific terminology. This is probably best read as the register of a combative desire to appropriate and make differently usable, as part of an alternative epistemological and even ontological effort, the language of error. Nevertheless, it can disconcert often enough too, as the shaman dons the antiseptic gloves of the laboratory.

V

The poisoned chalice of Ted Hughes's prose is elevated effortfully, then, above error; and the effort, I have suggested, sometimes shows at the levels of style and argument. It is a relief, always, to turn to the grace and subtlety of those simply memorable statements made more casually about poets he admires.

On Keith Douglas: 'inside each line an entirely fresh melody starts up, forges a quick path against our expectation, and leaves the line as a trace of its passage, while a quite different melody, from some unexpected angle, inscribes another flourish beneath it, followed by another just as surprising'.[25] Hughes here demonstrates a talent for the closest of close reading, in both the accuracy of sympathetic analysis and the specificity of aural attention. He suggestively evokes the almost aleatory nature of Douglas's music, which many have found difficult to hear at all. He conveys its ultra-modern restlessness, appreciating the risky adventure of a rhythm subverting itself in the very act of articulation. In addition, forging a path and leaving a trace could be implicitly military metaphors and therefore empathetically appropriate to the poet of such work as 'How to Kill' who was himself killed during the Second World War at the age of 24, leaving his angular lines as the trace of his own passage.

On Emily Dickinson: despite their trust in the life she loves, her poems constantly approach 'almost a final revelation of horrible Nothingness … remaining true to this, she could make up her mind about nothing. It stared through her life. Registering everywhere and in everything the icy chill of its nearness, she did not know what to think'.[26] This turns Dickinson inside out in the way her poems sometimes turn themselves, carrying what initially appears to be warmth to a sudden freezing point, or opening gaping chasms in what had seemed solid ground. The scepticism of what Hughes believes her sense of Nothingness prompts her to ('she could make up her mind about nothing') is so intrinsic to her poems that we might think of it as forming both the rationale of her (lack of) punctuation and the reason for her vast productivity. Hughes phrases this with a little flicker of ambiguity: she did not know what to think about anything; or, she knew exactly what to think about nothing, since she thought about nothing else. And he reads that response as itself an act of attention virtually religious in its devotion, producing the (eventually) published liturgy of an intense privacy, a negative revelation.

On Dylan Thomas in his letters: 'Somewhere inside his head was a miniature replica of the world, with heavens and hells to match, in a brilliant radiance, slightly caricature, but quite real: it tumbles through his prose.' This characterization of Thomas's microcosmic representation of an actual world which, by the vivid light of peculiar and peculiarly artful imagination, becomes alternatively actual, itself brilliantly replicates in critical prose the brilliant replications of its subject, even while intimating an element of critique. Then, meditating further on the way Thomas's letters form 'the best introduction to the way his poetry ought to be read', Hughes says: 'Everything we associate with a poem is its shadowy tenant and part of its meaning, no matter how New Critical purist we try to be'.[27] The generalization, made against a critical orthodoxy – *the* critical orthodoxy of the Cambridge curriculum which this critic had himself rejected – is all the more compelling because of the proof just given of this critic's own competence within the terms of that very orthodoxy. It is compelling in other ways too: and the phrase 'shadowy tenant' vividly summons the material – biographical or historical, for instance, the stuff of letters, or mythical-psychoanalytical, the stuff of Hughes's readings – which critical dispensations less narrow than the New Critical might lure from its resident dark corners in poems.

In Hughes's remarks on living poets in his letters there are varieties of both acuity and generosity of the kind we find elsewhere in the letters too. Generosity is outstandingly present in the unenviously complimentary letter he sent Seamus Heaney when he won the Nobel Prize in 1995.[28] But there is also occasionally an acerbic humour, expressed with excellent comic timing. Eliot's smile, for instance, is 'like someone recovering from some serious operation'; and, of Neruda, 'he read torrentially for about 25 minutes off a piece of paper about 3" by 4". Then he turned it over, & read on', where the comma is deliciously placed, and the ampersand appropriately and surely satirically urgent.[29]

With regard to Eliot, however, whom, 'The Poetic Self' makes plain, Hughes revered above all other moderns – indeed, it appears, above all other poets except Shakespeare – the satire is ultimately subdued to awe: 'when he spoke, I had the impression of a slicing, advancing, undeflectible force of terrific mass. My image for it was – like the bows of the Queen Mary'.[30] The 'image' here – for earned authority and a terrifyingly absolute singularity of aim – is itself made use of in a memorial poem for Hughes by Seamus Heaney, to whom Hughes had presumably said something similar in conversation. In 'Stern' in *District and Circle* (2006) the prose-style of a poet therefore becomes, fittingly, a new poem by another poet. A private conversation between poets turns into the public conversation of literary history, the register of a continuity of poets – Eliot, Hughes, Heaney – vigilantly looking out for one another, in several senses, as Heaney conceives of himself 'standing on a pierhead watching him / All the while watching me as he rows out'.

CHAPTER 11

Back Home: Bob Dylan, Now and Then

Ah, but I was so much older then
I'm younger than that now

'My Back Pages', *Another Side of Bob Dylan* (1964)

As Dylan approached his seventieth birthday on 24 May 2011, I had been listening for a while to *The Original Mono Recordings*, usually known as the Mono Box, and *The Witmark Demos: 1962-1964*, both released late in 2010. The Mono Box puts back into circulation mono versions of the first eight albums, from *Bob Dylan* in 1962 to *John Wesley Harding* in 1967; *The Witmark Demos*, volume 9 of Dylan's ongoing 'Bootleg Series', brings into official circulation for the first time an astonishing range of material – 47 songs in all, in less than three years – which Dylan recorded for his first publishing companies, Leeds Music and M. Witmark & Sons, only some of which were ever officially studio-recorded and released by Dylan himself. Many, however, have appeared over the years on bootleg recordings, as have a very large number of Dylan's other songs and variant versions and accounts of songs. Hence the title of this series, in Dylan's commandingly insouciant reclamation of his own copyright.

* * *

So as Dylan approached 70 I was thinking about his twenties. These albums, though, are the product also of Dylan in later life. The Bootleg Series has long since made him his own editor. This is not a neutral activity. It involves emotional, psychic and interpretative investment. Are we to read the Mono Box, for instance, only as Dylan's sudden, even unlikely, perhaps nostalgic, desire that we hear him in mono again after all these years, or is he implicitly offering this phase of his career as a completed arc, one that now comes with exceptionally high authorial approval and imprimatur? Or, should we read it as the definition of such an arc by an artist confident that his later, still continuing, work does not pale even in the light of this early incandescence? This would be an artist therefore also confident that, against many odds, his exceptionally lengthy career has resourcefully negotiated a not uncommon kind of twentieth-century American aesthetic catastrophe: that of the spectacular earlier career forever shadowing all subsequent work. Think of Orson Welles, Truman Capote, Marlon Brando, Peter Bogdanovich. The rubric for this successful negotiation would be one of Dylan's most teasing but also most provocative aphorisms about creativity: 'She knows there's no success like failure / And that failure's no success at all'. She is someone therefore, this artist who don't look back, who knows what Samuel Beckett knows too when he offers the acerbically ambivalent advice – is it heartening or disheartening? – to 'Fail better'.

* * *

Thinking about the Bootleg Series is to think not only about paradox but oxymoron, since a legal bootleg is a contradiction in terms, one that inevitably disciplines to the usual market forces what had once been excitingly clandestine, contraband, *samizdat*. The Bootleg Series makes for a wholly different economy in the Dylan oeuvre. In the light of this, I want to think about some occasions of Dylan, mainly but not exclusively in his twenties. Not a thesis but a few notions, notes and queries – and quotations.

* * *

Dylan was 19 when he made his first album: but at least part of him was as old as the blues singers he was imitating, and that is older than the hills among which they sat. Jesse Fuller, Bukka White, Blind Lemon Jefferson: magically remote, darkly attractive names when I first read them on the sleeve of that album when I was 13 or 14. But when I first learnt how to listen to it, I found the songs of these remote bluesmen suddenly intimate with my own adolescent moods and thoughts, which were also often thoughts not about age but certainly about death. At 13, 14, 15: it is the time it first really gets to you, isn't it? And Dylan at 19 just hits that: he feels his way into, he inhabits, dying in his youth. The first record includes songs called 'In My Time of Dyin'', 'Fixin' To Die' and 'See That My Grave Is Kept Clean'.

* * *

Dylan is acting of course, or singing-acting, sometimes even a bit melodramatically: but he is still really nailing it too, with astonishingly commanding verve. And the heart-meltingly lovely 'Song to Woody'

165

suggests that in his life, as well as in the art he was absorbing, Dylan was learning about endings as he was only just beginning. Leaving Minnesota for New York really *was* to visit the dying Woody Guthrie in New Jersey State Hospital in Morristown – which Dylan did on his very first day in the city. 'Song to Woody', Dave van Ronk tells us in his wonderful, exhilaratingly good-humoured memoir *The Mayor of MacDougal Street*, was exactly what its title says: a song written specifically to sing to Woody in the hospital. Van Ronk, who had good and frequent reason to find Dylan exasperating, pays generous, humbled tribute to his willingness to make many lengthy, unglamorous bus trips across the New Jersey turnpike to visit a man with the truly terrible, protracted and incurable Huntington's Chorea. Much as van Ronk and his Greenwich Village pals loved Woody's songs, he says, they were not about to do *that*.

* * *

The hospital was actually a sort of mental institution and very distressing to the 19-year-old Zimmerman. Dylan was telling lots of stories about himself then, but this was a true one, and in fact he did not tell it much. I have always thought it was Robert Zimmerman who made those trips, though, not Bob Dylan, and that they helped Robert Zimmerman to become Bob Dylan. They showed him what was necessary. Not just Guthrie's songs and Guthrie's image, as Dylan perceived them and received them, but also the reality of Guthrie as a dying man. This was part of the self-conception or self-invention. What else is he saying when he talks to the journalist about death so insistently in *Dont Look Back*? 'You do your job in the face of that and how seriously you take yourself, you decide for yourself'. The name 'Bob Dylan' is the name of a job too, and it is variously adaptable: and one of its adaptations is as a mechanism for taking a self seriously in the face of mortality.

* * *

You can read this – hear this – not only in 'Song to Woody' and 'Last Thoughts on Woody Guthrie' but also in the astounding Carnegie Chapter Hall 1961 concert version of 'This Land is Your Land', available on the *No Direction Home* album. The song had been Guthrie's tacit rebuke and alternative to Irving Berlin's chauvinist 'God Bless America'; but Dylan turns what is usually a rousing democratic anthem into something mournfully close to threnody. Even so early in his career, in his first concert outside small folk-club appearances, this unconcernedly ran the risk of affront. Dylan's account of 'This Land is Your Land' is one of the most melancholy things he has ever done, and one of his most exquisitely heartfelt performances. It is not just that he is thinking about, and honouring, the man who wrote the song. It is that he is thinking while he sings – you can hear him doing the thinking while he is doing the singing – about what possible contemporary relevance these lyrics written in 1940 might have in 1961, with their idealistic vision of uncomplicatedly pristine heritage and solidarity ('This land was made for you and me'). A couple of years later, in the bizarre speech he made when collecting the Tom Paine award from the National Emergency Civil Liberties Committee in New York in 1963 – a speech for which he subsequently wrote a lengthy letter of excruciated apology – Dylan makes overt what is implicit in his interpretation of the song: 'it has sure changed in the time Woody's been here and the time I've been here. It is not that easy any more. People seem to have more fears'. Even so, you could say that, interpreting the song in this way, Dylan is tacitly attending to anxious complications in the original. There, in verses usually dropped from the version sung in the 1960s (and dropped by Dylan too), confidence in the land's reclamation is undermined by the confrontation with both a forbidding wall labelled 'Private Property' and a hungry queue outside a Relief Office 'in the shadow of the steeple', which appears to implicate the Church too in the repression of the poor. If Dylan's account of the song denies to his early-1960s audience the opportunity to relax into conventional left-liberal pieties, it also challenges the whole idea of piety in the public sphere and registers a profound suspicion of the self-satisfaction that often accompanies it. And this is certainly to have been wise before his time. 'In *Beyond Good and Evil* Nietzsche talks about feeling old at the beginning of his life', Dylan says in *Chronicles*: 'I felt like that, too'.

* * *

Thinking about the importance of Guthrie to Dylan, it is revealingly instructive that, although Dylan sang Guthrie songs a great deal in concert in the early 1960s – to the extent of becoming, he said, 'a Woody Guthrie jukebox' – he did not actually record one officially until much later; possibly out of a combination of obeisance, tact and self-preservation. When he wrote songs himself which had, or took on, 'anthemic' cultural status, they were not at all songs of uncomplicated heritage or solidarity, even if their first audiences, including Joan Baez, may have read them or heard them like that. 'Blowin' in the Wind' and 'The Times They Are A-Changin'' are anxiously riddled with complication. The former asks questions to which there is, unsettlingly, no answer; or, should there chance to be one, it is blown away irretrievably in the wind. This is poignantly underwritten by the refrain's edgy off-rhyme of 'friend' and 'wind' and perhaps even by the locution 'my friend' itself, which is often no indication of true friendship whatever. Witness, for instance, the way it becomes politically manipulative rhetorical gambit and then, in the immediately subsequent line, perkily impudent riposte in 'I Shall Be Free' on the same album as 'Blowin' in the Wind', *The Freewheelin' Bob Dylan*, in 1963:

> Well, my telephone rang it would not stop
> It's President Kennedy callin' me up
> He said, 'My friend Bob, what do we need to make the country grow?'
> I said, 'My friend, John, Brigitte Bardot'.

'The Times They Are A-Changin'' extends repeated invitations – 'Come gather round people / Wherever you roam'; 'Come mothers and fathers / Throughout the land' – to acknowledge disconcerting actualities: 'And admit that the waters / Around you have grown'; 'And don't criticize / What you can't understand'. There is not much comfort of solidarity there, especially when the invitation is issued with what sounds like callowly presumptuous, even aggressive, authority, and when any putative solidarity between those invited into the circle of gatherers-round is undermined by the almost vindictive pleasure the song appears to take in its register of inter-generational conflict.

* * *

Writing the numerals 13, 14, 15, I think of Dylan's numerals in his early piece, 'My Life in a Stolen Moment', first published in the programme for his concert in New York Town Hall in 1963. He ran away from home, he tells us there, at the ages of 10, 12, 13, 15, 15½, 17 and 18: 'I been caught and brought back all but once'. (That '15½' is terrific: not only because it registers, with comic hyperbole, the urgency of the desire but also because it makes us think about what Robert Lowell calls 'the pathos of a child's fractions'.) That is a lot of running, but it is also a lot of being brought back. Dylan's computation does not hold much literal truth although, it seems, it does hold some: but it still carries figurative truth. Dylan just seems to have managed a more spectacular version of what everyone has to manage in order to live an adult life: getting away from the first place and people and finding a different place and different people. You have no direction home, first, and you may even say to yourself, 'Don't look back'. But then, not long afterwards, you set yourself the paradoxical project of bringing it all back home, partly because unsuspected kinds of obligation or affection suddenly seem involved in all of this too. You get 88 'matching songs' for the word 'home' in the Dylan online concordance. The name of the father is rejected, certainly, and the father is rejected in some of the songs too, notably 'Highway 61 Revisited', where the name of the biblical patriarch Abraham is abbreviated across a line-break to 'Abe', the form by which Robert Zimmerman's father was usually known. And this father, having initially doubted God's seriousness, appears, after the threat of divine retribution, willing to do His dreadful will without much demur:

> Oh God said to Abraham, 'Kill me a son'
> Abe says, 'Man, you must be puttin' me on'
> God say, 'No'. Abe say, 'What?'
> God say, 'You can do what you want Abe, but
> The next time you see me comin' you better run'
> Well Abe says, 'Where do you want this killin' done?'
> God says, 'Out on Highway 61'.

The streetwise, vernacular comedy of this biblical appropriation does not really hide its anti-paternal animosity. But, 'My Life in a Stolen Moment' tells us – disarmingly, given that it has just told us of its author's get-away attempts – 'I wrote my first song to my mother an' titled it "To Mother"'; and then suddenly, very arrestingly, 'Lonesome Day Blues' on *'Love and Theft'* so many years later in 2001 offers this apparent *non sequitur*:

> I'm forty miles from the mill –
> I'm droppin' it into overdrive
> I'm forty miles from the mill –
> I'm droppin' it into overdrive
> Settin' my dial on the radio
> I wish my mother was still alive.

Eric Lott's psychoanalytic reading of the song in the *Cambridge Companion to Bob Dylan* proposes that this is not at all a *non sequitur*, in fact, because the radio dial is the maternal nipple. I almost believe this; and in a song whose transitions are pretty unfathomable, the apparently unaccommodated, piercing commonplace of the desire calls a lot of attention to itself. Is 'Lonesome Day Blues' designed in fact primarily to create an opportunity for that line, and to cover its tracks too?

* * *

I wonder if these polarities of risky escape and persistent attachment or even longing – the Homeric pattern actually, the Odyssean one of voyage and *nostos* – are not the consistent polarities of Dylan's imagination, its deepest signatures, through an extensive thematics of politics, sex, love, religion, family and music itself. Dylan may contain multitudes, in the orthodox Whitmanian-American manner, but beneath all that could it be that he moves to the music of a dual motion? 'O my name it ain't nothin' / My age it means less': maybe so, but still 'The country I come from / Is called the mid-West'. You may be going somewhere, or nowhere, even into anonymity; and the place you come from may not have a name, exactly, but just a conventionally inexact way of being 'called'. But it is still where you come from and you say so in a song even after you have had the call to change your name, after you have discovered that you have a 'calling'. And in this case the calling involves another kind of going back: to the song by Dominic Behan, 'The Patriot Game', which opens, 'My name is O'Hanlon / I've just turned sixteen', whose lyric structure and melody 'With God on Our Side' brings so discerningly to a new home. This alternation is a kind of heartbeat in Dylan, systole and diastole. And in Dylan the work always is work of the body: the work of thorax and larynx and breath, the musculature of hands on an instrument, lips on another instrument, a body pulsing with energy. Lyric poetry holds a contract with the body, the lyre is in the hand: cerebral lyric is a contradiction in terms. Dylan's carnal lyric is essence of lyric: a body swayed to music, a brightening glance.

* * *

Systole and diastole. 'Well, it's always been my nature to take chances / My right hand drawing back while my left hand advances'. This would make much more ordinary sense if it read, 'it's never been my nature to take chances', since advancing one hand while you knowingly draw back the other seems, in its revision of the expression that the right hand does not know what the left hand is doing, the very gesture of evasiveness, disingenuousness, complicatedly self-preservative calculation. But that is not the way Dylan writes/sings it; and it is therefore not the way he reads the gesture. He – or at least the song's persona, which is a caveat we must always enter with Dylan, who has invented a name for himself – gives in the same motion in which he takes away, and this is to 'take chances' too; and what that taking chances upon is a song like this one, 'Angelina', which he then refuses the chance of becoming part of the record he has recorded it for. Dylan's artistic perversity is extreme, and this tremendous song was omitted from *Shot of Love* in 1981; you have to hunt it down on the Bootleg Series. The gesture is also an odd one for a right-handed man to figure as self-revelation. Drawing your right hand back while you advance your left is to replace dexterity with the awkward or even, at the root of the Latin opposition between 'dexter' and 'sinister', with something more morally suspect; and 'my left hand advances', where the strong present indicative contrasts with the tentative participial 'drawing back', makes it seem that the hand moves without conscious agency. The gesture therefore sounds menacing. Dylan is not ever very right-on and certainly seditious, contrarian; and in interview and anecdote, and mid-1960s stage persona, he has sometimes carried an air of menace. But sinister? Suze Rotolo could not live with his darkness, she tells us in her emotionally complex book *A Freewheelin' Time*; and in an interview she says that when she read Françoise Gilot on Picasso she recognized an exactly comparable, and also unlivable-with, 'sense of entitlement'. In *Chronicles* Dylan makes Picasso a precursor and exemplar: 'Picasso had fractured the art world and cracked it wide open. I wanted to be like that'. This is a confession of astonishingly over-reaching ambition that would seem laughably self-regarding and self-deluding in anyone else I can think of. That it does not in Dylan is the measure of the way the ambition had been so amply fulfilled before he let us know he had had it. Leonard Cohen just hits the mark and speaks the truth when, unenviously, he admires Dylan as 'the Picasso of song'.

* * *

So perhaps genius must be allowed its entitlement; or is it just a particular style of masculine genius that requires or demands it? When Dylan makes the observation about Picasso he also, much less attractively, admires his way with women. Suze Rotolo generously although not wholly forgivingly retrospectively permits Dylan his entitlement, allowing that the songs may be sourced there, or at least given their permission or passport there. Entitlement perhaps inevitably goes along with giving yourself the title: and *Bob Dylan* is the title of the first record as well as the title the singer had recently given himself. But entitlement is presumption, arrogance and large self-permission. What does it permit Dylan? It permits him, initially, to move on those blues singers and to move on Woody Guthrie. 'Move' as in 'make your move', but also in the sense in which Richard Ellmann uses the word in his book *Eminent Domain* (1967), anticipating and influencing Harold Bloom: 'Writers *move* upon other writers not as genial successors but as violent expropriators, knocking down established boundaries to seize by the force of youth, or of age, what they require. They do not borrow, they override.' As if, in other words, they are entitled to do so. 'By the force of youth, or of age': Dylan was at it then, and he is still at it now. This is not insouciant, exactly, but it is not completely calculating, either, since it has the air of improvisation, or it did then. But it does refuse to know its place; and by that refusal it makes a new place for itself, and it makes a name for itself.

* * *

Dylan is explicitly reflective about this as early as '11 Outlined Epitaphs', the poem-sequence on the sleeve of *The Times They Are A-Changin'* in 1963, where he makes the process seem less rapacious:

> Yes, I am a thief of thoughts
> not, I pray, a stealer of souls
> I have built an' rebuilt
> upon what is waitin'
> for the sand on the beaches
> carves many castles

> on what has been opened
> before my time
> a word, a story, a tune, a line
> keys in the wind t'unlock my mind
> an' t'grant my closet thoughts backyard air

This metaphoric profusion is undisciplined, but may be allowed to signal the depth of self-recognition; and what we now know of Dylan and religion casts on the words 'pray' and 'souls' new light, in which they seem less neutral than they did then. Artistic theft, both its aesthetics and its ethics, is something Dylan has thought hard and anxiously about from the beginning and not only when he entitled an album *'Love and Theft'*, putting his title in inverted commas to signal that it also was stolen; even if with some love, it must be, and in a way that certainly drew more than customary attention to an academic study published by a university press, Eric Lott's *Love and Theft: Blackface Minstrelsy and the American Working Class*. Accusations of plagiarism have been levelled at Dylan's later work in particular, both his songs and his paintings. His admission of theft at such an early stage should be brought into the reckoning here; and so should the distinction he makes between being 'a thief of thoughts' and 'a stealer of souls', and his apparently devout aspiration to maintain it.

* * *

At 20 Dylan was a bit coy about his age. There is that very funny moment in the radio interview with Cynthia Gooding in 1962. She has seen Dylan play rock-and-roll three years earlier in Minneapolis, so she really should not be up for his self-mythologizing here. You do hear some wary scepticism in her voice, but she is more or less up for it. She sounds a bit in love with him actually when she asks, 'You must be twenty years old now, aren't you?' And Dylan – taken aback but deadpan, a bit rueful – says, 'Yeah, I must be twenty'. Gooding, in genuine or mock exasperation, asks, *'Are* you?' 'Yeah,' says Dylan, 'I'm twenty, I'm twenty', making the repetition sound more dubious than corroborative. Why does he do this? Because he is being Bob Dylan. Robert Zimmerman is twenty, that is for sure: but Bob Dylan is whatever age he chooses to be, or whatever age seems appropriate at the time, because he is making it up as he goes along, and he is certainly not twenty when he sings Blind Lemon Jefferson. Or, as he famously says in the Halloween concert in 1964, giving the game away, but concealing himself yet again too, 'It's Halloween. I have my Bob Dylan mask on. I'm masquerading'. And he relishes the word, drawing the single syllable of 'mask', with the abrupt click of its final 'k', out languorously into the French gerund of 'masquerading', with its charade and its implied licentiousness. He giggles when he says it, and it sounds like a marijuana giggle: but no wonder he giggles after that. 'How came ye muffled in so hush a masque?' – Keats, 'Ode on Indolence', with a query addressed to Bob Dylan. And while we are on the topic of the mask: I cannot find anything in *Beyond Good and Evil* about Nietzsche's feeling old at the beginning of his life, but I have chanced upon this: 'there is not only guile behind a mask – there is so much graciousness in cunning'. Nietzsche, clearly thinking (against the grain) about Bob Dylan.

* * *

Such coincidences, or co-incidings, occur regularly, in my experience, for anyone literary listening to Dylan. See, outstandingly, Mark Ford wondering whether there has ever been 'a finer description' of Dylan's 1966 tour with the Band than a passage written by Ralph Waldo Emerson in 1844, in his essay 'The Poet', where, says Ford, he 'predicts the imminent arrival of a genius whose vision will consummate the new reality of the new republic'. Even Emerson's enthusiasm for Whitman waned; but he prophesies, with his pen, the eventual advent of Dylan:

> Doubt not, o poet, but persist. Say, 'It is in me, and shall out'. Stand there, baulked and dumb, stuttering and stammering, hissed and hooted, stand and strive, until, at last, rage draw out of thee that *dream*-power which every night shows thee is thine own; a power transcending all limit and privacy, and by virtue of which a man is the conductor of the whole river of electricity.

* * *

So, shortly after listening to *Blonde on Blonde* on the Mono Box, it chanced that I read Boris Pasternak's Yuri Zhivago describing Russian folksong:

> An old Russian folk-song is like water in a weir. It looks as if it were still and were no longer flowing but in its depths it is ceaselessly rushing through the sluice-gates and its stillness is an illusion. By every possible means – by repetitions and similes – it attempts to stop or to slow down the gradual unfolding of its theme, until it reaches some mysterious point, then it suddenly reveals itself. In this insane attempt to stop the flow of time, a sorrowful, self-restraining spirit finds its expression.

This is a description of Russian folksong, but it is also a description – an inwardly exact one, the best I have ever read – of 'Sad-Eyed Lady of the Lowlands'. This is mere coincidence, of course, and one that occurs, as far as I know, only in the mind of this listener and reader. But then I remember that Dylan's forebears were Russian Ashkenazi Jews. 'Some people tell me / I got the blood of the land in my voice', Dylan sings on 'I Feel A Change Comin' On' on *Together Through Life* in 2009. But which land? The new republic, or the very old regime? And how far back does a voice – does Dylan's voice – go? When he sings, in 'I and I' on *Infidels* in 1983, 'Someone else is speakin' with my mouth, but I'm listenin' only to my heart / I've made shoes for everyone, even you, while I still go barefoot', he is brilliantly evoking the unspecifiable derivation of his singing voice and also, in the specific metaphor for song-making, establishing a connection with those of his Russian forebears who, we learn from the biographies, worked in, or managed, a shoe factory in Odessa until they fled to America in the aftermath of a pogrom.

* * *

But – to pick up my theme after what has possibly not really been a detour – why would Cynthia Gooding collude with Dylan's self-mythologizing? Why would anyone? His Jewishness matters here, I think. Suze Rotolo tells us she discovered it only when his draft card fell out of his wallet: but she was just 17 when they met, and her background was Italian-American. But many people in the New York folk music world were Jewish. Was there a form of tacit recognition going on? Dave van Ronk, shrewd but forgiving, insists that everyone was busily self-inventing then and nobody cared much, and cared much less than Dylan assumed. Van Ronk tells a funny story about Dylan literally falling off his stool when he discovers that Jack Elliott, the cowboy singer and buddy of Woody's, is actually – or was – Elliot Adnopoz, son of a wealthy Jewish surgeon. That was also, of course, the moment van Ronk, who says he previously did suspect it, knew that Dylan was Jewish.

* * *

Still, Dylan did care. Of course Jewish people do change their names, especially when they go into American show business. Another Zimmermann [*sic*], Ethel Agnes, changed hers to Ethel Merman. In the very full account of the name change he gives in *Chronicles* – which I would not see much reason to doubt if it were not accompanied by a completely bizarre account of the end of the name Robert Zimmerman – Dylan does not even mention motivation. How far has anti-Semitism been a consideration for him? Michael Jones, in a scrupulously well-researched essay in *The Political Art of Bob Dylan*, thinks it inheres in the cry of 'Judas!' in Manchester in 1966. I am not so sure about that, since in an English culture then almost unimaginably more Christian than now, 'Judas' meant 'traitor' much more readily than it implied 'Jew'. In *Chronicles* Dylan makes a clearly still resentful point of telling us that when he formed bands at school they would be stolen from him by people with greater local family connections who could organize payment. Is anti-Semitism implicit in this story, since the 'family connections' of someone called 'Zimmerman' presumably did not extend very far in Hibbing, Minnesota? Anti-Semitism is overt when, elsewhere in *Chronicles*, Dylan recalls sitting after a meal in a circle of singer-songwriters in Johnny Cash's house. They pass the guitar around and do a party piece, receiving complimentary comment afterwards. It sounds attractively sociable, if a little competitive, until Dylan sings 'Lay, Lady, Lay' and June Carter Cash's cousin Joe asks, as his only comment, 'You don't eat pork, do you?' Kris Kristofferson, Dylan says, 'almost swallowed his fork'. Dylan, calling Joe Carter 'sir', admits that he does not eat pork and quotes a remark about eating pork that he had heard Malcolm X make in a radio broadcast several years earlier. 'There was an awkward momentary silence', Dylan says, 'that you could have cut with one of the knives off the dinner table'. (And we remember what 'Talkin' New York' on *Bob Dylan* tells us: that a lot of people don't have much food on their table but they got a lot of forks and knives and they gotta cut somethin'.)

* * *

This is a fascinating, ramifying moment. Dylan has sung a country song he has written, one that appears on an album on which he shares a duet with Johnny Cash, king of country music and host of this meal and entertainment. Cash has also composed an admiring poem about Dylan for the album's sleeve; and this was an album met with horror by some of Dylan's first fans because country music is the music of rednecks, reactionary and terminally unhip. Joe Carter, of the well-known country music act the Carter Family, which Johnny Cash has married into, behaves exactly according to the conventional idea of a redneck and clearly believes that this is *his* music and that Dylan, the Jewish Dylan, is an appropriating outsider, without rights: he is not entitled to be here. Joe is manifestly behaving with extreme discourtesy to his host and with something even worse to Dylan himself. Dylan responds with a surely barbed imitation of country manners – that apparently deferential, in fact scathing, 'sir' – and with a tacit reference to the leader of the Nation of Muslims who himself did not eat pork but who was also tainted with anti-Semitism. On *Nashville Skyline*, though, Dylan makes great country music and makes country music new, and very influentially so. So it is most definitely his music; and so is blues music and folk music and rock music and gospel music, all the musics Dylan has adopted and reinvented: out of love, not out of exploitative opportunism; or, yes, out of love and theft. His entitlement is his genius for making these musics his own; and his race has nothing to do with it. Origin has nothing to do with it; destination does. Later in *Chronicles* Dylan tells us that the great blues singer Robert Johnson learned to play guitar from a man named Ike Zinnerman – 'a mysterious character not in any of the history books'. Although this sounds altogether too conveniently and skittishly Dylanesque to be true, Ike Zinnerman is in fact historical: you can even Google the unique photograph of him. But surely Dylan's bringing the name up and its near-coincidence with his own original name make a clever, subtle, sly joke about the whole idea of origin as permanent definition, its sinister nonsense. Or, as the ebullient 'Country Pie' on *Nashville Skyline* has it, with comprehensive tolerance, 'Raspberry, strawberry, lemon and lime / What do I care? / Blueberry, apple, cherry, pumpkin and plum / Call me for dinner, honey, I'll be there' – that song which decisively favours over the forgettable Joe Carter another much more memorable old Joe: Old Saxophone Joe, who may or may not eat pork but who does, as it happens, have a hogshead up on his toe.

* * *

You can see Dylan in the act of making himself up in Andy Warhol's 'Screen Test', filmed in the Factory in New York in January 1965 and now available on YouTube. Whatever else they may have been, the Screen Tests were also theatres of cruelty, exercises in Warholian manipulation, provocation and control, since no one can bear to be looked at and to have to look back – and at Andy Warhol's camera! – for so long, especially when instructed neither to move nor to blink. Dylan's Test, as it appears on YouTube, lasts about three minutes and twenty seconds, but this duplicates some footage. Dylan is inscrutable and beautiful as he looks and looks and then disobediently withdraws his look and looks again, twitching and shrugging a bit. Impassiveness lapses briefly into boredom and, just for a moment, into what looks like wry bafflement that he has agreed to this. Unlike some other subjects of the Tests, though, who veer between assurance and embarrassment, he remains perfectly self-possessed. He knows about looking and he has, of course, The Look. (You get *170* 'matching songs' for the word 'look' in the concordance.) His beauty has to do with the way intelligence and self-knowledge shine in his skin, and the way he is thinking about what to reveal; the way his body does the thinking as well as the looking. He certainly looks self-aware, but he does not look sufficiently that to look *knowing* – because he is inventing the look, he is still making it up as he goes along: it is experimental, approximate, mobile. It is the look the Mono Box songs from *Bob Dylan* to *John Wesley Harding* wear on their faces too. I think Dylan's songs lose that look subsequently; which is not at all to say they lose too much, and maybe there are gains also; and in any case who does not lose their looks? But Dylan's avoidance of the American aesthetic catastrophe does not completely release him from the curse that what the later songs must always see when they look in the mirror, as the Mono Box may acknowledge, is these earlier songs, whatever their 'postman' says.

When he calls himself that – 'I'm just the postman, I deliver the songs' – Dylan is finding an original metaphor for Romantic and post-Romantic concepts of inspiration. These are remarkably persistent: both Seamus Heaney and Paul Muldoon, for instance, have their versions of them. We have to regard such metaphors, then, as more than just tropes, to think that they do genuinely define the way some poets feel about their creativity. The metaphors can never tell anything like a whole truth, though, since so much of the work of such writers exhibits in its manuscript variations its footwork or spadework also. Dylan's songs reveal the extent of their author's homework in their adaptations of, and allusions to, already existing tunes, motifs and lyrics; and in some of the more recent songs this can even produce a disconcertingly laborious patchwork. Nevertheless, I wonder if Dylan's figure carries more than conventional weight, protecting a genuine mystery and not just our access to it, since in his interviews – quite unlike those of, say, Seamus Heaney and Paul Muldoon – he hardly ever has anything of interest to say, and rarely has anything at all to say, about where the songs come from. This is true even of the lengthy conversation with Cameron Crowe which forms the basis of the song-by-song liner notes for the career retrospective *Biograph* (1985); and in Dylan's interview with Paul Zollo, designed for a book, *Song-Writers on Song-Writing* (2003), in which numerous songwriters do talk revealingly about their compositional processes, Dylan almost entirely sidesteps the questions and even, Zollo tells us, plays 'a small Peruvian flute' while making his 'responses'.

* * *

In *Chronicles*, Dylan does, to an extent, talk about his songs, especially those on *Oh Mercy*, but even here he does so by means of obliquity, suggestion, subjunctives and conditionals, as though he has very limited authority to speak, and he never discusses their sources, origins or occasions. And when he talks most beautifully and memorably about them it is to confirm a sense that he is more or less passive before their invitations. Of 'Disease of Conceit', for instance: 'the song rose up until I could read the look in its eyes. In the quiet of the evening I didn't have to hunt far for it'; and of 'Shooting Star': 'I felt like I didn't write it so much as I inherited it'. In fact, he says most about his own songs in *Chronicles* when he is not talking about them at all but when he is talking, rivetingly, about the songs of Brecht and Weill and Robert Johnson, and the paintings of Red Grooms. Allen Ginsberg, in a phrase from his unpublished journals quoted by Stephen Scobie, notes of a *Rolling Thunder* performance, 'Dylan overtaken / by his songs'. That seems a permanent condition.

* * *

Some things do vanish with the look, though, things I still love, which is why I love the Mono Box. There is the fact that, as Mike Marqusee says and demonstrates in his excellent book *Wicked Messenger: Bob Dylan and the 1960s*, these songs bear 'an umbilical relation to the turmoil of their times'. I take this to be axiomatic; and it gives these songs, at least for anyone who was around and so much younger then, an aura or density which is, of its nature, unrepeatable. Dylan himself appears to think this too in *Chronicles*, where he phrases the thought as – why not? – a form of mystical theology or magic when, of his 1960s work, he says that he then had 'power and dominion over the spirits. I had it once, and once was enough'. Any melancholy of loss here appears to be subsumed in and countered by the mystic's or magician's knowledge of the personal cost involved. I do not know if 'umbilical relations' are responsible in these songs for what I miss from the later ones. But what I love in them is a certain form of sadness; a certain form of spontaneity, and of spontaneous humour; a certain perfection of enunciation, as though he is carving his voice on the air; a certain absolute rhythmic self-assurance and authority, accompanied by a near-perfection of editorial control; a certain oblique candour, actually, for all the masquerade; a certain instinctive delight in his own creative capacity, which seems to surprise him before it surprises us, and leaves us surprised and then delighted by his surprise. A certain form, I suppose, of being brilliant and young, of being brilliantly young. 'I was young when I left home': I believe that, it is just the truth, and it is a great way to start a song, since everything in any listener wants to know what happened next. And 'I was so much older then, / I'm younger than that now': I believe that too, since it makes apostasy seem inevitable, necessary, the way you must go to get anywhere else at all. 'May you stay forever young', though: I do not believe that, not really. It is believably elegiac, certainly, since the literal impossibility of its desire's ever being fulfilled is the measure of the depth of its tender paternal love, which is also the measure of a shared mortality. But figuratively such desire seems just a velleity, close kin to regret. Eternal youth would not be self-evidently an enduring virtue, and it really should not be an enduring state of mind. Youth's a stuff will not endure: that is a melancholy absolute. Besides, it is a banal tune.

* * *

During the Rolling Thunder tour when Dylan and Baez are on stage together someone yells out, 'You make a lovely couple'. Baez was never just the beautiful, intense, fragile conscience of America, although she was certainly that too sometimes, and maybe still is: but it is with an entirely personal pained reproach that she snarls back, destroying the moment and the proffered sentiment, 'A lovely couple o' *whutt?*' Whoever the poor guy was who said it must have been devastated: imagine being castigated from the stage by Joan Baez. He could console himself though with the thought that she intended it for Dylan far more than for him; and perhaps it was well merited, since Dylan's having her there at all, ten years after they had been together as lovers, seems to have been a complicated – although also possibly to some degree hapless – combination of come-on and put-on: not only for Baez herself, who should have resisted, but also for an almost inevitably voyeuristic audience. This narcissism, altogether the wrong kind of looking and invitation to look, is the salient feature and failure of the director and star of the movie made out of that tour, *Renaldo and Clara*. Renaldo is the one Bob Dylan I can live without.

* * *

But if you have lived with Dylan for years the way I have, if you have gone together through life, you and he also make a couple of something. This is a coupledom, even if only one of you knows it. But a couple of what? I remember Michael Neve discussing Dylan years ago in the *London Review of Books* and reaching for Hazlitt on Hamlet, the character Hamlet: 'Hamlet is a name, his speeches and sayings but the idle coinage of the poet's brain. What then, are they not real? They are as real as our own thoughts. Their reality is in the reader's mind. It is *we* who are Hamlet'. Like Hamlet, Bob Dylan is a name, and his songs are the coinage of a poet's brain. The same for me, then, with Dylan: as real as my own thoughts.

CHAPTER 12

In Retrospect:
Christopher Logue,
Anne Carson, David Jones

I
Sea of Space: Christopher Logue's *Cold Calls: War Music continued*
(2005)

When Keats first looked into Chapman's Homer, his response was a magnificent sonnet celebrating the power of translation; but despite the word 'looking' in his title ('On First Looking into Chapman's Homer'), which has its eye on reading, the poem also celebrates the power of the oral. Of Homer's original, Keats says, 'Yet never did I breathe its pure serene / Till I heard Chapman speak out loud and bold'. Keats, that is, absorbs new knowledge and discovers new repose by becoming attuned to an air alive with new sonorities. Keats may mean this literally, since his first experience of Chapman was of reading his version aloud with Cowden Clarke. Pope too, a subsequent illustrious translator of Homer, thought that 'Homer makes us hearers, and Virgil leaves us readers'. Perhaps all three poets instinctively perceived what some classical scholars have since held about the oral-improvisatory nature of Homer's poems.

Cold Calls was intended, the blurb tells us, as the 'penultimate' instalment of Christopher Logue's long-running, intermittently published version of the *Iliad*, which began with *Patroclus* in 1962 and whose overall title is *War Music*. However, since Logue died in December 2011, we should probably assume that this is in fact the ultimate instalment. In a way perhaps encouraged by the tradition of the oral connected with the *Iliad*, Logue's sequence had its own origin in performance, as a radio broadcast prepared with the classicist Donald Carne-Ross; and *War Music* has, over the years, consistently offered itself as a performing as well as a printed text. As a consequence, the poem almost always has an ear-grabbing immediacy and urgency, sometimes emphasized, even exaggerated, by typography and layout.

The sequence has had influential admirers and classicist detractors. The former tend to find the latter pedantically incapable of recognizing the actual poetic effort being undertaken, but I am not sure that the issue is so clear. The argument is that Logue is not making a version of the original in any traditionally recognized and sanctioned sense, but offering an 'account' of it. This is Logue's own word; and although it does not, of itself, tell us much about authorial intention, it has been taken as an indication that Logue is taking liberties with an original in a way given permission in modern practices of poetic translation most prominently by the example of Ezra Pound. T. S. Eliot, particularly the Eliot of 'Coriolan', seems to me to be part of Logue's conception too, but it is clear that Pound – whom Logue's Hector quotes at one point – is the most significant mentor of the enterprise, notably in his method of what he called the 'luminous detail'. There are many striking, sometimes isolated or islanded fragments in Christopher Logue's Homer, and some of these breathe a late modernist serene. There is this, for instance, which, following and exemplifying Logue's overall title for the sequence, makes war a metaphorical music:

> To the sigh of the string, see Panda's shot float off;
> To the slap of the string on the stave, float on
> Over the strip for a beat, a beat; and then
> Carry a tunnel the length of a lipstick through Quist's neck.

This has a great deal of Logue the Homeric translator in it. There is the familiar ghost of Pound in its wavering anapaestic rhythms, its variations of pentameter and hexameter and its recall of the alliterative metres adapted in Pound's version of *The Seafarer*. There is the quasi-cinematic directive to the reader ('see') that is partly controlling of response but also partly the proposal of collaborative re-creation and cajolingly involving as narrative method. There is the joltingly anachronistic unsuitability of comparison ('a tunnel the length of a lipstick') that, on reflection, must be permitted its weirdly discrepant appropriateness: the lipstick is the right size for the wound, at least if this is a wound made by a bullet rather than an arrow, and the lipstick, like the wound, makes a red smear. The ironizing aestheticism of such evocation and analogy, its sheer exquisiteness, enforces even greater recoil from the hideous violence of the action. This is 'war music' indeed, and anyone seeking an anthology of luminous details may confidently be directed to Logue's Homer. *Cold Calls* has a memorable one, delicate and precise in its evocation and with a whisper of Yeats's 'In Memory of Eva Gore-Booth and Con Markiewicz':

> And now the light of evening has begun
> To shawl across the plain:
> Blue gray, gold gray, blue gold,
> Translucent nothingnesses
> Readying our space,
> Within the deep, unchanging sea of space,
> For Hesper's entrance and the silver wrap.

Such long perspectives open up here, as Logue measures 'our space', the scene of the relentless human catastrophe of the *Iliad*, against the cosmic serene of space itself with its mythologized Romantic evening star, and as the whole is given a sudden concluding contemporary edge by the metaphor of a cinematic 'wrap'. The coming of evening dark is viewed as the completion of a scene, as though this space is derived after all not only from the machinery of Hesperus and Greco-Roman mythology but from the Stanley Kubrick of *2001: A Space Odyssey*.

Writing to a modernist aesthetic of the detail, however, with the radical pruning which that involves, is necessarily to fail to give weight to one essential attribute of the *Iliad*: its sheer, unrelenting, necessary momentum, its cumulative, absolute pressure and intensity. The lack of interest in, or respect for, essential attributes of the original suggested by this is, however, carried much further in Logue's frequent disregard of, and divergences from, Homer. Notably, his version has crudities reflecting nothing that I can see in Homer, where they would be so tonally disruptive as to undermine all point and purpose. Thersites, for instance, tells Agamemnon that anyone in receipt of his unwonted generosity would be so surprised as to 'jump / Down the eye-hole of his own knob', and someone called Molo tugs at the dead Patroclus's penis, squeaking 'Achilles' love!' Molo is a name (like 'Panda' and Quist') nowhere in Homer, of course, and, throughout, Logue invents strange, un-Homeric names of, to me, uninterpretable significance. These become more plentiful as the sequence progresses, and *Cold Calls* introduces, among others, Deckalin, Mowgag, Meep and Nyro. Along with apparently deconstructive interferences of this kind, *War Music* sometimes also collocates episodes from different books of the *Iliad*, making it difficult to know where we are in the narrative or to what purpose the collocation has been made. Logue's sequence, even more radically – as it were – invents episodes with no basis whatever in Homer. In these ways, and in others, *War Music* is pointed in its refusal of pathos, unlike such great modern *Iliad*-dependent poems as Auden's 'The Shield of Achilles' and Cavafy's 'The Horses of Achilles'.

Simone Weil finely, and famously, wrote that 'the true hero ... of the *Iliad* is force', and so it is; and Logue's Odysseus appears more or less to cite Weil when he says, with staccato definitiveness, 'We are God's own. Our law is his. Is force'. The emphasis on force is emphatically sustained in *War Music* and epitomized in Menelaos's blunt absoluteness when he chants his self-motivating hatred of the enemy he wants to kill: 'I want to shout into his broken face: / You are dead. You are no longer in this world'. The *Iliad*, however, would be virtually unreadable if it were a poem only about force, and Simone Weil writes too about what is 'painfully contrastive' in it. In fact, its acts of violence, while always accepted as necessary in the ethical code espoused by both Greeks and Trojans, are interrupted by moments in which the corpse-strewn ground is cleared, sometimes literally, for the expression of things not to be comprehended under the rubric of force.

Some of these are associated with women. There is, above all, Andromache's plea to her husband Hector when their young son Astyanax is convincingly terrified by his father's helmet, and her subsequent prophetic lament in which Hector's death is foreseen. Other such contrastive moments in the *Iliad* prominently include those 'necrologues' in which, at the point of death, hitherto unidentified warriors are suddenly granted brief obituaries – fleeting, fragmentary biographies. The effect is to provoke in the reader a desolately chastened sense of waste: it would be bad enough anyway, but the necrologues twist the knife. 'These infrequent moments of grace,' Weil says, 'suffice to convey with deep regret just what violence has killed and will kill again'. The selectivity of Logue's treatment of the *Iliad* finds no space, however, for any of these things; and these things have meant a great deal to many generations of the poem's readers.

In addition to such omissions, there are what Logue calls in his spirited, eminently readable autobiography *Prince Charming* (2001) his 're-compositions' of Homer's poem. Homer's gods come in for a lot of this. In the *Iliad* they are cynically manipulative, whimsical and malevolent; and in Zeus and Hera we are presented with the aboriginally scratchy marriage. The gods have, however, their cloudy, empyrean grandeur too, and the contrast is important. Logue consistently brings them down several notches in the direction of bathos and banality. Aphrodite, for instance, is to be discovered 'repositioning a spaghetti shoulder-strap' and can be found in *Cold Calls* 'dressed / In grey silk lounge pajamas piped with gold / And snakeskin flip-flops', as though she is treading a camp catwalk rather than walking the fields of Elysium. *War Music* also appears to map Catholicism onto the Homeric religion. Aphrodite is 'Our Lady of the Thong'; Zeus is never called Zeus, but always 'God' and is pronominally capitalized as 'He' and 'Him' and referred to as 'the King of Heaven' and 'the Lord our God'; Poseidon is 'Pope of the Oceans'; Agamemnon 'dips his hands in holy water'; Achilles celebrates a kind of Mass and recites a version of the Lord's Prayer on behalf of Patroclus; Athena considers herself a member of 'the Holy Family'.

It is hard to know exactly how to interpret this analogizing, which seems more hectic travesty than 'recomposition' – whatever that means – but it does supply a major element of derogation in Logue's poem. It proposes, I suppose, that the way the gods behave to humans, always and everywhere, is a species of whimsical torment; but it also suggests an element of covert authorial involvement, since we learn from *Prince Charming* of Logue's Catholic education at the hands of the Christian Brothers. Surprisingly, given the track record of that confraternity, this appears to have been happy enough. Even so, I think we can read this prominent aspect of *War Music* as a kind of spilt anti-Catholicism, a humanist ridiculing of the concepts of metaphysics and eschatology themselves.

There is in all of this an imp of the perverse, and almost a kind of Logueian *peripeteia*. In *War Music*, that is, we encounter not a reversal of fortune but of legitimate readerly expectation. An example occurs at the end of *Cold Calls*, where a petulant Achilles refuses at considerable length to return to battle; and so of course we do not get the death of Hector or the meeting of Priam and Achilles, which are both crucial, frequently alluded to and often reinvented episodes in Homer. In this regard, it is worth recalling that in the late 1950s and early 1960s, when he was conceiving his sequence, Logue was involved in the poetry and jazz movement. He was also a very visible Aldermaston anti-nuclear marcher in 1958: *Prince Charming* publishes a photograph of him there with Kenneth Tynan and Doris Lessing, and the latter was, Logue tells us, one of the spurs to his first engagement with Homer. Both of these things put their social and political pressure on *War Music* at least as much as Pound's influence puts its poetic one.

We might read Logue's Homer, then, as a jazz improvisation on an original melody, one that sometimes strays a very long way indeed from its source, and in a spirit of unruly insubordination. The dissent inherent in this may derive from a scandalized disgust at Homer's apparent celebration of a militarism inevitably associated in British history and culture with the masculinist ethos that it promoted in generations of schoolboys. So Logue's anti-pathos should be seen as offering a responsible critique of a Homeric pathos too readily collusive with that militarism, the aesthetic sugar to its imperialist pill. *War Music* takes a marked political edge from its inclusion of numerous anachronistic references to recent military engagements (Gallipoli, Alamein, Iwo Jima, Stalingrad). In this, the poem recalls not so much Pound as Picasso, his *Massacre in Korea*, in which naked soldiers wearing visors carry both Greco-Roman swords and stylized machine-guns. One of Logue's warriors is presented in exactly such dual perspective:

> The Uzi shuddering warm against your hip
> Happy in danger in a dangerous place
> Yourself another self you found at Troy.

The relation of *War Music* to its original is comparable to that of Picasso's painting to Goya and Manet: both homage and desecration.

Logue's term 'account', then, takes on a connotation in addition to 'interpretation'. It proposes that *War Music* offers a reckoning of the *Iliad*, a calling of it to account. Christopher Logue, who was once, as *Prince Charming* tells us in a memorable sequence, an insubordinate, and imprisoned, soldier in the British Army, appears, in virtually the same act of suspicious scrutiny, both obsessively admiring of, and deeply repelled by, his original. He becomes thereby a traducer as well as a translator, defacing the monument, refusing to bow to the icon. *War Music*, in its profound self-division and self-laceration, is disconcertingly unstable in its representations, wildly discordant in its tonal registers, and hardly Homer: but it is, still, an 'account' of the *Iliad* in which the light from Achilles' helmet may be seen – and heard – 'screaming across three thousand years', where 'screaming' is very much the required and definitive word, the *mot juste*.

II
Aligned and Adverse: Anne Carson's *Nox* (2009)

Anne Carson, an academic classicist, is a poet of unlikely similitudes. While this does involve her placing of the classical and the contemporary in suggestive relationship, as we might anticipate, this has hardly of itself been peculiar, original or even particularly notable since the moment of Modernism. Her most well-sanctioned use of 'mythical' modernist structure is probably *Autobiography of Red*, a long narrative poem published in 1998. This maps onto an account of compulsive gay adolescent desire, turmoil and violence a long lyric poem about Geryon and Herakles by the Greek poet Stesichoros. Even so, this classical doubling is the only well-sanctioned thing about this work; and elsewhere Carson's classicist readings of the contemporary give rise to at least as much estrangement as recognition. Hers is work that consistently alerts us to the inevitability of disjunction, non-correspondence and destabilization, and to the arduous artifice involved in literary attempts to structure patterns of meaning across divergent historical epochs.

In addition, Carson is constantly herself alert to the provisionality of her procedures. Epistemological anxiety, even distress, seems deeply to inform her methods and forms, and hers is an aesthetic of the oblique, the wried and the skewed, signalled by unpredictable crossings, transits, collocations and juxtapositions. Her central points of reference and allusion – touchstones of a kind, to whom frequent reference is made – are joltingly eclectic: Beckett, Gertrude Stein and Virginia Woolf, as we might almost expect, but also Emily Brontë, George Eliot and Simone Weil. Some of her scenarios or mises-en-scène seem almost calculated to provoke, baffle or astound: Virginia Woolf and Thucydides hold a conversation during a TV programme about the Peloponnesian War; ekphrastic poem-annotations on Edward Hopper are accompanied by ethical and theological reflections by St Augustine; a ruinous marital relationship is framed by a set of quotations from relatively obscure texts by Keats, including his annotations of *Paradise Lost* and work he intended to publish under the pseudonym Lucy Vaughan Lloyd of China Walk, Lambeth; Longinus dreams about Antonioni in an essay which attempts to read out of the encounter a contemporary sublime; a piece called 'Irony Is Not Enough' is subtitled 'Essay on My Life as Catherine Deneuve' in a way indicating that a certain dry, even desiccated, comedy sometimes attaches to these similitudes, or discrepancies; and, most extensively, in the critical study *Economy of the Unlost* (1999), Paul Celan and Simonides of Keos – whose best-known poem is the epitaph for the Lacedaemonians fallen at Thermopylae – are juxtaposed under the rubrics of both lyric economy and ultimate human depredation.

Economy of the Unlost offers, in its prefatory 'note on method', a rationale for its author's characteristic procedures. Deciding that there is 'too much self' in her writing, Carson says that her aim is to reach a state of 'not settling'. Readers will initially almost inevitably resist the unlikely collocation made by *Economy of the Unlost*, since no poet of modernity seems more an instance of, and witness to, ethical and aesthetic exceptionality than Paul Celan. Carson's defence of not settling comes, though, itself to unsettle resistance. 'With and against, aligned and adverse,' she says, 'each is placed like a surface on which the other may come into focus. Sometimes you can see a celestial object better by looking at something else, with it, in the sky'. Some of the similitudes in Carson's work more generally do seem to me to remain disconcertingly ineffective, their capacity for comparative sharpening of vision unproven, and the gnomic, dark sayings to which they give rise resisting the intelligence all too successfully. But *Economy of the Unlost* supplies, in its close readings, a sustained justification of method. The comparisons and equivalents become, as the thematizing of 'economy' develops its rigours of scrutiny and insight, richly apposite and fruitful in a set of brilliantly ramifying considerations of the work of both poets. Carson's treatment of Celan's 'Matiere de Bretagne' in particular is, simply, a revelation.

Her insouciant flouting of the customary academic protocols when she introduces into a critical study her anxiety about exposing too much 'self' in her writing both suggests and underwrites a further set of similitudes in her work. Prose, even literary-critical or scholarly prose, is never clearly separated off from poetry, so that genre in Carson is itself fluidly subject to destabilization. Thus, *Plainwater* (1995) defines itself as 'essays and poetry', *Decreation* (2005) as 'poetry, essays, opera'; *Autobiography of Red* is subtitled 'a novel in verse' and *The Beauty of the Husband* (2001) as 'a fictional essay in 29 tangos'. The imaginative and the critical or philosophical impulses in this writer form a single creative urge or push. This has made for some controversy regarding her status as 'poet', and any concern with prosody does seem to me intermittent, at best. Better, probably, to think of her work in both prose and verse as 'writing', in the way David Jones in his preface to *In Parenthesis* invites us to consider that work, implicitly proposing for the word a peculiar, newly heightened or italicized valency.

All this provocative and often difficult instability in Anne Carson serves, when it works most effectively, a genuinely, disturbingly, initially disorientatingly novel form of perception and interpretation in which some recognizable things are perturbed into unpredictable and unforeseeably profitable relationship. Her first book, *Eros the Bittersweet* (1986), sets a sort of programme by offering a study of the forms of 'erotic paradox' taken by 'glukupikros', the 'sweet bitter', in classical Greek love poetry and especially in Sappho, whom Carson extensively and hauntingly later translated in *If Not, Winter: Fragments of Sappho* (2002). *Eros the Bittersweet*, arguing and annotating the similarity between, or the inseparability of, the sweet and the bitter in erotic experience, also argues a comparability between the way Eros acts on the mind of a lover and the way knowing acts on the mind of a thinker, the intimate crossing in the imaginative and affective life of the erotic and the intellectual. This shows some indebtedness to French models occasionally referred to in her work (Derrida, Lacan, Bachelard), but for Carson it is also associated with some of the virtuous effects of the aorist in Greek grammar, which conveys aspect as well as tense, allowing, for instance, for a sense of origin or future consequence even as it registers termination. In 'The Glass Essay' in *Glass and God* (1998) she appears to define one such effect when she refers to 'a sudden sense of every object / existing in space on its own shadow'. This is exactly the effect given to the objects, and subjects, of her own finest writing, which gives us access to a world of unexpected doubles, shadows, depths, strange alternative patterns and metamorphoses within or alongside ordinary appearance, experience, emotion and schedule. This is a world in which, notably, the erotic is likely to veer or warp at any moment into the mystical, a warping in which we may certainly read the shadowy shape of a possibly still retained but also individually, personally feminized authorial Catholicism. The erotic itself is likely to take fluidly unorthodox forms, as the work is drawn as much to gender as to genre instability, everywhere undermining any notion of the normative in human sexuality. Some of Carson's work bends the usual co-ordinates out of alignment in a way that allows new light to enter; new light, or what she calls in *Men in the Off Hours*, a desirably 'inadvertent lucidity'.

Among the things intimately involved in all of this are both an attitude to death and a needy desire to register subjectivity, sometimes deeply distressed subjectivity, in terms other than those made available by romantic and post-romantic modes of poetic self-expression, self-exposure and self-recognition – 'confessionalism' and its variants, latterly – whose probably inevitable egotism Carson clearly suspects and disdains. Even so, her work articulates a great deal of distressing biographical material. This has to do prominently with her immediate, first family: a fraught relationship with a father who is eventually hospitalized with long-term dementia; a difficult relationship with a nevertheless adored mother; and, beyond these not completely uncommon difficulties, the more exotic one of a relationship with (or to) a brother whom she hadn't seen for over twenty years before his death. This brother, Michael, appears in several texts in Carson's work, notably 'Water Margins: An Essay on Swimming by My Brother' in *Plainwater* (1995). We learn there that thinking about him provokes 'a sadness … in me that I have never quite put down'.

Nox is a long elegy for Michael Carson, who died in Copenhagen in 2000, in which the burden of this sadness, newly and differently sharpened by death, is given remarkable shape. We learn Michael's story as the poem advances, although elements of it have also been made available in some of the earlier work. He disappeared in 1978, as an alternative to imprisonment (we are not told for what crime, but we do hear that he has dealt in drugs). He wanders – sometimes more or less destitute – in Europe and India for many years, marries at least twice and has had a lover called Anna who dies young and was far more important to him than either of his marital partners. Over the course of more than twenty years he has written postcards home occasionally, giving no return address, but has not written at all for the seven years prior to his death, during which time his mother has also died. He has only ever written one full-length letter to her, on the occasion of the lover Anna's death. Fragments of this letter are reproduced in *Nox*, and the mother's grief and unappeasable yearning are a constant focus of attention. She eventually comes to believe (wrongly) that Michael is dead because when she prays for him 'nothing comes back'. He has made only a handful of phone calls to his sister, the poet, since his disappearance, asking for money. She learns of his death only several weeks after the funeral.

Formally, *Nox* is one of the most extraordinary, most unlikely elegies ever written: a series of lexical glosses with numbered commentaries on Catullus no. CI, 'Multas per gentes', the elegy for his own brother who also died and was buried far from home, the poem which famously concludes, 'ave atque vale'. Not only generically, but materially too, *Nox* is an astounding production. A prefatory note tells us that Robert Currie assisted in its 'design and realization'; and what he appears to have done is to have reproduced – superbly – a homemade scrapbook by Carson in the form of a lengthy, concertina'd scroll housed inside a cardboard box. (A *Paris Review* interview with Carson conducted in 2002 lets us know that a version of the work as a homemade object already existed then, almost ten years before its publication.) The format of the poem therefore has an element of the artist's book about it, but a reproducible one; and Carson is, or has been, a maker of drawings as well as writings. *Nox* includes various extra-textual elements – drawings, pastels, collages, photographs – and peculiar textual elements too: combinations of typescript and reproduced hand-written material; blotched or badly copied text; corrected text; crossings-out making some text illegible; typos; words written in wax made legible only by pencil shadings; reproduced letters and excised stamps; handwritten alterations to typed texts. The continuous, ravelled paper of the text may also remind us of papyrus roll, which may be appropriate to the work's genre – or pastiche-genre – as a commentary on a classical poem. The boxed text also seems to me a material realization or dramatization of the equivalence proposed by Robert Lowell in his blank-verse sonnet 'Reading Myself': 'this open book … my open coffin'. If we understand it like this, then it is also Carson's material dramatization of the truth that all elegy is self-elegy too, that it is Margaret you mourn for. Inevitable self-involvement, self-awareness and self-attention are themselves the focus of keen scrutiny in this conceptually misgiving writerly performance.

Nox proceeds by offering, always on its left-hand pages – its sinister side? – a gloss on every word in Catullus's poem, while the right-hand sheets, and often both left and right together, contain the numbered items of 'commentary' and all the other materials I have mentioned. The 'commentary' gives us the brother's story and the poet's reaction to it, and to him. The necessity that we read both texts more or less simultaneously means that our reading is constantly interrupted or disrupted by oscillations of attention. The glosses read very slowly, as glosses do, with their briefly declarative explications and phrasal exemplars, while the commentaries are much faster and their sophistications of syntax always have a certain rhetorical element. Language itself, with its slippery provocations and dispersals, is therefore heavily foregrounded in this work.

We gradually come to realize, though, that the moods and emotions of the commentaries bleed into, or contaminate, the glosses. In no sense neutrally definitional, they have, as it were, been interfered with authorially. As a result, almost every gloss includes, in its exemplary cases, the word 'nox' or one of its grammatical cognates, together with a translation of the example. These supply such emotionally charged and resonant phrases as 'the vast plain of night' under 'aequora', 'to vanish by night into nothing' under 'vectus' and, under 'atque', 'just like him I was a negotiator with the night'. The word that supplies the book's title therefore sounds a sort of cumulative funerary knell as the work progresses.

This foregrounded linguistic disruption is accompanied by a deep scepticism about any truth that this elegy may have to tell about the person elegized. This is conveyed partly by means of a scholarly, if fragmentary, meditation on the relationship between history and elegy as it is perceived by both the hardly known early Greek writer Hekataion and by the very well-known Greek historian Herodotus. *Nox*, therefore, an already generically unclassifiable work, also finds space, as much of Carson's imaginative work does, for an essay in literary criticism. This can itself be intensely poetic, becoming so, for instance, when it reflects on the way Hekataion meditates on the emblem of the phoenix. He finds in it, Carson says, 'the immense fragility of his own flying – composed as it is of these ceaselessly passing shadows carried backwards by the very motion that devours them, his motion, his asking'. That must be an emblem for the undertaking that is *Nox* itself too, this text finding an image for its own exploratory procedures as it is compelled aesthetically forward by a backwards-facing memorial necessity or obligation. As such, the image harmonizes fruitfully but also plangently with the possibility which Carson discovers in *Decreation* in a synoptic essay on three mystics (as she perceives them): Sappho; Marguerite Porete, the medieval French author of *The Mirror of Simple Souls* who was burnt at the stake as a heretic; and Simone Weil. Their writings manifest, Carson says, in a way implying her own intense desire for such a thing too, 'a sort of dream of distance in which the self is displaced from the centre of the work and the teller disappears into the telling'. *Nox* really does work as a mode of writing exceptionally at the service of writerly self-displacement.

As such, it also possesses – extraordinarily, given its desolating material and the inevitable melancholia of elegy – an element of comedy, a sad comedy of discrepancy. In his one letter to his mother, fragmentarily reproduced in thick block capitals, Michael says of Anna, his lover killed by an epileptic attack, 'Like wind in your hair she had epilepsy her life was hell sometimes flipping like a fish'. The irregular punctuation or bad grammar of this contributes to its poignancy. It suggests too though that brother, like sister, was a maker of strikingly unlikely but dramatically inventive similes. It therefore suggests some likeness in the midst of huge sibling disparities of life, career and fate; and, perhaps as sign or code of such recognition, a page of the text of *Nox* accompanying Michael's letter and its simile is watermarked with the word 'like' scrawled six times in increasing size. One of the most basic modes of poetic likeness is the riddle, which falls under the aegis of comedy; and one of the glosses to the word 'per' in *Nox* offers 'a riddle, enigma or dark fact'. *Nox* itself darkly testifies to Michael Carson's nature as all three. But the work itself also offers its readers a riddle: why is an elegy like a gloss and commentary on a classical text; or, why might the one be written as the other?

Involved in the answer is what Carson tells us about her attempts to translate Catullus no. CI. Her version, previously published in *Men in the Off Hours*, appears late in *Nox*, and she tells us she finds it unsatisfactory. 'Nothing in English', she says,

> can capture the passionate, slow surface of a Roman elegy. No one (even in Latin) can approximate Catullan diction, which at its most sorrowful has an air of deep festivity, like one of those trees that turns all its leaves over, silver, in the wind … I came to think of translating as a room, not exactly an unknown room, where one gropes for the light switch. I guess it never ends. A brother never ends. I prowl him. He does not end.

No one would ever claim that there is festivity in *Nox*. If a dead brother is like a dead language, he can be recovered only in traces, fragments, memorial ruins, hauntings, approximations and vanishings. So much so, in fact, that Carson's version of Catullus translates 'ave atque vale' with relentless finality as 'Farewell and farewell': a double insistence, a collapsing of Catullus's distinction between greeting and going into a further, unillusioned similitude; a collapsing justifiable as a translation because Catullus presents his poem as a graveside address, where all hail is inevitably farewell too. Michael Carson, whose escape from Canada necessitated a false passport, lacks even a name in death. He has no gravestone, and his ashes have been scattered on the sea. But there is in *Nox* the play of language, form and material structure which themselves, and of themselves, make it clear that something, at least, may be carried over, carried forward, translated, something that may supply 'a lock against oblivion'. Troping Plutarch on Herodotus, Carson calls her own 'something', her memorial invention for her brother, 'a headstand', as if she, as author and translator, is a sort of jongleur before the feast, and feats, of language(s). Towards the poem's conclusion she also reproduces Michael's own 'ave atque vale' in his letter home: 'Love you. Love you.' This is a doubling of yet another kind, offered, we must assume, in tacit penitence as well as grateful affection. In the end, *Nox* doubles its elegy with a sort of love poem too. It is a brilliant, very moving invention that will reward numerous rereadings.

III
David Jones Revisited (2010)

David Jones's long poems *In Parenthesis* (1937) and *The Anathemata* (1952) have been unavailable for several years, a saddening state of affairs for any admirer: so it is excellent to be able to welcome them back in the handsome new Faber editions published in 2010. Jones's third poetic sequence, *The Sleeping Lord and Other Fragments* (1974), has remained in print; but the final necessary volume, his collection of essays on art, religion, aesthetics and culture, *Epoch and Artist* (1959), is available only from Faber Finds, the print-on-demand service. Useful as this is, it means that nobody is going to come across it by serendipity, that long-sanctioned form of readerly discovery, already greatly eroded by online ordering and Kindle's introduction of the intangible, unlendable text.

Serendipity was how I first came across *In Parenthesis*, when I went to Oxford for an interview to read English in the late 1960s. I found it in the Paperback Bookshop on Broad Street and thought it looked a bit like *The Waste Land*, which I knew pretty well, and *Ulysses*, which I did not but had glanced through several times in mixed excitement and bafflement. In any case, it had an introduction by T. S. Eliot who commented on the affinity between Jones and Joyce, Pound and himself; and at the time Eliot was more or less God's literary representative on earth for me.

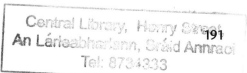

As chance had it, my tutor when I got to Oxford, Reggie Alton, knew *In Parenthesis* and was also keen on Jones's artwork – the paintings, engravings, drawings and late letterings – and he lent me a catalogue. I wrote an essay on the poem in my first year and eventually wrote a postgraduate thesis on *The Anathemata*. Jones therefore never seemed to me any more recherché than Eliot or Joyce: but then I also shared with him some at least of what he calls the problematical 'unshared backgrounds' of readers of modern literature, especially a traditional Catholic education in which the Latin liturgy was prominent (Jones himself was a convert to the religion). Other elements of Jones's constant literary allusiveness, however – notably the Welsh mythological material – I had to bone up on just like most other people.

But there is no point in denying or ignoring the difficulties presented by unshared cultural co-ordinates; and they are presumably, at least partly, why these books have fallen out of print. Despite some excellent critical work on Jones over the years, he has never been absorbed adequately by literary tradition and he has hardly been taken on at all by university literary syllabuses. Neither has he benefited from what is often a stimulus to seeking out a writer's work, a full-scale biography, although the Canadian scholar Thomas Dilworth has been at work on one for many years. Coming to the end of a lengthy career as a university teacher of English, I therefore find it almost impossible to conceive of introducing Jones to contemporary undergraduates, even though over the years I have occasionally acted as an examiner for doctoral theses on him, and some current doctoral students of my own, writing on other things altogether, seem to have found their way to him.

There is nothing wrong with that kind of readership: fit audience though few. But, rereading these poems again in 2010, I still find myself regretting that Jones has not been more thoroughly or widely absorbed. It probably would not have surprised the writer himself: *The Anathemata* begins 'at the sagging end and chapter's close' and, towards its own close, it asks an anguished question of its own materials whose enervatedly dejected rhythm seems almost the question's own despairing answer:

> Failing
> > (finished?) West
> > your food once.

At the poem's opening, and at this moment too, what is being recalled is the Latin Roman Catholic liturgy; but despite his question here, Jones would have found it inconceivable that the Catholic Church itself would abandon that liturgy and its language not very long after the poem was published. The reactionary signals given out by this kind of plaintiveness took for Jones the form taken in other modernist poets too: an attraction to the extreme right-wing politics of the 1930s. This is profoundly unappealing, even if it was, it seems, relatively short-lived in

Jones's case. In fact, though, his work everywhere offers a counter to such reactionary modes and forms. It represents an enormous work of cultural reclamation and constitutes a celebration, in the teeth of termination, of all sorts of cherished things. These are frequently evoked with sensuous relish and with a kind of permanent, buoyantly – and boyishly – unabashed innocence. The word 'anathemata', as Jones defines it in his lengthy preface to that poem, is, etymologically, a word ambivalently poised between commination and celebration; and Jones's whole effort is to retrieve, perhaps for one final time, what would otherwise irrevocably be banished from modern consciousness and conscience.

The labour of retrieval, the commemorative *pietas*, is immense and intense, and Jones's texts bristle and cascade with footnotes uncovering the sources of his astonishingly wide reading. Some of those to *In Parenthesis* in particular are themselves virtually prose poems too; and many also carry a fascinating social and military history, often by recalling specific vocabularies, hardly recoverable elsewhere. The laboursome recovery also demands enormous patience; and, you might say, an aesthetic of patience is very deeply inscribed in Jones's literary and artistic forms, which took many years of slow composition. It is hard to know where the reciprocal patience all of this demands from a reader might be found in a time of such massive, exponential technological change as ours, when the fluctuating attentiveness encouraged by the Net seems almost a model of attentiveness as inattention, attentiveness as the new restlessness. This is a vastly accelerated form of that 'civilisational change' which also exercised and anguished Jones; 'even while we watch the boatman mending his sail,' he says in the preface to *In Parenthesis*, 'the petroleum is hurting the sea'. His work, especially *The Anathemata*, asks not only where 'we' begin and what our proper end might be, but how we might continue to recognize ourselves in the universe of the 'technocrats'; and, as the hurtful petroleum suggests, there is also an ecological concern implicit in a great deal of David Jones and rendered beautifully explicit in some of the poems of the *Sleeping Lord* sequence. Their more obviously striking contemporary relevance, together with their dramatizations of Jones's constant preoccupations as an opposition between Roman and Celtic world views, and their heightened lyric and rhythmic energies, make them probably the best place for any reader new to Jones to begin.

Of the two poems back in print, however, *In Parenthesis* is by far the more approachable. This is because, before it is anything else, *In Parenthesis* is a narrative, and a very affecting one. It may tell almost the generic story of a private soldier – Jones names his self-representation John Ball – in the early stages of the First World War, as his platoon sails from England to France and then moves slowly to the Front to be devastated in the battle of Mametz on the Somme in 1916. Although characterization is sketchy, it is also distinctive, and we feel for these men in their affections, anxieties and final terrors. The intermittent dialogue in the cockney and Welsh accents of Jones's regiment, the Royal Welch [*sic*] Fusiliers, is vibrant, spirited, warm and sometimes racy ('It's as cold as the Arctic Bear's arse' is, I am afraid, an expression my children all picked up from David Jones, via their father, at far too early an age). The nightmare of the put-upon private soldier, alleviated only but deeply by intense male companionship, is exceptionally rendered, although elements of it are shared with the poetry of Isaac Rosenberg and the prose of Frederic Manning's underrated *Her Privates We*.

Although this narrative has considerable momentum, Christopher Reid in conversation with me has recommended reading *In Parenthesis* backwards as well as forwards – starting at Part 7 and working back to Part 1 – as a way of better appreciating the narrative's individuality and poignancy. Despite an epiphanic economy learnt in part from early Joyce, and a kind of painterly particularity all his own, Jones's narrative can, on a first reading, seem slow, with longeurs and indirections: and this is largely because it is intertwined with a great deal of material drawn from literary, liturgical and mythological sources, prominent among which are the Roman Catholic liturgy of Good Friday, the Welsh tales collected in the *Mabinogion*, Malory, the early Welsh heroic poem *Y Gododdin, Henry V, The Rime of the Ancient Mariner* and *The Hunting of the Snark*. Some of these allusive passages are better known than most of Jones, since they have seemed obvious stand-alone pieces to anthologists: the passage at the end of the poem known as 'The Queen of the Woods', for instance; 'Dai's Boast', in which a private soldier celebrates a long tradition of military loyalty and attachment; and a passage in which the eagles of the Anglo-Saxon poem 'The Battle of Maldon' metamorphose into the 'rat of no-man's-land'. But such passages have also been at the centre of interpretative debate. Long ago Paul Fussell admiringly but sceptically wrote about the poem's 'honourable miscarriage', believing that no satisfactory fit had been achieved between realistic narrative and literary-mythological allusion. There are other ways of understanding this fit, or lack of it; and this is a debate every new reader will enter. An umpteenth reading convinces me that it is a debate still worth entering because this is a poem of intense, singular literary satisfaction.

It is harder to know how *The Anathemata*, a hugely demanding work, will find a new readership. Auden, who, like Eliot, greatly admired it and reviewed it at length, liked its crossword-puzzle element; although when I had the grant-aided opportunity to do this crossword I discovered that even the polymathic Auden had got some of the answers wrong. When you do the crossword you discover a radically anthropocentric view of life, even if this poet knows that 'anthropos is not always kind'; and some of what centres man for David Jones is now dated or dubious. The poem's anthropology and archaeology are necessarily of their moment; its theology and aesthetic and cultural theory are indebted to the neo-Thomist scholasticism of the Maritain school which is, it seems, of little contemporary interest even to Catholic theologians, however ingeniously and inventively Jones makes it sing in *Epoch and Artist*. It is crucial to Jones's anthropology, for instance, that man is 'the only sign-making animal', and this view must now compete with such zoological information as that conveyed in David Attenborough's truly astounding television films about animal and ornithological ways of being in the world. It is also a poem that regards Christian Incarnation as fact, not myth, even if Incarnation is approached again and again in mythological modes; and a brief Googling session suggests that Jones's most attentive current readers appear to be, at least in some form of the definition, Christians. Nevertheless, the open-minded reader will recognize that *The Anathemata* dramatizes its interests with palpable, impassioned vibrancy. The poem is manifestly propelled by the urgency of this poet's and artist's affections.

One instance. When I visited Lascaux, *The Anathemata* came to my mind. (For conservation reasons most people may now see only a replica of the original cave, but it is an extremely good one.) Jones conveys the awe-inspiring otherness of the cave paintings as well as their unmatched artistry. Born from a primal, vulnerable necessity – the need for food and clothing – the animal images were, it seems, a form of placatory, restorative or sympathetic magic. Jones meets their revelatory, bewildering otherness with an otherness of his own, a form of writing remarkably combining nursery rhyme, aesthetic theory, and sacramental theology:

> And see how they run, the juxtaposed forms, brighting the vaults of Lascaux; how the linear is wedded to volume, how they do, within, in an unbloody manner, under the forms of brown haematite and black manganese on the graved lime-face, what is done, without,
> > far on the windy tundra
> at the kill
> that the kindred may have life.

This kind of linguistic coalescence is poetry; and poetry is the reward for anyone patient enough with David Jones's own bewildering but also revelatory otherness, with the unique eventfulness of his writing.

Notes

Notes to Introduction

1 T. S. Eliot, in a letter to E. Martin Browne, cited in Seamus Heaney, *The Government of the Tongue* (London: Faber and Faber, 1988), 107.
2 T. S. Eliot, *On Poetry and Poets* (1957; London: Faber and Faber, 1969), 20.
3 Theodor W. Adorno, *The Adorno Reader*, ed. Brian O'Connor (Oxford: Blackwell, 2000), 210.
4 Theodor W. Adorno, *Negative Dialectics* (New York: Continuum Publishing Company, 1973), 362.
5 Seamus Heaney, *The Redress of Poetry: Oxford Lectures* (London: Faber and Faber, 1995), 9.
6 Heaney, *The Government of the Tongue*, 92, xix.
7 See Neil Corcoran (ed.), *Do You, Mr Jones? Bob Dylan with the Poets and Professors* (London: Chatto and Windus, 2002).
8 Heaney, *The Government of the Tongue*, xiii.
9 Walter Benjamin, *One-Way Street and Other Writings* (London: NLB, 1979), 65.

Notes to Chapter 1

1 Quotations from Thomas are taken from *The Annotated Collected Poems*, ed. Edna Longley (Tarset: Bloodaxe Books, 2008).
2 Wilfred Owen, *Selected Letters*, ed. John Bell (Oxford: Oxford University Press, 1985), 306.
3 Quotations from Owen are taken from *Wilfred Owen: The Complete Poems and Fragments*, ed. Jon Stallworthy (London and Oxford: Chatto and Windus/ Oxford University Press, 1983).
4 Quotations from Sassoon are taken from Siegfried Sassoon, *The War Poems* (London: Faber and Faber, 1983).
5 Dominic Hibberd, *Wilfred Owen: A New Biography* (London: Weidenfeld and Nicholson, 2002).
6 James Fenton, *The Strength of Poetry* (Oxford: Oxford University Press, 2001), 32.
7 Peter Howarth, *British Poetry in the Age of Modernism* (Cambridge: Cambridge University Press, 2005), 196.

8 Quoted in Hibberd, *Wilfred Owen*, 317.

9 Douglas Kerr, *Wilfred Owen's Voices* (Oxford: Clarendon Press, 1993), 277–95.

10 Jahan Ramazani, *Poetry of Mourning: The Modern Elegy from Hardy to Heaney* (Chicago: University of Chicago Press, 1994), 69.

11 Kerr, *Wilfred Owen's Voices*, 295.

12 Owen, *Selected Letters*, 353.

13 Siegfried Sassoon, *The Complete Memoirs of George Sherston* (1937; London: Faber and Faber, 1972), 496.

14 Owen, *Selected Letters*, 305.

15 Ezra Pound, *Selected Letters 1907-1941*, ed. D. D. Paige (1950; New York: New Directions, 1971), 40.

16 Quoted in *The Poems and Plays of Isaac Rosenberg*, ed. Vivien Noakes (Oxford: Oxford University Press, 2004), xlvi. Quotations from Rosenberg's poems are taken from this edition.

17 Ibid., xx.

18 Ibid., xlv.

19 D. W. Harding, *Experience into Words* (1963; Cambridge: Cambridge University Press, 1982), 97.

20 Quotations from Gurney are taken from *The Collected Poems of Ivor Gurney*, ed. P. J. Kavanagh (Oxford: Oxford University Press, 1982).

Notes to Chapter 2

1 Quoted in *The Poems and Plays of Isaac Rosenberg*, ed. Vivien Noakes (Oxford: Oxford University Press, 2004), 356. All quotations from the poems are taken from this edition.

2 See Jean Moorcroft Wilson, *Isaac Rosenberg: The Making of a Great War Poet: A New Life* (2008; London: Phoenix, 2009), *passim.*

3 *The Collected Works of Isaac Rosenberg*, ed. Ian Parsons (London: Chatto and Windus, 1979), 239.

4 Ibid., 255.

5 Ibid., 227.

6 Ibid., 230.

7 Ibid., 230.

8 Ibid., 303.

9 Geoffrey Hill, *Collected Critical Writings* (Oxford: Oxford University Press, 2008), 456.

10 *The Collected Works of Isaac Rosenberg*, 237.

11 *The Poems and Plays of Isaac Rosenberg*, xviii.

12 Hill, *Collected Critical Writings*, 454.

13 *The Collected Works of Isaac Rosenberg*, 268.

14 Cited by James Wood, *The Broken Estate: Essays on Literature and Belief* (1999; new edn, New York: Picador, 2010), 146.

15 Eliot in the *Criterion*, cited by Anthony Julius, *T. S. Eliot, Anti-Semitism and Literary Form* (1995; new edn, London: Thames and Hudson, 2003), 101–2.

16 Ibid., 102.

17 Wood, *The Broken Estate*, 146.

18 *The Collected Works of Isaac Rosenberg*, 242.

Notes to Chapter 3

1 Samuel Taylor Coleridge, *Lectures and Notes on Shakspere and Other English Poets* (1883; London: George Bell and Sons, 1904), 531.
2 Ian Hamilton, *Robert Lowell: A Biography* (1982; London: Faber and Faber, 1983), 289.
3 Nadezhda Mandelstam, quoted in Robert Lowell, *Collected Poems*, ed. Frank Bidart and David Ganzweiler (London: Faber and Faber, 2003), 1156.
4 I am using the version by Richard Pevear and Larissa Volokhonsky in their 'new translation' of *Doctor Zhivago* (London: Harvill Secker, 2010).
5 Boris Pasternak, *Selected Poems*, trans. Jon Stallworthy and Peter France (1983; Harmondsworth: Penguin Books, 1984), 154.
6 *Words in Air: The Complete Correspondence between Elizabeth Bishop and Robert Lowell*, ed. Thomas Travisano and Saskia Hamilton (London: Faber and Faber, 2008), 271.
7 Lowell, *Collected Poems*, 195.
8 Peter Robinson, *Poetry & Translation: The Art of the Impossible* (Liverpool: Liverpool University Press, 2010), 35.
9 Paul Muldoon, *The End of the Poem: Oxford Lectures on Poetry* (London: Faber and Faber, 2006), 194.
10 John Dryden, *Selected Criticism*, ed. James Kinsley and George Parfitt (Oxford: Clarendon Press, 1970), 186.
11 *The Letters of Robert Lowell*, ed. Saskia Hamilton (New York: Farrar Straus and Giroux, 2005), 327.
12 Ibid., 357.
13 Lowell slightly revised the *Imitations* version for its appearance in Olga Carlisle's anthology *Poets on Street Corners* in 1968. This is the version published in Lowell's *Collected Poems*, which I am discussing in this chapter.
14 Quoted in Lowell, *Collected Poems*, 1056.
15 See Zbigniew Herbert, *The Collected Poems, 1956-1998* (New York: Ecco, 2007), 186-7.
16 I have wondered whether Bob Dylan's refrain in his great, terrible, vindictive song 'Idiot Wind' on *Blood on the Tracks* (1975) draws on this line: 'You're an idiot, babe / It's a wonder that you still know how to breathe'.
17 See J. M. Coetzee, 'Zbigniew Herbert and the Figure of the Censor', *Giving Offense: Essays on Censorship* (Chicago and London: University of Chicago Press, 1996), 147-62.
18 See *Hamlet*, ed. Ann Thompson and Neil Taylor (London: The Arden Shakespeare: Thomson Learning, 2006), 371.
19 Zbigniew Herbert, *The Collected Prose, 1948-1998*, ed. Alissa Valles (New York: Ecco, 2010), 186.
20 Walter Benjamin, *Illuminations*, ed. Hannah Arendt (1970; London: Fontana 1973), 73.
21 Quoted by Charles Tomlinson in the introduction to his *Translations* (Oxford: Oxford University Press, 1983).
22 C. P. Cavafy, *Collected Poems*, trans Daniel Mendelsohn (New York: Alfred A. Knopf, 2009).

Notes to Chapter 4

1 Cited in Richard Finneran, Jared Curtis and Ann Saddlemyer (eds.), *The Tower (1928): Manuscript Materials* (Ithaca, NY and London: Cornell University Press, 2007), unpaginated. All subsequent references to Yeats's manuscripts for the poem are to this edition.

2 Cited in Curtis B. Bradford, *Yeats at Work* (Carbondale, Ill.: South Illinois University Press, 1965), 9.

3 See the account of the visit, including George's disgusted letter to Thomas MacGreevy, in R. F. Foster, *W. B. Yeats: A Life*, vol. 2, *The Arch-Poet* (Oxford: Oxford University Press, 2003), 319 ff.

4 *The Gonne-Yeats Letters, 1893-1938*, ed. Anna MacBride White and A. Norman Jeffares (1992; New York and London: W. W. Norton and Company, 1993), 445.

5 See Derek Roper, 'Yeats's Quattrocento Finger', *Yeats Annual*, 17 (2007), 181–96.

6 See Yeats's letter to Dorothy Wellesley (13 August 1936), in Dorothy Wellesley (ed.), *Letters on Poetry from W. B. Yeats to Dorothy Wellesley* (Oxford: Oxford University Press, 1940).

7 Helen Vendler, *Our Secret Discipline: Yeats and Lyric Form* (Oxford: Oxford University Press, 2007), 281.

8 Harold Bloom, *Yeats* (Oxford: Oxford University Press, 1970), 369.

9 Seamus Heaney, *Among Schoolchildren: A Lecture Dedicated to the Memory of John Malone* (Belfast: John Malone Memorial Committee, 1983), 15.

10 All quotations are taken from Delmore Schwartz's untitled essay in James Hall and Martin Steinmann (eds.), *The Permanence of Yeats* (1950; New York: Collier Books, 1961), 293–5. In a posthumous selection of his essays the piece is entitled 'An Unwritten Book': see *Selected Essays of Delmore Schwartz*, ed. Dwight Macdonald (Chicago and London: University of Chicago Press, 1970), 81–101.

11 All quotations are taken from the essay on 'Among School Children', in Cleanth Brooks, *The Well-Wrought Urn: Studies in the Structure of Poetry* (London: Dobson, 1949).

12 Frank Kermode, *Romantic Image* (1957; London: Fontana, 1971), 71.

13 Ibid., 63.

14 See Elizabeth Butler Cullingford, *Gender and History in Yeats's Love Poetry* (Cambridge: Cambridge University Press, 1993).

15 All quotations are taken from Kermode, *Romantic Image*, ch. 4, 'The Dancer' and ch. 5, 'The Tree'.

16 All quotations are taken from 'Image and Emblem in Yeats', in Paul de Man, *The Rhetoric of Romanticism* (New York: Columbia University Press, 1984), 145–238.

17 Seamus Heaney, *Preoccupations: Selected Prose, 1968-1978* (London: Faber and Faber, 1980), 113. See also ch. 5, below.

18 Helen Vendler, *Our Secret Discipline: Yeats and Lyric Form*, 94.

19 All quotations are taken from Vendler's reading of 'Among School Children', ibid., 279–89.

20 Ted Hughes, *Winter Pollen* (London: Faber and Faber, 1994), 81. See ch. 10, below.

21 Sister Marybride Ryan OP, 'The Paddler's Heritage: Yeats's Visit to St Otteran's School, 1926', *Yeats Annual*, 7 (1990), 208.
22 Sister Ryan died in Grand Rapids, Michigan in 2010 at the age of 97. The on-line obituary supplied by her Dominican convent tells us that she had a PhD in English, and ends with another of her poems, an affecting one called 'Homing'. Manifestly, Sister Ryan was no 'paddler'; but then viewed rightly no one ever is and in any case the ugly duckling in the fable becomes the swan.

Notes to Chapter 5

1 Richard Ellmann, *Eminent Domain: Yeats among Wilde, Joyce, Pound, Eliot, and Auden* (Oxford: Oxford University Press, 1967), 3.
2 Harold Bloom, *Yeats* (Oxford and New York: Oxford University Press, 1970).
3 See Neil Corcoran, *English Poetry since 1940* (London and New York: Longman, 1993), xv and Naomi Segal, *The Adulteress's Child: Authorship and Desire in the Nineteenth-Century Novel* (Cambridge: Polity Press, 1992), 11.
4 Christopher Ricks, *Allusion to the Poets* (Oxford: Oxford University Press, 2002), 5–6.
5 Harold Bloom, *The Anxiety of Influence* (Oxford: Oxford University Press, 1973), 153.
6 Terence Brown, *The Life of W. B. Yeats* (Oxford: Blackwell, 1999), 381.
7 These essays are collected in Seamus Heaney, *Preoccupations: Selected Prose, 1968-1978* (London: Faber and Faber, 1980).
8 This essay was published in P. J. Drudy (ed.), *Irish Studies*, vol. 1 (Cambridge: Cambridge University Press, 1980), 1–20.
9 Seamus Heaney, *The Place of Writing* (Atlanta, Ga.: Scholars Press, n.d. [1988]); Heaney, *Finders Keepers: Selected Prose, 1971-2001* (London: Faber and Faber, 2002).
10 Seamus Heaney, *The Redress of Poetry* (London: Faber and Faber, 1995), 160, 147.
11 Seamus Heaney, 'William Butler Yeats (1865–1939)', in Seamus Deane (ed.), *The Field Day Anthology of Irish Writing*, 3 vols (Derry: Field Day Publications, 1991), vol. 2, pp. 783–90 and Heaney, 'Introduction', *W. B. Yeats: Poems Selected by Seamus Heaney* (London: Faber and Faber, 2000).
12 Seamus Heaney, *Opened Ground: Poems 1966-1996* (London: Faber and Faber, 1998), 445–67.
13 Peter McDonald, 'Faiths and Fidelities: Heaney and Longley in Mid-Career', in Fran Brearton and Eamonn Hughes (eds), *Last Before America: Irish and American Writing: Essays in Honour of Michael Allen* (Belfast: Blackstaff Press, 2001), 15.
14 Seamus Deane, *Heroic Style: The Tradition of an Idea* (Derry: Field Day Publications, 1984), reprinted in Seamus Deane et al., *Ireland's Field Day* (London: Hutchinson, 1985), 50 and 'General Introduction', *The Field Day Anthology of Irish Writing*, vol. 1, p. xxvi.
15 Paul Muldoon, 'Sweeney Peregrine', *London Review of Books*, 1–14 November 1984, 20.
16 Neil Corcoran, 'A Languorous Cutting Edge: Muldoon versus Heaney?', *Poets*

of *Modern Ireland: Text, Context, Intertext* (Cardiff: University of Wales Press, 1999), 121–36.

17 Rui Carvalho Homem, 'On Elegies, Eclogues, Translations, Transfusions: An Interview with Seamus Heaney', *European English Messenger*, 10(2) (2001), 30. ('But "The Master" is specifically about meeting with my hero, Czesław Miłosz. Many people think it is about Yeats because it is set in a tower and so on.')

18 Heaney, *Preoccupations*, 100.

19 Ibid., 101.

20 The whole story of the ordering of the poems in the *Collected Poems* is brilliantly told in Gould's article 'W. B. Yeats and the Resurrection of the Author', *The Library*, 16(2) (June 1994), 101–34.

21 Quoted in Heaney, *Preoccupations*, 107.

22 George Moore, *Hail and Farewell: Ave, Salve, Vale*, ed. Richard Cave (Gerrards Cross: Colin Smythe, 1976), 540. This is Moore's 1933 version of the original 1911 text.

23 Heaney, *Preoccupations*, 108.

24 Ibid., 108–9.

25 Heaney, *Opened Ground*, 454–5.

26 'Nobel poet discloses his despair at Bloody Sunday', *Sunday Times*, 2 February 1997, 3.

27 Blake Morrison, *Seamus Heaney* (London: Methuen, 1982), 79.

28 Heaney, 'A tale of two islands', in Drudy, *Irish Studies*, vol. 1, p. 11.

29 It is striking that the same imagery recurs in the penultimate poem (no. xlvii) of the 'Squarings' sequence in *Seeing Things*, which figures potential and fulfilment – in life, or in poetry – as the sensing of things in an 'offing': 'The emptier it stood, the more compelled / The eye that scanned it. / But once you turned your back on it, your back // Was suddenly all eyes like Argus's.'

30 Brown, *The Life of W. B. Yeats*, 275.

31 Seamus Heaney, *The Government of the Tongue* (London: Faber and Faber, 1988), 92 and *The Redress of Poetry: Oxford Lectures* (London: Faber and Faber, 1995), 8, 9. The phrase 'strong enough to help' is quoted from George Seferis, as I note in my introduction.

32 *The Field Day Anthology of Irish Writing*, vol. 2, p. 790. In a study of the influence of Yeats's stanzaic poems on contemporary Northern Irish poetry Peter McDonald also emphasizes the resourcefulness with which these poets adapt or accommodate the Yeatsian structures: Heaney, Derek Mahon, Michael Longley and Paul Muldoon, he says, 'offer a use of Yeats's forms which is something other than either ideological grudge or formalist imitation'. See Peter McDonald, *Serious Poetry: Form and Authority from Yeats to Hill* (Oxford: Clarendon Press, 2002), 166.

33 Fiona Stafford, *Starting Lines in Scottish, Irish, and English Poetry: From Burns to Heaney* (Oxford: Oxford University Press, 2000), 294, where she quotes from Heaney's 'Foreword', in Niall Macmonagle (ed.), *Lifelines: An Anthology of Poems Chosen by Famous People* (Harmondsworth: Penguin Books, 1993).

34 Julia Kristeva, 'Revolution in Poetic Language' (1974), reprinted in Toril Moi (ed.), *The Kristeva Reader* (Oxford: Blackwell, 1986), 89–136, 111. She has in mind the way the sign-system of the novel, for instance, is formed 'as the redistribution of several different sign-systems: carnival, courtly poetry, scholastic discourse'.

Notes to Chapter 6

1 Christopher Ricks, *Dylan's Visions of Sin* (London: Viking, 2003), 222.
2 Bizarrely, he says that he had not realized until he got there that Gaelic was the only spoken tongue of most islanders; this despite the fact that he had accepted a publisher's commission for the trip and the book.
3 Philip Larkin, *Further Requirements: Interviews, Broadcasts, Statements and Book Reviews, 1952-85*, ed. Anthony Thwaite (London: Faber and Faber, 2001), 18.
4 Louis MacNeice, *The Dark Tower and Other Radio Scripts* (London: Faber and Faber, 1947), 15.
5 MacNeice knew Bowen and took over the magnificent Regent's Park house she had lived in when she gave it up. The house, 2 Clarence Terrace, is fictionalized in *The Death of the Heart*.
6 An outstanding literary representation of this anxiety is the gondola journey taken by von Aschenbach to the Lido, initially entirely against his will, at the beginning of Thomas Mann's *Death in Venice*. The gondolier's palpable malevolence there finds a near equivalent in both Bowen and MacNeice, who would almost certainly, of course, have known the story.
7 Louis MacNeice, *The Poetry of W. B. Yeats* (1941; London: Faber and Faber, 1967), 146.
8 MacNeice himself ought to have used the word 'psittacism' in an undergraduate paper of his which he quotes, a little self-approvingly perhaps, in his book *Modern Poetry*, where he says that 'we must know how to be *new*, as contrasted with repetition – psittacosis – on the one hand and with escape from tradition – aphasia – on the other'. Psittacosis is actually a contagious disease of birds, transmissible, especially from parrots, to human beings as a form of pneumonia. Desirable as it is to avoid it, it cannot therefore be what the young, forgivably peacocking MacNeice actually meant. He meant 'psittacism'. Strangely, he got it right when he more or less repeated the remark in the essay 'Poetry Today', of 1935. See Alan Heuser (ed.), *Selected Literary Criticism of Louis MacNeice* (Oxford: Clarendon Press, 1987), 13.
9 Quoted in Peter McDonald, *Serious Poetry: Form and Authority from Yeats to Hill* (Oxford: Clarendon Press, 2002), 179.
10 Tom Paulin, 'The Man from No Part: Louis MacNeice', *Ireland and the English Crisis* (Newcastle upon Tyne: Bloodaxe, 1984), 76.
11 MacNeice, *The Poetry of W. B. Yeats*, 145–8.
12 See 'Tendencies in Modern Poetry', *The Listener* (27 July 1939), 185–6.
13 Magritte's painting has strong literary associations too. On the mantelpiece in front of the mirror is a punctiliously, even hyper-really, painted edition of *Les Aventures d'Arthur Gordon Pym*, Baudelaire's translation of Edgar Allen Poe's *The Narrative of Arthur Gordon Pym of Nantucket*.

Notes to Chapter 7

1 Quoted in D. J. Enright (ed.), *Poetry of the 1950s* (Tokyo: The Kenkyusha Press, 1955), 17.

2 W. B. Yeats, *The Oxford Book of Modern Verse* (Oxford: Oxford University Press, 1936), viii.

3 See John Hollander, *The Gazer's Spirit: Poems Speaking to Silent Works of Art* (Chicago and London: University of Chicago Press, 1995), *passim*.

4 See James A. W. Heffernan, *Museum of Words: The Poetics of Ekphrasis from Homer to Ashbery* (Chicago and London: University of Chicago Press, 1993), *passim*.

5 W. B. Yeats, *Essays and Introductions* (London and Basingstoke: Macmillan, 1961), 244.

6 Heffernan, *Museum of Words*, 23.

7 In thinking about the possibilities of ekphrasis I have been helped by Elizabeth Bergmann Loizeaux's *Twentieth-Century Poetry and the Visual Arts* (Cambridge: Cambridge University Press, 2008). Professor Loizeaux is also the author of the excellent *Yeats and the Visual Arts* (New Brunswick, NJ: Rutgers University Press, 1987).

8 An exploded view is a diagram or technical drawing showing the relationship between, or order of assembly of, an object's various parts.

9 See www.felimegan.ie/longley.html.

10 Fran Brearton, *Reading Michael Longley* (Tarset: Bloodaxe Books, 2006), 117, 120.

11 In fact, de Hooch made a series of paintings during his time in Delft from 1652 to 1660, and Hugh Haughton thinks that in this poem Mahon has others in mind too. See Hugh Haughton, *The Poetry of Derek Mahon* (Oxford: Oxford University Press, 2007), 156.

12 See Peter C. Sutton, *Pieter de Hooch, 1629-1684* (New Haven, Conn. and London: Yale University Press, 1998), 124.

13 What I say here is given a slightly different inflection in an excellent reading of the poem by Stephen Cheeke, who discovers in it 'an uneasy acknowledgement of a tribal allegiance, a distrustful submission to the nostalgia that masks ideology in the sanctified forms of memory and art'. See *Writing for Art: The Aesthetics of Ekphrasis* (Manchester: Manchester University Press, 2008), 34.

14 This can be accessed online at www.flanagan-art.com.

15 See Rand Brandes and Michael J. Durkan, *Seamus Heaney: A Bibliography, 1959-2003* (London: Faber and Faber, 2008), 75 and www.felimegan.ie/review.html#.

16 The story of the press is told, with wonderful illustrations, in Brian Lalor, *Ink-Stained Hands: Graphic Studio Dublin and the Origins of Fine-Art Printmaking in Ireland* (Dublin: The Lilliput Press, 2011).

17 See Dennis O'Driscoll, *Stepping Stones: Interviews with Seamus Heaney* (London: Faber and Faber, 2008), especially 333–6.

18 Seamus Heaney's *A Personal Selection* (Belfast: Ulster Museum, 1982) is unpaginated.

19 Richard Long has made a series of mud hand circles. A photograph of one of them

can be viewed at www.richardlong.org/Exhibitions/2011exhibitupgrades/ mudhandcirc.html, and, of course, on the dust jacket of this book.

20 The large portrait, which is very impressively hung in the Ulster Museum in Belfast, can be viewed at www.nmni.com/images/CollectionImages/record_ photos/BELUM/U/002001-003000/002101-002200/U2107_INT_mcguire_10. jpg.

21 O'Driscoll, *Stepping Stones*, 327.

Notes to Chapter 8

1 Wikipedia says that the magazine was edited by William Peskett, with Trevor McMahon and Robert Johnstone.

2 Paul Muldoon, 'Caprice des Dieux', *Times Literary Supplement*, 11 May 1984, 516. Why Muldoon has never reprinted this wonderfully witty and wicked little poem is another of the mysteries.

3 Neil Corcoran, 'A Languorous Cutting Edge: Muldoon versus Heaney?', *Poets of Modern Ireland: Text, Context, Intertext* (Cardiff: University of Wales Press, 1999), 121–36.

4 See 'Paul Muldoon in Conversation with Neil Corcoran', in Elmer Kennedy-Andrews (ed.), *Paul Muldoon: Poetry, Prose, Drama* (Gerrards Cross: Colin Smythe, 2006), 165–87.

5 Although no poem by Heaney carries this title, we learn from his conversations with Dennis O'Driscoll that the Marian visitation is in fact coded into 'The Mud Vision' in *The Haw Lantern*. Heaney says that the poem is 'set in the Irish midlands, but the actual memory behind it was of thronged roads and gardens around a housing estate in Co. Tyrone in the late 1950s, when the Virgin Mary was supposed to have appeared to a woman in Ardboe'. See Dennis O'Driscoll, *Stepping Stones: Interviews with Seamus Heaney* (London: Faber and Faber, 2008), 286.

6 See John Lyon, '"All That": Muldoon and the Vanity of Interpretation', in Tim Kendall and Peter McDonald (eds.), *Paul Muldoon: Critical Essays* (Liverpool: Liverpool University Press, 2004), 110–24.

7 Clair Wills, *Reading Paul Muldoon* (Newcastle upon Tyne: Bloodaxe Books, 1998).

Notes to Chapter 9

1 Frank O'Hara, *Jackson Pollock* (New York: George Braziller, 1959), 22.

2 Frank O'Hara, *Art Chronicles, 1954-1966* (New York: George Braziller, 1975; rev. edn, 1990), 67.

3 O'Hara, *Jackson Pollock*, 23.

4 Susan Sontag, 'Notes on Camp' (1964), reprinted in *A Susan Sontag Reader* (Harmondsworth: Penguin Books, 1982), 106.

5 In his essay 'French Frank' Rod Mengham discusses the importance of 'the Paris–New York axis' in O'Hara and the way it acts as an implicit rebuke to American cold war isolationism. In fact, thinks Mengham, O'Hara 'is reading

contemporary American culture through French poetry, and it is specifically in the poetry of Pierre Reverdy that he finds something exceptionally significant that he can make use of in his attempt to resist the triumphalism attached to American art'. See Robert Hampson and Will Montgomery (eds.), *Frank O'Hara Now: New Essays on the New York Poet* (Liverpool: Liverpool University Press, 2010), 53.

6 Mark Ford, 'Introduction', in Frank O'Hara, *'Why I Am Not a Painter' and Other Poems*, ed. Mark Ford (Manchester: Carcanet, 2003), 8.

7 John Ashbery, 'Introduction', in *The Collected Poems of Frank O'Hara*, ed. Donald Allen (New York: Alfred A. Knopf, 1979), viii–ix.

8 In his remarkable book *Digressions on Some Poems by Frank O'Hara* (New York: Farrar, Straus and Giroux, 2003) Joe LeSueur tells us that 'A Step Away from Them' was written the day after Jackson Pollock's funeral.

9 O'Hara, *Art Chronicles, 1954-1966*, 40.

10 'About Zhivago and His Poems', *The Collected Poems of Frank O'Hara*, 509.

11 *A Susan Sontag Reader*, 107.

12 O'Hara, *Standing Still and Walking in New York*, ed. Donald Allen (Bolinas: Grey Fox Press, n.d.), 62.

13 Ibid., 46.

14 LeSueur, *Digressions on Some Poems by Frank O'Hara*, 194.

15 In the film *No Direction Home*, directed by Martin Scorsese (2005), Dylan cites 'Strange Fruit' as an influence: not on his songs themselves, but on his lack of concern about audience reaction to them.

16 This is Holiday's claim in her notoriously unreliable but completely fascinating autobiography *Lady Sings the Blues* (1956; New York, Harlem Moon/Broadway Books, 2006), but the claim is disputed by David Margolick in his book *Strange Fruit: The Biography of a Song* (New York: Ecco Press, 2001).

17 She can be seen performing it at www.youtube.com/watch?v=h4ZyuULy9zs.

18 Cited in David Lehman, *The Last Avant-Garde: The Making of the New York School of Poets* (1998; New York: Anchor Books, 1999), 196.

19 Reprinted in Norman Mailer, *Advertisements for Myself* (New York: Putnam, 1981).

20 Billie Holiday (with William Dufty), *Lady Sings the Blues*, 110.

21 Cited in Margolick, *Strange Fruit*. Holiday, he says, 'sensed, and resented, Hammond's condescension'.

Notes to Chapter 10

1 William Hazlitt, *The Fight and Other Writings*, ed. Tom Paulin and David Chandler (London: Penguin Books, 2000), 393.

2 Ted Hughes, *Tales of the Early World* (London: Faber and Faber, 1988), 80.

3 Ted Hughes, *Winter Pollen*, ed. William Scammell (London: Faber and Faber, 1994), 178.

4 Ibid., 317, 319.

5 *Letters of Ted Hughes*, ed. Christopher Reid (London: Faber and Faber, 2007), 170.

6 Ibid., 711–12.

7 See Neil Corcoran, *Shakespeare and the Modern Poet* (Cambridge: Cambridge University Press, 2010).

8 For his definition of *Gaudete*, see Ted Hughes, *Difficulties of a Bridegroom: Collected Short Stories* (London: Faber and Faber, 1995), ix.

9 A very useful version of the narrative is recovered from various sources in an appendix to Keith Sagar, *The Laughter of Foxes: A Study of Ted Hughes* (Liverpool: Liverpool University Press, 2000), 170–80.

10 *Letters of Ted Hughes*, 34.

11 Ibid., 108.

12 Ibid., 189.

13 Hughes, *Winter Pollen*, 496–7.

14 Ibid., 9.

15 *Letters of Ted Hughes*, 474.

16 Ibid., 644.

17 Ibid., 704.

18 See, for instance, ibid., 719.

19 Neil Roberts, *Ted Hughes: A Literary Life* (Basingstoke: Palgrave Macmillan, 2006), 168.

20 Ted Hughes, *The Dreamfighter and Other Creation Tales* (London: Faber and Faber, 2003), 50.

21 Hughes, *Winter Pollen*, 149.

22 John Carey (ed.), *William Golding: The Man and his Books* (London: Faber and Faber, 1986), 166; Ted Hughes, *Shakespeare and the Goddess of Complete Being* (London: Faber and Faber, 1992; rev. edn, 1993), 47.

23 W. B. Yeats, *Essays and Introductions* (London: The Macmillan Press, 1961), 107.

24 Hughes, *Winter Pollen*, 205.

25 Keith Douglas, *Complete Poems*, ed. Desmond Graham, with a new introduction by Ted Hughes (Oxford: Oxford University Press, 1987), xxi.

26 Hughes, *Winter Pollen*, 158.

27 Ibid., 79; 81.

28 *Letters of Ted Hughes*, 683.

29 Ibid., 159–60; 247.

30 Ibid., 645.

Sources for Chapter 11

Bob Dylan

Books
Chronicles: Volume One (London: Simon and Schuster, 2004).
Lyrics, 1962–2001 (London: Simon and Schuster, 2004).
'My Life in a Stolen Moment' and 'Last Thoughts on Woody Guthrie', *Writings and Drawings* (London: Jonathan Cape, 1973).

CDs
'Angelina', in *The Bootleg Series*, vols 1–3: *(Rare & Unreleased) 1961-1991* (1991).

Biograph (1985).
Bob Dylan Live 1964, Concert at Philharmonic Hall, The Bootleg Series, vol. 6 (2004).
Infidels (1983).
'Love and Theft' (2001).
Nashville Skyline (1969).
No Direction Home: The Soundtrack, The Bootleg Series, vol. 7 (2005).
Oh Mercy (1989).
The Original Mono Recordings (2010).
Together Through Life (2009).
The Witmark Demos: 1962-1964, The Bootleg Series, vol. 9 (2010).

Films

Bob Dylan Screen Test, Andy Warhol's Factory, 23 January 1965. www.youtube.
com/watch?v=M--oHOn4a0U.
Dont Look Back [*sic*], a documentary film by D. A. Pennebaker of Dylan's 1965
concert tour of the United Kingdom. De luxe edition available on Sony/
BMG DVD, documentary 82876832139 (2006).
Renaldo and Clara (1978), not available on DVD.

On-line concordance

www.bobdylan.com/songs.

Other Authors

Beckett, Samuel, *Worstward Ho* (London: John Calder, 1983).
'Bob Dylan and the NECLC' (www.corliss-lamont.org/dylan.htm), which collects
the extraordinary documents in the case of Dylan's Tom Paine award,
including his long letter (or poem?) of apology.
Cohen, Leonard, 1985 interview (www.youtube.com/watch?v=NXP7uDNbvUY).
Ellmann, Richard, *Eminent Domain: Yeats among Wilde, Joyce, Pound, Eliot and
Auden* (New York: Oxford University Press, 1967).
Emerson, Ralph Waldo, 'The Poet', in *The Essential Writings of Ralph Waldo
Emerson*, ed. Brooks Atkinson (New York: Random House: The Modern
Library, 2000).
Ford, Mark, 'Trust Yourself: Emerson and Dylan', in Neil Corcoran (ed.), *Do
You, Mr Jones: Bob Dylan with the Poets and Professors* (London: Chatto and
Windus, 2002).
Gooding, Cynthia, *Folksinger's Choice*, live radio performance with Bob Dylan, 11
March 1962 (Leftfield Media CD, 2010).
Hazlitt, William, 'Hamlet', *Characters of Shakespeare's Plays* (London and Toronto:
J. M. Dent & Sons: Everyman's Library, 1906).
Jones, Michael, 'Judas and the Many Betrayals of Bob Dylan', in David Boucher
and Gary Browning (eds.), *The Political Art of Bob Dylan*, rev. edn (Exeter:
Imprint Academic, 2009).
Lott, Eric, *Love and Theft: Blackface Minstrelsy and the American Working Class*
(New York and Oxford: Oxford University Press, 1993).
— '"Love and Theft" (2001)', in Kevin J. H. Dettmar (ed.), *The Cambridge
Companion to Bob Dylan* (Cambridge: Cambridge University Press, 2009).
Lowell, Robert, 'Harriet, I', *Notebook* (London: Faber and Faber, 1970).

Marqusee, Mark, *Wicked Messenger: Bob Dylan and the 1960s*, rev. version of *Chimes of Freedom* (New York: Seven Stories Press, 2005).

Neve, Michael, 'Queen Mary', *London Review of Books*, vol. 6 no. 24, 20 December 1984.

Nietzsche, Friedrich, *Beyond Good and Evil*, trans R. J. Hollingdale, rev. edn (London: Penguin, 2003).

Pasternak, Boris, *Doctor Zhivago*, trans Manya Harari and Max Hayward (New York and London: Alfred A. Knopf: Everyman's Library, 1991).

Rotolo, Suze, *A Freewheelin' Time: A Memoir of Greenwich Village in the Sixties* (London: Aurum Press, 2009).

— 'Tomorrow is a long time' (Suze Rotolo interviewed by Richard Williams), *Guardian*, 16 August 2008.

Scobie, Stephen, *Alias Bob Dylan Revisited* (Markham, Ont.: Red Deer Press, 2004).

van Ronk, Dave and Elijah Ward, *The Mayor of Macdougal Street: A Memoir* (Cambridge, Mass.: Da Capo Press, 2005).

Zollo, Paul, *Song-writers On Song-writing*, 4th edn (Cambridge, Mass.: Da Capo Press, 2003).

Index